The Psychology Major's Handbook

Second Edition

TARA L. KUTHER
Western Connecticut State University

THOMSON
WADSWORTH
Australia • Canada • Mexico • Singapore • Spain • United Kingdom • United States

THOMSON
WADSWORTH

Publisher: Vicki Knight
Editorial Assistant: Juliet Case
Technology Project Manager: Darin Derstine
Marketing Manager: Dory Schaeffer
Marketing Communications Manager: Brian Chaffee
Project Manager, Editorial Production: Karol Jurado
Art Director: Vernon Boes
Print Buyer: Judy Inouye
Permissions Editor: Joohee Lee
Production Service: Matrix Productions Inc.
Copy Editor: Carol Dean
Cover Designer: Denise Davidson
Cover Image: Indivision/DEX Image
Compositor: Cadmus
Text and Cover Printer: Transcontinental Printing/Louiseville

Printed in Canada
3 4 5 6 7 09 08 07

For more information about our products, contact us at:
Thomson Learning Academic Resource Center
1-800-423-0563

For permission to use material from this text or product, submit a request online at **http://www.thomsonrights.com.**

Any additional questions about permissions can be submitted by email to **thomsonrights@thomson.com.**

Library of Congress Control Number: 2005923582

ISBN 13: 978-0-534-53387-8
ISBN 10: 0-534-53387-6

Thomson Higher Education
10 Davis Drive
Belmont, CA 94002-3098
USA

Asia (including India)
Thomson Learning
5 Shenton Way
#01-01 UIC Building
Singapore 068808

Australia/New Zealand
Thomson Learning Australia
102 Dodds Street
Southbank, Victoria 3006
Australia

Canada
Thomson Nelson
1120 Birchmount Road
Toronto, Ontario M1K 5G4
Canada

UK/Europe/Middle East/Africa
Thomson Learning
High Holborn House
50–51 Bedford Row
London WC1R 4LR
United Kingdom

Latin America
Thomson Learning
Seneca, 53
Colonia Polanco
11560 Mexico
D.F. Mexico

Spain (including Portugal)
Thomson Paraninfo
Calle Magallanes, 25
28015 Madrid, Spain

About the Author

To TK and CK

Tara L. Kuther is Associate Professor of Psychology at Western Connecticut State University. She earned her PhD in developmental psychology from Fordham University and teaches courses in child, adolescent, and adult development. Dr. Kuther is Chair of the Instructional Resource Award Task Force of the Office of Teaching Resources in Psychology (OTRP) of the Society for Teaching of Psychology, Division 2 of the American Psychological Association. She is also active in the Council on Undergraduate Research as a psychology counselor. Dr. Kuther is the author of several books, including *Careers in Psychology: Opportunities in a Changing World* (with Robert Morgan) and *Graduate Study in Psychology: Your Guide to Success*. Her research examines risky behavior during adolescence and early adulthood, moral development, and ethical issues in research and teaching. To learn more about Dr. Kuther's work, visit her website at http://tarakuther.com

Brief Contents

Contents

Chapter 7

What Can I Do With a Bachelor's Degree in Psychology? 124

Chapter 8

Chapter 9

What Can I Do With a Graduate Degree in Psychology? 162

Preface

Psychology is an overwhelmingly popular major, with more than 75,000 baccalaureate degrees awarded each year. *The Psychology Major's Handbook* is intended for a range of students, including prospective and declared psychology majors. My goal in writing this book is to offer undergraduate students practical information to help them make informed decisions about whether to pursue psychology as a major and a career, as well as to help students develop an active learning style, hone their study skills, and become more self-aware through a variety of explorative exercises. In the second edition of *The Psychology Major's Handbook,* I have added quizzes, exercises, and checklists to each chapter to help readers employ the techniques described in this book and take an active role in their professional development. Students should consider this book another resource to use in addition to their advisors. *The Psychology Major's Handbook* complements a variety of psychology courses, including introductory psychology, careers in psychology, methodology courses, capstone courses, seminars for psychology majors, and any courses that require writing or in which the instructor wishes to promote active learning and conscientious study habits. New college students are often surprised by the autonomy required of students. Perhaps the biggest difference between high school and college is that college requires students to take an active role in their education.

This book is organized to accompany students on their journey from Introductory Psychology through the college years. Chapter 1 introduces students to the scope of psychology, including subspecialties and the wide range of places where psychologists work. Chapter 2 addresses the challenge of choosing a college major by discussing the importance of developing self-awareness through journal writing and self-assessment exercises. Readers are encouraged to consider their skills, abilities, and interests when determining whether psychology is the right choice. Each subsequent chapter closes with journal exercises that encourage readers to learn about themselves and apply the chapter material to their own lives.

Chapters 3 through 6 are intended to accompany students through the college years, serving as a resource to review periodically. Chapter 3 examines the skills that are honed in college and helps students identify and take advantage of the resources at their schools so that they can get the most from their college years. Specifically, the chapter covers how to develop relationships with faculty and how to get research and field experience. The chapter also surveys the range of presentation and publication opportunities available to undergraduates in psychology. Chapter 4 emphasizes study skills as the key to success in college and provides detailed tips and strategies to improve time management, reading, note taking, studying, and test taking. Chapter 5 examines the psychology term paper or literature review: how to choose a topic, narrow it, locate information, understand the format of research articles, take notes, avoid plagiarism, write the first draft, and revise it. In Chapter 6, the empirical paper is demystified. Readers learn about the structure of an empirical paper, what to include in each section, and American Psychological Association (APA) style; a template illustrating APA style is provided at the end of the chapter.

Chapters 7 through 10 offer specific information for psychology majors and students who are considering psychology as a major. Chapter 7 addresses the pervasive myth that there are no jobs available for psychology majors. Readers learn about the value of a liberal arts degree, what employers look for, how to acquire useful skills, and jobs for psychology majors in business, human resources, and the social service fields. Learning about jobs is one thing; getting them is another. Chapter 8 provides advice on how to obtain a job after graduation: finding positions, completing applications, résumés, cover letters, and interviews.

Chapter 9 provides information about careers that require a graduate degree, takes a close look at the master's degree with specialties in psychology and related fields, and discusses the job outlook and salary prospects. The differences among doctoral degrees—the PhD, PsyD, and EdD—are also examined. Careers, employment settings, and salaries for holders of doctoral degrees are presented, as well the impact of managed care on psychologists. The final chapter, Chapter 10, provides advice for students who are interested in attending graduate school. Discussion includes training models (e.g., scientist-practitioner) and the differences between clinical and counseling programs. Readers are encouraged to examine their reasons for applying to graduate school. Specific advice is provided on gathering program information, evaluating programs, preparing for the Graduate Record Exam (GRE), completing admissions essays, obtaining recommendation letters, and succeeding in interviews. Like earlier chapters, Chapter 10 presents exercises as a means for self-exploration and to help readers determine their priorities.

Acknowledgments

The *Psychology Major's Handbook* was not a solitary endeavor. I am most appreciative of the constructive comments and helpful suggestions I have received from reviewers: Leonard Mark, Miami University; Frank Vattano, Colorado State University; Peggy Skinner, South Plains College; and Holly Straub, University of South Dakota. Wherever possible, I have incorporated their suggestions and feel that the book has improved as a result.

In addition, I thank my editor at Wadsworth, Vicki Knight, for her keen insight, diligence, and warm guidance. Thanks to Vinny Prohaska and Erin McDonald for reviewing and commenting on drafts of the first edition. I thank Drew Appleby for sharing some of his class activities and ideas. Much of what appears in these pages has come from interaction with my wonderful students and colleagues at Western Connecticut State University, without whom this book would not be possible. Philip and Irene Kuther have provided unwavering support and guidance throughout my education and career. Finally, I thank Tom Kelly for his all-around encouragement and friendship throughout the completion of this project and always.

Dear Student,

Welcome to the world of psychology! *The Psychology Major's Handbook* is intended to accompany you on your journey through college. A comprehensive book such as this can sometimes be overwhelming, so here are some guideposts to help you find your way:

- If you're wondering, "What's psychology?" check out Chapter 1, which explains the scope of psychology, including the many subspecialties and the wide range of places where psychologists work.
- Not sure what to major in or whether psychology is for you? In Chapter 2, you'll learn about yourself through journal exercises and activities that will help you identify your skills, abilities, and interests.
- Ever wonder exactly what you're getting out of college? Feeling confused because of a lack of guidance? Chapter 3 explains the hidden curriculum in college: how you can take control of your education by getting involved with faculty, research, and field experience.
- Does it seem as if you study and study and still don't get the grades you want? In Chapter 4 you'll learn about essential study skills, including time management tips, suggestions on how to read more effectively, advice on note taking, study tips, and guidance for taking tests with ease.
- Have a big paper assignment and don't know where to start? Turn to Chapter 5 for tips on how to choose a paper topic, where to get ideas, how to find information, take notes, write the paper, and revise it.
- Taking experimental psychology or a laboratory class and don't know how to write a lab report? Chapter 6 demystifies the empirical paper or research article. You'll learn about the special structure of empirical articles, what to include in each section, and APA style. A template appears at the end to help you conquer APA style.
- Want to major in psychology but have no clue about what to do after graduation? Chapter 7 dispels the myth that psychology majors are unemployable. You'll learn about the value of a liberal arts degree, what employers look for, how to acquire useful skills, and jobs for psychology majors in business, human resources, and the social service fields.
- Getting close to graduation and want to find a job? Turn to Chapter 8 and learn how to obtain a job after graduation. Everything you need to know is covered, including how to find positions, complete applications, prepare a résumé, write cover letters, and ace interviews.
- Think you might want to continue your education, but aren't sure of the choices? In Chapter 9 you'll learn about graduate degrees in psychology and the variety of careers available to holders of graduate degrees in psychology. You'll also have an opportunity to take a close look at the master's degree: reasons for obtaining one, your choices of fields, and the

job outlook and salary information for recipients of master's degrees. You'll take a similar look at the doctoral degree and the differences among PhD, PsyD, and EdD degrees. Chapter 9 also covers careers, employment settings, and salaries for holders of doctoral degrees, and the impact of managed care on psychologists.

- So you think graduate school is for you? Chapter 10 tells you how to gather program information, evaluate programs, prepare for the GRE, complete admissions essays, obtain recommendation letters, and handle interviews.

CHAPTER 1

WHAT IS PSYCHOLOGY?

CHAPTER GUIDE

Close your eyes and imagine a psychologist. What do you see? What activities compose the field of psychology? Does your image include any of the following?

- Conducting research with monkeys
- Monitoring a magnetic resonance imaging (MRI) machine to understand what parts of the brain are active when people view pictures of various items and situations
- Creating and administering a survey on employee perceptions of their work environments
- Developing and evaluating interventions for families with histories of domestic violence
- Helping educators learn about how the mind works and how to teach most effectively
- Counseling clients who suffer from depression
- Teaching physicians how to understand the emotions that accompany illness and to communicate more effectively with patients
- Developing and implementing training programs for employees
- Helping police departments by providing information about criminal behavior, assisting officers in managing stress, and understanding the limitations of eyewitness testimony

Generally when we think of the field of psychology, we tend to think of professionals who conduct therapy in private practice settings. Would it surprise you to learn that all the activities just mentioned are within the field of psychology? We are exposed to psychology each day through our experiences with television, radio, books, and the Internet. However, there are many misconceptions about psychology and what psychologists do. Psychology is a diverse discipline, much more so than as depicted in the media and on television.

The Scope of Psychology

A formal, though broad, definition of psychology is the scientific study of mind and behavior. Behavior refers to anything an animal or a person does, feels, or thinks. Many students are surprised to learn that some psychologists work with animals. Psychologists often study animal physiology and behavior to extend what they learn to humans.

Psychology is concerned with how the brain, the environment, psychological functioning, and behavior relate to and influence one another. Topics of psychological study include social relationships, the brain and the chemicals that influence it, vision, human development, the causes of normative and atypical behavior, and many others. Psychologists apply scientific methods of observation, data collection, analysis, and interpretation to learn more about what makes people and animals behave as they do. Psychologists generate hypotheses, or guesses, about what might cause a particular behavior or phenomenon and then conduct careful research to test these hypotheses. Psychologists also work directly with people. Psychologists who engage in private practice apply the findings of research in their work with people.

Psychologists conduct a variety of activities in many settings. You're probably most aware of them as service providers, supplying psychological therapy and treatment to clients. However, only about one-half of psychologists work in service provider roles. What do the rest do? Some psychologists are employed as professors at universities, community colleges, and high schools. Others work as researchers in university, hospital, corporate, and government settings. Psychologists work as administrators, managing hospitals, mental health clinics, nonprofit organizations, government agencies, businesses, schools, and other facilities. Most psychologists perform in more than one of these roles. For example, a psychologist who works as a college professor might also have a private practice or conduct research for a social service agency.

You have already seen that a wide range of topics fall under the umbrella of psychology. Following are some of the more common specialties within psychology. All of these require graduate level training, education beyond the bachelor's degree. In each of these areas, you'll find psychologists who spend most of their time conducting research to expand the knowledge base, those who practice or apply research findings to help people and communities, and those who do both—as scientist-practitioners. In addition, more than one-third of psychologists teach and conduct research at colleges and universities.

Clinical Psychology

Clinical psychologists study and treat persons with emotional, behavioral, and psychological disorders. Researchers in this area study questions such as how to best treat a particular diagnosis (e.g., determining which therapy works best). You're probably familiar with the practitioner role of a clinical psychologist because it is commonly depicted on television. In practice, clinical psychologists assess and treat people who are experiencing psychological problems and disorders. These problems may range from normative difficulties such as dealing with grief or a crisis to more serious and chronic disorders such as schizophrenia and mood disorders.

Clinical psychologists work in universities as professors and researchers. They also work in healthcare settings including hospitals, mental health centers, and private practice. Some clinical psychologists specialize in particular populations such as children or older adults. Others specialize in particular problems such as depression or anxiety. Still others work as generalists, dealing with all ages and all types of problems.

Counseling Psychology

Counseling psychologists engage in many of the same activities as do clinical psychologists but focus their activities on normative functioning rather than on psychological disorders. They conduct research on how to help people deal with everyday life issues and transitions such as divorce, remarriage, career changes, and transitions to and from college. Practicing counseling psychologists help people adjust to life changes and transitions and provide vocational assessments and career guidance. Many counseling psychologists work in academic settings as professors and researchers. Others work in community settings such as mental health clinics, halfway houses, college counseling centers, and social service agencies.

Developmental Psychology

Developmental psychologists study human development across the life span. In academic settings, they teach and conduct research on the emotional, intellectual, and physical development of children, adolescents, and adults. Research topics include a diverse array of issues such as whether most adults experience a midlife crisis, how babies learn to crawl, and what factors influence adolescent drug use.

Developmental psychologists also work in applied settings such as child care centers, pediatric hospitals, and geriatric centers. They work as consultants for parenting magazines, toy companies, and children's television programs. Some developmental psychologists assess children to ensure that they are timely in meeting developmental milestones. Applied developmental psychologists also provide assessments and develop interventions for all phases of life (e.g., an applied developmental psychologist might provide advice on how to design a nursing home that meets the needs of older adults). Other developmental psychologists create and evaluate intervention programs like Head Start, a prominent child development and educational enrichment program that has served low-income children and their families since the mid-1960s.

Educational Psychology

Educational psychologists study the process of education and how people learn. They also develop methods and materials to increase the efficiency and effectiveness of educational programs and curricula designed for people of all ages. Educational psychologists work in academic settings and conduct research on learning and instruction. Some study how people learn to read or complete math problems. Others train teachers and develop methods of instruction to enhance the educational setting.

Experimental Psychology

Experimental psychologists conduct research and teach a variety of topics including learning, sensation, perception, human performance, motivation, memory, language, thinking, and communication. Many study human cognition: how we take in, store, retrieve, and apply knowledge. Other experimental psychologists study animals to apply what they learn to humans or simply because animal behavior is interesting. Most experimental psychologists are employed in academic settings, teaching and conducting research. Others work as researchers for businesses, corporations, and the government.

Forensic Psychology

Forensic psychologists study legal issues from a psychological perspective. They conduct research on such issues as the reliability of eyewitness testimony, juror selection, and how to interview eyewitnesses without contaminating their testimony. Forensic psychologists provide expert testimony on cases in criminal, civil, and family courts. They may evaluate prisoners, assist in making parole decisions, and assess defendants to determine whether they are competent to provide testimony. Forensic psychologists work not only with lawyers and judges but also with police departments to select, train, and evaluate police officers.

Health Psychology

Health psychologists study how psychological, biological, and social factors influence health and illness. They conduct research on health-related topics such as whether relaxation techniques and social support can help people overcome illnesses more quickly, and how to change people's attitudes about smoking. Health psychologists design, assess, and modify programs to promote health and wellness (e.g., stress management, smoking cessation, weight loss). They work in academic and research settings such as universities and medical schools, as well as in applied settings such as hospitals and clinics.

Human Factors Psychology

Human factors or engineering psychologists study how people interact with machines, environments, and products. They conduct research on how people understand and use machines to increase safety, efficiency, and productivity. Human factors psychologists might work on designing computer monitors to prevent user fatigue and eyestrain, or they might arrange the instruments on car dashboards to enhance access and safety. Human factors psychologists develop, evaluate, and modify military equipment, airplanes, computer terminals, and consumer products. Most human factors psychologists work in industry and government; some work in academic settings.

Industrial-Organizational Psychology

Industrial and organizational psychologists apply psychological principles to the workplace. They are concerned with the relation between people and work. Industrial and organizational psychologists often work for companies, corporations, and the government, studying how to recruit, select, train, and evaluate employees. They conduct applied research on issues such as what personality factors make a good employee, how to improve worker productivity, and the characteristics of effective leaders. Industrial and organizational psychologists develop programs to improve employee morale and make the workplace more efficient and pleasant. Others teach and conduct research as members of academic departments in psychology and business.

Neuropsychology

Neuropsychologists examine the relation between the brain and behavior. How do neurotransmitters influence our behavior? What part of the brain is responsible for motivation, language, and emotion? Neuropsychologists conduct research to answer questions about how the brain influences our emotions and behavior. They teach and conduct research in academic settings, as well as train neuropsychologists, medical doctors, and clinical psychologists. Some neuropsychologists assess and treat persons with brain injuries within neurology, neurosurgery, psychiatric, and pediatric units of hospitals and in clinics.

Psychometrics and Quantitative Psychology

Quantitative psychologists study and develop new methods and techniques for acquiring, analyzing, and applying information. A psychometrician may create or revise psychological tests, intelligence tests, and aptitude tests. Quantitative psychologists help other researchers in designing, conducting, and interpreting experiments. Quantitative psychologists and psychometricians work primarily in research and academic settings.

Social Psychology

Social psychologists study how people interact with each other and how they are influenced by the social environment. They conduct research on personality theories, attitude formation and change, persuasion and conformity, and how people relate to one another, including attraction, prejudice, group dynamics, teamwork, and aggression. Social psychologists work in academic settings as teachers and researchers, but they also work for corporations and advertising agencies, conducting marketing research and studying how consumers view products.

School Psychology

School psychologists work to foster the intellectual, emotional, educational, and social development of children. They apply psychological principles to the school environment. School psychologists conduct research on educational topics such as how the classroom climate influences student learning and how to promote appropriate behavior in the classroom. They work in schools to assess and counsel students, interact with parents and teachers, and develop behavioral interventions.

As you can see, psychology is diverse and involves much more than therapists and leather sofas. Instead, the field of psychology offers a variety of careers in direct service, academics, government, and business. Not all psychologists conduct therapy or even study people. What all the subfields of psychology have in common is a concern with understanding the causes of behavior.

Differences among Psychologists, Psychiatrists, Social Workers, and Counselors

So, you think you might want a career that allows you to help people? Many occupations permit you to help others improve their lives. Chapters 7 and 9 discuss career options in psychology at the bachelor's, master's, and doctoral levels, as well as graduate study in psychology and related fields. Students often wonder how psychologists differ from psychiatrists, social workers, and counselors. Let's take a moment to examine the differences among psychologists, psychiatrists, social workers, and counselors.

Psychologist

A psychologist is a mental health professional with a doctor of philosophy (PhD) or a doctor of psychology (PsyD) degree. A doctoral degree is obtained by attending graduate school for about 5 to 7 years beyond the bachelor's degree. (For more detailed information about graduate training in psychology, see Chapter 9.) As we've discussed, there are many types of psychologists, but the areas of applied psychology typically are clinical, counseling, and school psychology. Psychologists who provide direct service assess and treat clients' psychological and emotional problems through talking therapies and behavior management programs. In some states, such as New Mexico and Louisiana, psychologists can prescribe medication (Holloway, 2004).

Psychiatrist

A psychiatrist holds a doctor of medicine (MD) degree. He or she has gone to medical school, just as your family physician has. After 4 years of medical school, psychiatrists complete a 3-year residency program in psychiatry during which they learn how to diagnose and treat mental illnesses. Psychiatrists tend to work with clients with serious psychological disorders such as schizophrenia. They are trained in emergency and crisis evaluations, inpatient and outpatient treatment, and medication. Because of their medical training, psychiatrists are more likely than psychologists to treat psychological disorders and mental illnesses by prescribing medication.

Social Worker

A social worker is a mental health professional who usually holds a master of social work (MSW) degree but may also hold a doctorate in social work. Social workers help individuals, families, groups, and communities to develop their skills and the ability to use their own and community resources to resolve personal and social problems. They help people adjust to normative transitions and life-threatening illnesses, and work in hospital and community settings.

Counselor

There are many types of counselors; nearly all hold master's degrees entailing 2 years of course work and about 600 hours of supervised clinical experience. Nearly all states have some form of counselor credentialing. Holders of master's degrees in counseling can conduct therapy independently and may seek licensure or certification. Counselors help clients take active roles in improving their lives. They may help clients find careers that they love (career counselors), learn how to become more motivated students (guidance counselors), learn ways of coping with addictions (certified alcohol and substance abuse counselors), and with other problems.

ETHICS IN PSYCHOLOGY

Psychologists directly and indirectly affect people through conducting research, writing, teaching, or providing therapy. Therefore, psychologists' attention to ethics, or principled conduct, is paramount. Each of the types of psychologists and mental health professionals we have discussed is confronted with ethical challenges. For example, psychologists who provide therapy must balance challenging their clients to confront issues plaguing them with the need to protect them from self-harm. Establishing professional boundaries with clients is another challenge that practicing psychologists face; for example, is it ever appropriate to hug a client?

Psychologists in each of the subfields face ethical issues that are unique to their fields. For example, forensic psychologists might assess a defendant to determine his or her capacity to stand trial. In this situation, who is the client? To whom is the forensic psychologist responsible—the court, the defendant, or the prosecuting attorney? Consider an industrial-organizational psychologist working in a business setting who must advise employers in making decisions about whom to lay off. Should the psychologist consider an individual's performance alone or also consider his or her personal life? Should the employee's marital and family status influence the decision?

Psychologists who conduct research encounter another set of ethical issues. How do psychologists balance the benefits of research against the possible harm that can occur to participants—the mental, emotional, and physical risks of research participation? One critical way in which participants' rights are protected is the federal requirement that researchers seek informed consent from participants before conducting a study. Informed consent is a participant's informed, rational, and voluntary agreement to participate. *Informed* means that it must be given with a knowledge of the risks and benefits of participation. Researchers are obligated to explain the scope of the research and whether a potential for harm exists. *Rational* means that it must be given by a person capable of making a reasoned decision. Parents provide permission for their minor children to participate because we assume that minors are not able to meet the rational criteria of informed consent. Finally, *voluntary* means that it must be given freely and without coercion.

Researchers' responsibilities continue after the research is completed. Scientists' work can ultimately impact society. In reporting results, psychologists should be mindful of the social and political implications of their work (SCRD, 1991). Researchers must consider how their findings will be portrayed in the media and must work to correct misinterpretations. They must attempt to foresee the inferences that people may draw about their findings and be prepared to correct misconceptions.

OVERVIEW OF *THE PSYCHOLOGY MAJOR'S HANDBOOK*

Now that we've discussed the diverse nature of psychology and the differences among several careers in the helping professions, let's talk about what you can expect from this book. Your first step in choosing a major and preparing for a career is to learn to know yourself. Chapter 2 will introduce you to new ways of getting to know yourself. A major theme of this book is that *you* play a major role in determining your success in college and beyond. Chapter 3 will show you how to take an active role in your education and shape your own future. Regardless of your major, you'll need to learn how to study and how to write papers. Chapters 4, 5, and 6 will introduce you to time management and study tips, as well as to information about how to write college papers—specifically, psychology papers.

The last portion of the book offers practical information for psychology majors. What can you do with a bachelor's degree in psychology and how do you look for a job after graduation? Chapters 7 and 8 will answer these and other questions. In Chapter 9 you'll learn what careers are available with a graduate degree in psychology (and related fields). Finally, Chapter 10 will provide you with an overview of how to apply to graduate school.

EXERCISE 1.1
Psychology in the Media

Locate a magazine article or web site describing psychology research findings.

1. Provide a brief summary of the findings.
2. Explain what subfield of psychology the research represents.
3. Identify one potential ethical issue related to the research topic.
4. Reconsider the findings described in the article. What further questions do you have? What questions should be addressed next? If you were the researcher whose work was mentioned in article, what would you try to learn next?

EXERCISE 1.2
Internet Scavenger Hunt

Use the Internet to answer each of the following questions about specialties in psychology. Provide the search terms used, the web site, and your response.

1. In what states can psychologists prescribe medication?
2. How is forensic psychology different from psychology and the law?
3. What is a specialist degree in school psychology? Why earn one?
4. During World War II, psychologists used their skills in new ways to help the war effort. In what ways did they contribute? What field of psychology developed from these contributions?
5. What is Principle A of the American Psychological Association ethics code?
6. What subfield(s) is(are) concerned with a biopsychosocial model? What is a biopsychosocial model?

7. When was the PsyD degree born?
8. Discuss two subfields of experimental psychology.
9. Identify three ways in which psychologists can contribute to businesses and corporations.
10. What is *Eye on Psi Chi*? What did it replace?

Suggested Readings

Kuther, T. L., & Morgan, R. D. (2004). *Careers in psychology: Opportunities in a changing world*. Belmont, CA: Wadsworth.

Ruscio, J. (2002). *Clear thinking with psychology—Separating sense from nonsense*. Belmont, CA: Wadsworth.

Smith, R. A. (2002). *Challenging your preconceptions—Thinking critically about psychology*. Belmont, CA: Wadsworth.

Sternberg, R. J. (1997). *Career paths in psychology: Where your degree can take you*. Washington, DC: American Psychological Association.

Web Resources

The following web sites are hot-linked at *The Psychology Major's Handbook* web site at *http://info.wadsworth.com/kuther*

American Psychological Association

http://www.apa.org

The web site for the American Psychological Association, the largest professional organization for psychologists.

About Psychology

http://psychology.about.com

Shelly Wu, about.com's guide to psychology, regularly provides articles about all areas of psychology and maintains the most up-to-date psychology links on the Internet.

Psychology: Scientific Problem Solvers . . . Careers for the 21st Century

http://www.apa.org/students/brochure/index.html

This online brochure, from the American Psychological Association, provides an excellent overview of the diverse fields within psychology, complete with interviews with established professionals in each field.

Psych Web

http://www.psywww.com/index.html

This web site is a portal to psychology-related material for students and professors. You'll find links to pages on careers in psychology, psychological classics on the web, and a plethora of web sites devoted to psychology.

Classics in the History of Psychology

http://psychclassics.yorku.ca/

On this web site you'll find the full text of classic books on psychology, from Sigmund Freud to B. F. Skinner and others.

Psi Chi: The National Honor Society in Psychology

http://www.psichi.org

The Psi Chi web site offers a variety of resources for psychology students, including full-text access to all the articles published in *Eye on Psi Chi*, the organization's quarterly newsletter. Articles cover areas of psychology, career preparation, personal growth, and other subjects.

CHAPTER 2

Choosing a Major: Is Psychology for You?

Chapter Guide

If you're like most students, one of the most difficult decisions that you face is choosing a college major. How do you decide what to do with your life? Deciding on a major can be tough if you believe that your undergraduate major determines your career; fortunately, this isn't true. Choosing a major is not the same as choosing a lifelong career, yet this myth persists. For example, many people assume that students who major in the arts, humanities, or social sciences (e.g., psychology) either are not qualified for any type of job or are qualified only for careers in those specific areas. Actually, students who earn undergraduate degrees in sociology, history, psychology, and similar majors find jobs in business, research, human resources, teaching, the military, and a variety of other occupations. (See Chapter 7 for more information about careers with a bachelor's degree in psychology.) Your major will not limit you to only one career choice.

Within 10 years after graduation, most people are working in careers that are not directly connected to their undergraduate majors. In addition, new types of jobs are emerging each year, and most of us have no way of knowing what these jobs will be or what type of education will be needed in order to qualify for them. For example, 15 years ago, most people had never heard of a web designer (someone who creates web pages and designs Internet sites). It's likely that other careers will evolve over the coming years. Consequently, career counselors recommend that college students focus on developing general, transferable skills, such as writing, speaking, computer competence, problem solving, and team building, that employers want and that graduates will need in order to adjust to a rapidly changing world. Choose a major that reflects *your* interests and abilities and provides you with opportunities to develop and hone skills that are useful in a variety of careers. The exercises in this chapter will help you to learn more about yourself; assess your interests, skills, and abilities; and determine which major is right for you.

WRITING AND SELF-AWARENESS

The first step in choosing a major is understanding yourself. Reflective and personal writing are important tools to help you understand yourself. Consider keeping a journal, a record of self-reflective writing. Although journal writing often evokes images of an adolescent girl locked away in her bedroom secretively scribbling into a locked volume, "Dear Diary," this picture is far from the truth. A diary is a daily recording of events, but a journal is so much more. A journal is a collection of your creative activity and can take many forms: a notebook, a computer file, a personal digital assistant (PDA) file, or even a web log. It is a place where you can reflect on yourself and on your experiences, goals, dreams, and anxieties. Your journal is a private learning space, a place where you can make discoveries about yourself—and understanding yourself is critical to choosing a major that you'll love.

Why Write?

Believe it or not, I was skeptical about the power of self-reflective writing—until I tried it. Here are some benefits of journal writing, or the reasons for you to consider keeping a journal.

Self-Exploration Journal writing offers a chance to explore your own thoughts. Sometimes we're not aware of our true thoughts and feelings until we capture them with the written word. Writing is a way of learning about yourself and the world around you. It forces you to focus your thoughts, providing an opportunity to identify your opinions and values. It also helps you to clarify your sense of identity and learn about yourself.

Therapy After a long day or a difficult experience, your journal provides a place for reflection. It's a private opportunity to let out feelings of frustration, anger, or anxiety. Writing about your deepest thoughts and feelings, or even about everyday mundane matters, can help you to release pent-up stress, which is vital for your emotional and physical health. What's even better is that a journal will never say, "I told you so." Don't censor yourself in your journal; just get it all out onto the written page and you'll feel better. You'll find that you will be better able to concentrate after you've cleared your head by journal writing.

Get Organized Writing is an organizational tool. A journal can be a place to gather your thoughts, brainstorm ideas, and plan. Don't set any expectations for your journal. It doesn't have to be filled with descriptions of monumental experiences. Journal entries don't have to be well written or scholarly. Don't let these myths rob you of the chance to benefit from journal writing. Perhaps the easiest way to begin keeping a journal is to use it as a place to record lists of immediate tasks to be accomplished as well as long-term plans. In this way, a journal can help to organize your daily life. With regular use, writing will become a habit and expand beyond everyday topics to include self-reflection, planning, and goal setting. You can write about your goals and document the steps needed to achieve them, as well as about your progress.

Solve Problems Writing is an effective tool for problem solving because writing is thinking. The next time you find yourself confronted with a problem or a big decision, try writing about it. Explain the problem in words: What do you know about it? Discuss your feelings about the problem and analyze it. You may find that your writing leads you to brainstorm potential solutions. Then your writing might shift toward analyzing each solution. Expressing ideas in written form requires a different thought process than does thinking. We think in new ways when we write. This allows us to conceptualize problems differently and find solutions more quickly.

Enhance Communication The more often you write, the more your writing will improve. Journal writing strengthens communication skills, both oral and written. It provides practice in identifying and expressing ideas, which is one of your major goals as a college student.

Unleash Your Creativity Writing offers a creative outlet, a place to generate stories, essays, and poetry. If you're having a tough time thinking up ideas for class papers or essays, your journal is the place to turn. Through writing we become more creative. There are a variety of techniques and exercises that can help you to find your center of creativity and inspire new ways of thinking and expressing yourself. Check out the exercises in this chapter and throughout this book. Also, take note of the web resources at the end of this chapter for places where you can learn how to record your ideas.

Record Your Experience A journal provides a record of your life. Days, weeks, and months pass all too quickly. Memory is fallible. A journal helps you to remember events, experiences, feelings, and intentions. It offers a place to record accomplishments, hopes, and dreams as well as to retain details that you would probably otherwise forget. From a therapeutic perspective, looking back over old journals allows an opportunity to reflect on patterns of experience, interaction, and emotion, providing insight into yourself and your perspective on life. How have you changed and grown? Review your journal for insights into yourself.

Starting a Journal

"OK, you've convinced me. How do I start?"

First, find a place to record your thoughts. Your journal can take many forms. Some students prefer to keep their journals as word processing files on a computer. Others write in bound composition books or simply keep folders of journal entries. You can keep your journal on your PDA or perhaps even create a web log or an online journal using web log software like that found on livejournal.com (http://www.livejournal.com), typepad.org (http://www.typepad.org), blogger.com (http://www.blogger.com), or a similar site. The cardinal rule of journal writing is to remember that your journal is for you. Don't let spelling, handwriting, and grammar be major concerns. Put your feelings and experiences down in writing any way that you can. No one else will review or grade it.

What Should You Write About?

There are no rules when it comes to journals. You can write about anything that comes to mind, such as poetry, story ideas, and reflections, as well as more everyday items such as lists of accomplishments and tasks to be completed. Even everyday frustrations can be topics for your writing. Take time to observe your life. If you're having difficulty, try writing about the trouble you're experiencing in starting a journal. Write down your thoughts as they come, even if you're writing that you don't know what to write. Try describing events that are happening to you or around you from a third-person perspective. For example, begin writing with the phrase, "It was a time when . . . ," and then describe the event in detail using as many of your senses as possible. What sounds, smells, sights, and feelings were present? Pretend that you're an outside observer and use pronouns such as *he* and *she*. This exercise can help you to put things into perspective; it is especially effective when writing about life changes (like the transition to college), relationships (like that argument with your boyfriend or girlfriend), and events that you have found upsetting (like finding out that you didn't do so well on that test). Throughout this book, you'll find plenty of topics and ideas to write about in your journal, which will help you learn more about yourself and make plans for your future.

When Should You Write?

The goal of keeping a journal is to catch your thoughts. The more often you write in your journal, the more you'll learn about yourself. Take your journal with you. If you have 15 minutes between classes, write in your journal. You might even write about what you've learned in your prior class and how it relates to your experience. Try writing at bedtime or right after waking up. It doesn't take much time. You'll be surprised at how much you can write in just a few minutes. The key is to avoid censoring yourself. Allow yourself to be thoughtful and write what's on your mind. Explore your thoughts about a specific topic or about life in general. Try to get into the habit of writing each day, even if it is just a short entry. Also, try to write some longer entries because they will give you an opportunity to develop your thoughts and discover insights about yourself.

Give journal writing a shot in whatever format works for you—whether it is a handwritten page, a computer file, a PDA file, or a web log. Writing will help you to explore who you are and who you hope to become. In your journal, the mundane can become profound. Take a chance and explore yourself through writing.

SELF-ASSESSMENT

Understanding yourself is critical to choosing a major that intrigues you. Journal writing is an important start, but selecting a major requires a more thorough self-assessment. It sounds technical, but self-assessment is the process by which you examine your skills, abilities, motivations, interests, values, experience, and accomplishments. In other words, it's how you learn about yourself. Through self-assessment you can build a firm foundation of knowledge about yourself and then use this knowledge to make sound decisions about your major. The exercises in this chapter will help you to better understand yourself, but remember that self-awareness will not be achieved instantaneously. It takes hard work, soul-searching, and time.

Assess Your Personality and Attitudinal Traits

Who are you? What personality characteristics best describe you? Understanding your unique personality will help you to choose a major that is right for you. After you graduate, knowledge about your personality traits will help you to find a position or career that meshes with these characteristics and is rewarding and fulfilling. Exercise 2.1 will help you obtain a better understanding of your personality, which is essential in choosing a major that you'll be happy with. Consider writing in your journal about what you learn about yourself after completing Exercise 2.1.

Exercise 2.1
Assessing Your Personality Traits

Check off the traits that describe you, including additional traits if needed. Take your time to think about each one and be honest with yourself. Then complete the questions below.

❑ Academic
❑ Active
❑ Accurate
❑ Adaptable
❑ Adept
❑ Adventurous
❑ Affectionate
❑ Aggressive
❑ Alert
❑ Ambitious
❑ Analytical
❑ Appreciative
❑ Articulate
❑ Artistic
❑ Assertive
❑ Astute
❑ Athletic
❑ Attentive
❑ Balanced
❑ Brave
❑ Broad-minded
❑ Businesslike
❑ Calm
❑ Candid
❑ Capable
❑ Caring
❑ Cautious
❑ Charitable
❑ Cheerful
❑ Clean
❑ Clear
❑ Competent
❑ Competitive
❑ Congenial
❑ Conscientious
❑ Conservative
❑ Considerate
❑ Consistent
❑ Conventional
❑ Cooperative
❑ Courageous
❑ Creative
❑ Critical
❑ Curious
❑ Daring
❑ Decisive
❑ Deliberate
❑ Delicate
❑ Democratic
❑ Dependable
❑ Detail-oriented
❑ Diligent
❑ Discreet
❑ Distinctive
❑ Dominant
❑ Dynamic
❑ Eager
❑ Easygoing
❑ Effective
❑ Efficient

❑ Eloquent
❑ Emotional
❑ Empathetic
❑ Extroverted
❑ Farsighted
❑ Feeling
❑ Firm
❑ Flexible
❑ Forceful
❑ Formal
❑ Frank
❑ Frugal
❑ Future-oriented
❑ Generous
❑ Gentle
❑ Good-natured
❑ Gregarious
❑ Hardy
❑ Helpful
❑ Honest
❑ Hopeful
❑ Humorous
❑ Idealistic
❑ Imaginative
❑ Impersonal
❑ Independent
❑ Individualistic
❑ Industrious
❑ Informal
❑ Initiator
❑ Innovative
❑ Intellectual
❑ Intelligent
❑ Introverted
❑ Intuitive
❑ Inventive
❑ Jovial
❑ Judicious
❑ Just
❑ Kind
❑ Liberal
❑ Likable
❑ Literary
❑ Logical
❑ Loyal
❑ Mature
❑ Methodical
❑ Meticulous
❑ Mistrustful
❑ Modest
❑ Motivated
❑ Nurturant
❑ Objective
❑ Observant
❑ Open-minded
❑ Opportunistic
❑ Optimistic
❑ Orderly
❑ Organized
❑ Original
❑ Outgoing
❑ Patient
❑ Peaceable
❑ Perceptive
❑ Persistent
❑ Practical
❑ Productive
❑ Progressive
❑ Protective
❑ Prudent
❑ Punctual
❑ Quick
❑ Quiet
❑ Rational
❑ Realistic
❑ Receptive
❑ Reflective
❑ Relaxed
❑ Reliable
❑ Reserved
❑ Resourceful
❑ Responsible
❑ Responsible
❑ Risk-taker
❑ Sedentary
❑ Self-confidentl
❑ Self-controlled
❑ Self-disciplined
❑ Self-starter
❑ Sensible
❑ Sensitive
❑ Serious
❑ Sincere
❑ Sociable
❑ Sophisticated
❑ Stable
❑ Strong
❑ Strong-minded
❑ Structured
❑ Subjective
❑ Successful
❑ Tactful
❑ Talented
❑ Tenacious
❑ Thorough
❑ Thoughtful
❑ Tolerant
❑ Trusting
❑ Trustworthy
❑ Truthful
❑ Understanding
❑ Unexcitable
❑ Uninhibited
❑ Uninhibited
❑ Uninhibited
❑ Vigorous
❑ Warml
❑ Wholesomel
❑ Wise

Examine the list of personality descriptors that you have checked off. Carefully consider each one. How well does each adjective describe you? Choose the three that are the most important.

1. Why do these words describe you? Provide examples from your experience that illustrate how each word describes you.
2. Clear your mind and think back to when you were a child. Do you remember talking to friends and family about what you wanted to be when you grew up? Write about your memories. Consider the careers listed above. Why did you select those occupations? How have your views changed, if at all?
3. Compare your personality traits as described in question 1 with your views about occupations as a child and your views now. In what ways are your personality characteristics similar to those needed for the occupations that you find interesting?

A more precise way to use what you know about yourself to choose a major is to identify your Holland personality style. Your personality determines the work environment that you'll find most appealing. Holland (1959) proposed that people's personalities and the matching work environments can be loosely categorized into six groups. Which of the following personality types best describes you? You may find that your personality is a combination of several types.

Realistic Someone with a realistic personality type is athletically or mechanically inclined. He or she would probably prefer to work outdoors with tools, plants, or animals. Some of the traits that describe the realistic personality type include practical, candid, a nature lover, calm, reserved, restrained, independent, systematic, and persistent.

Investigative The investigative type enjoys learning, observing, problem solving, and analyzing information. Traits that describe the investigative type include curious, logical, observant, precise, intellectual, cautious, introspective, reserved, unbiased, and independent.

Artistic Imaginative and creative, the artistic personality type likes to work in unstructured situations that allow for creativity and innovation. Personality characteristics of the artistic type include intuitive, unconventional, moody, nonconforming, expressive, unique, pensive, spontaneous, compassionate, bold, direct, and idealistic.

Social The social personality type enjoys helping and training others. Characteristics that describe the social type include friendly, cooperative, idealistic, perceptive, outgoing, understanding, supportive, generous, dependable, forgiving, patient, compassionate, and eloquent.

Enterprising The enterprising personality type likes to work with people in persuasive, performance, or managerial situations to achieve goals that are organizational or economic in nature. Characteristics that describe the enterprising type include confident, assertive, determined, talkative, extroverted, energetic, animated, social, persuasive, fashionable, spontaneous, daring, accommodating, and optimistic.

Conventional The conventional personality type is well organized, has clerical or numerical ability, and likes to work with data and carry out tasks in detail. The conventional type can be described as meticulous, numerically inclined, conscientious, precise, adept, conforming, orderly, practical, frugal, structured, courteous, acquiescent, and persistent.

After reading these descriptions, you will probably have a good idea of where your interests lie. Most people find that one or two of the personality types fit them well. For a more precise assessment, consider taking the Self-Directed Search (Holland, 1994). The Self-Directed Search is a self-report questionnaire that assesses your personality type according to Holland's theory. Check with the career development office at your university to learn more about it; there's even an online version, which you can take for a fee at http://www.self-directed-search.com. Understanding your personality type may make it easier to choose a major because some majors are better suited to particular personalities than are others. Table 2.1 lists college majors organized by Holland personality type. Remember that this is just a guide to careers. Not all possible careers are listed, and the categories are much more fluid than they appear.

TABLE 2.1 **HOLLAND PERSONALITY TYPES AND COLLEGE MAJORS**

Realistic	Investigative	Artistic
Aerospace Engineering	Animal Science	Advertising
Agriculture/Forestry	Anthropology	Art History
Animal Science	Astronomy	Art Education
Architecture	Biochemistry	Architecture
Biosystems Engineering	Biological Sciences	Classics
Civil Engineering	Chemistry	Communications
Criminal Justice	Computer Science	English
Electrical Engineering	Engineering	Foreign Language
Engineering	Forestry	Graphic Design
Environmental Studies	Geography	History

(continued)

TABLE 2.1 **Holland Personality Types and College Majors (Continued)**

Realistic	Investigative	Artistic
Exercise Science	Geology	Interior Design
Geology	Mathematics	Journalism
Health and Physical Education	Medical Technology	Music
Industrial Engineering	Medicine	Music Education
Mechanical Engineering	Nursing	Speech/Drama
Medical Technology	Nutrition	
Nuclear Engineering	Pharmacy	
Plant and Soil Sciences	Philosophy	
Radiological Technology	Physical Therapy	
Recreation and Tourism Management	Physics	
Sports Management	Psychology	
	Sociology	
	Statistics	

Social	Enterprising	Conventional
Audiology	Advertising	Accounting
Counseling	Agricultural Economics	Business
Criminal Justice	Broadcasting	Computer Science
Elementary Education	Communications	Economics
History	Economics	Finance
Human Development	Finance	Mathematics
Human Services	Industrial Relations	Statistics
Library Sciences	Insurance	
Occupational therapy	Journalism	
Nursing	Law	
Nutrition	Management	
Philosophy	Marketing	
Political Science	Political Science	
Recreation and Physical Education	Public Administration	
Psychology	Speech	
Religious Studies		
Sociology		
Social Work		
Special Education		
Urban planning		

Adapted from Lock, 1988; University of Tennessee, n.d.

Assess Your Skills and Abilities

In addition to understanding your personality, your choice of major should reflect your skills and abilities. What are your skills? What activities do you do best? If you're unsure, try writing an experiential diary to get a better grip on your abilities. An experiential diary lists all the jobs, leadership positions, and extracurricular activities that you've engaged in and then lists all the tasks constituting each of these activities and jobs (DeGalan & Lambert, 1995). Once you've created this master list, write down all the skills required to perform the tasks on your list. For example, if your task was answering the phone, it probably entailed the following skills: communication skills (the effective use of language), problem solving, and the ability to direct inquiries. Also, identify specific skills that you've learned, such as the ability to use a computer programming language or speak a foreign language. Even with an experiential diary, it is sometimes difficult to list and remember all your skills and abilities. Exercise 2.2 will help you to better understand your capabilities.

EXERCISE 2.2

Assess Your Skills

Check off all the skills that apply to you; then complete the activity that follows.

- ❑ Acting or performing
- ❑ Administering
- ❑ Advising
- ❑ Analyzing Data
- ❑ Applying
- ❑ Arranging social functions
- ❑ Budgeting
- ❑ Calculating
- ❑ Checking for accuracy
- ❑ Coaching
- ❑ Collecting money
- ❑ Communicating
- ❑ Compiling statistics
- ❑ Conceptualizing
- ❑ Controlling
- ❑ Coordinating events
- ❑ Counseling
- ❑ Creating new ideas
- ❑ Decision-making
- ❑ Designing
- ❑ Dispensing information
- ❑ Dramatizing ideas or problems
- ❑ Editing
- ❑ Entertaining people
- ❑ Evaluating
- ❑ Expressing feelings
- ❑ Finding information
- ❑ Fund-raising
- ❑ Generalizing
- ❑ Goal setting
- ❑ Handling complaints
- ❑ Identifying problems
- ❑ Illustrating
- ❑ Implementing
- ❑ Improving
- ❑ Initiating with strangers
- ❑ Innovating
- ❑ Interpreting
- ❑ Interviewing
- ❑ Investigating problems
- ❑ Judging
- ❑ Leading

- ❑ Listening to others
- ❑ Managing
- ❑ Measuring
- ❑ Mediating
- ❑ Motivating
- ❑ Navigating
- ❑ Negotiating
- ❑ Observing
- ❑ Organizing
- ❑ Painting
- ❑ Persuading
- ❑ Photography
- ❑ Planning
- ❑ Problem Solving
- ❑ Programming
- ❑ Promoting
- ❑ Proofreading
- ❑ Questioning
- ❑ Reading
- ❑ Reasoning
- ❑ Recording
- ❑ Record keeping
- ❑ Recruiting
- ❑ Researching
- ❑ Scheduling
- ❑ Selling
- ❑ Singing
- ❑ Sketching
- ❑ Speaking
- ❑ Supervising
- ❑ Synthesizing information
- ❑ Teaching or training
- ❑ Team building
- ❑ Thinking logically
- ❑ Tolerating ambiguity
- ❑ Translating
- ❑ Troubleshooting
- ❑ Visualizing
- ❑ Writing

1. Look back over the skills that you have checked. Can you think of examples of how each skill has developed or how you've used it to achieve a goal? Based on these considerations, choose the top three to five skills and explain your choices. These skills are your strengths.
2. Now look at all the skills that you have checked, including those you didn't choose as your final set as well as those that you would have chosen but for which you couldn't think of supporting examples. Do any of these skills need further development? Which of these skills do you prefer using? Why? Which skills are you interested in using in the future? Why? Which skills do you dislike? Why?
3. Are there any skills that you don't currently have but would like to develop? Explain.

Assess Your Interests

What interests you? The happiest and most successful students choose majors that they find engaging. Many students decide on a major before considering their interests and values. They take courses for a semester or two and then realize that they've chosen a major in which they have minimal interest. Identifying your interests early in your college career can save you from changing majors and wasting time. What appeals to you?

An effective way of assessing your interests is to write about your personal history. In your journal, on scrap paper, or on a word processor, write about all the times you can think of when you have encountered a problem (regardless of its size) and taken action to solve that problem. In other words, write about all your accomplishments. List as many as you can. Don't stop when it becomes difficult, but probe further. If you're stumped, try freewriting about your achievements (yes, another use for your journal). Freewriting entails writing whatever comes to mind without censoring or editing it. Keep the ideas flowing or even write about the difficulty you're experiencing in coming up with ideas. Eventually you'll produce a number of interesting items to reflect on. Remember, the accomplishments that you list don't have to be enormous. Accomplishments can be small, and they don't have to be recognized by other people. Write about the achievements that are personally relevant to you and that you are proud of.

Next examine your accomplishments carefully. Which have brought you the most satisfaction? Which do you value the most highly? Why? This exercise helps you to identify your strengths and is a fantastic self-esteem builder. By understanding which achievements you cherish, you'll have a better idea of your interests and values, which is essential in choosing a major or career.

Values

Although choosing a major does not tie you to a particular career, it is useful to consider what career you aspire to in order to select a major and seek the educational experiences that will prepare you for it. What do you want out of life? How do you define success? Would you rather live in a city or in a rural area? Is personal time and flexibility important to you? Would you like a family (and if so, large or small)? Is financial success important? Values concern the things that are important to you, that you see as desirable in life. Spend time thinking through your priorities. Journal writing can help you to understand and clarify your values.

Putting It All Together

Now that you're aware of your personality traits, skills, interests, and values, put them all together to get a comprehensive view of yourself. Look through the lists and descriptions of majors in your college handbook. Do any seem to fit your set of traits, skills, and interests? Some majors and careers will require many of the personal traits and skills that you possess, and others will not match your self-description (DeGalan & Lambert, 1995). In your journal, list all the majors that sound interesting and seem to fit. Examine the courses required for each. Study your college handbook and the department web site to find information about the programs and opportunities for majors after graduation.

Speak with recent graduates to learn about their majors and their career experiences. If you don't know any recent graduates, visit your school's career center. Most college career centers maintain databases of recent graduates; you can contact a few graduates with different majors to learn more about their work. Also, visit the career center to seek advice. Tell the career counselor what you've learned about yourself by completing the worksheets in this chapter, and he or she can help you narrow your choice of majors.

Don't forget to talk with professors to learn more about potential majors. Visit the office of a professor whose class you enjoy to learn more about his or her work and about the field in general. Ask questions about the undergraduate major and what kinds of jobs recent graduates have obtained. Checklist 2.1 will help you to keep track of all these tasks.

CHECKLIST 2.1

Steps in Choosing a Major

- ❑ Assess your personality and attitudinal traits
- ❑ Assess your skills and abilities
- ❑ Assess your values and life goals
- ❑ Research majors
- ❑ Explore courses
- ❑ Talk with other students and recent graduates
- ❑ Visit the career center
- ❑ Talk with professors
- ❑ Compare alternatives
- ❑ Reflect on your choice
- ❑ Remember that your major is not your career

Once you have narrowed down your choice of majors to two (or even three), compare them with regard to the following:

Your level of interest
The curriculum (What kinds of classes are you required to take?)
Your skills and abilities (Is the major too easy or too challenging for you?)
Professors (How many are there? What do they study? What are they like?)
Your motivation to study the subject.
The kinds of jobs that graduates hold (Is it likely that the major will prepare you for the kind of career you desire?)

In short, consider the pros and cons of each major.

Finally, once you have chosen a possible major, again reflect on your choice. Freewrite about the following questions to be sure that you've made the choice that is right for you.

- Do I enjoy this subject?
- Can I perform well in this subject?

- Do I tend to seek out other students and faculty in this department for discussions and other informal interactions?
- How will this major prepare me for graduate study or employment?

Deciding on Psychology

Is psychology right for you? Only you can answer this question. Psychology offers many opportunities. As a psychology major, you will develop and expand your knowledge of human behavior. You'll become increasingly able to discriminate relevant from trivial information. You'll learn how to find and pull together (or *synthesize,* in "professor-speak") information from a variety of sources. You'll learn about psychological theories, concepts, and terms that will help you to understand and influence the world around you. If you study and take college seriously, you'll develop advanced critical thinking, communication, and interpersonal skills, which are valuable in all careers regardless of whether they are directly related to psychology.

What does majoring in psychology entail? Table 2.2 presents courses that you can expect to take as a psychology major. Some psychology courses are required for majors at nearly all schools, whereas others are electives found at a handful of schools. Of course, the exact titles of courses, requirements, and prerequisites can vary by institution. Chapter 7 provides more information about

TABLE 2.2 Common Psychology Courses

Abnormal Psychology	Educational Psychology	Psychology and Law
Adolescent Psychology	Experimental Psychology	Psychology of Adjustment
Adulthood and Aging	Family Psychology	Psychology of Creativity
Applied Psychology	Group Dynamics	Psychology of Gender
Behavior Modification	Health Psychology	Psychology of Learning
Careers in Psychology	History of Psychology	Psychology of Motivation
Child Psychology	Industrial Psychology	Psychology of Personality
Clinical Psychology	Introductory Psychology	Psychology of Women
Cognitive Psychology	Life-Span Development	Psychopharmacology
Cognitive Neuroscience	Organizational Psychology	Sensation and Perception
Consumer Psychology	Physiological Psychology	Social Psychology
Cross-Cultural Psychology	Psychological Statistics	Sports Psychology
Developmental Psychopathology	Psychological and Educational Testing	Research Methods

the skills and abilities that you'll develop as a psychology major, as well as employment opportunities for graduates with baccalaureate degrees in psychology.

Remember that this is your decision. In choosing your major, you are the only expert. No one else can do it for you, and no test provides all the answers. Although parents, friends, professors, and counselors might offer assistance and advice, ultimately this is your decision. Your major will not lock you into one career path—there are many roads, and a psychology major can be the first step toward a variety of careers.

SUGGESTED READINGS

Andrews, L. L. (1998). *How to choose a college major*. Chicago: NTC Publishing Group.

Johnston, S. M. (1998). *The career adventure: Your guide to personal assessment, career exploration, and decision making*. Upper Saddle River, NJ: Prentice Hall.

Kuther, T. L., & Morgan, R. D. (2004). *Careers in psychology: Opportunities in a changing world*. Belmont, CA: Wadsworth.

Reeves, D. L., & Bradbury, M. J. (1998). *Majors exploration: A search and find guide for college and career direction*. Upper Saddle River, NJ: Prentice Hall.

Lock, R. D. (2005). *Taking charge of your career direction—Career planning guide*, Book 1. Belmont, CA: Wadsworth.

WEB RESOURCES

The following web sites are hot-linked at *The Psychology Major's Handbook* web site at *http://info.wadsworth.com/kuther*

Career Assessment

http://www.quintcareers.com/career_assessment.html

This is an excellent and comprehensive site with articles, tools, and other resources for assessing your career interests.

Self-Directed Search

http://www.self-directed-search.com

Available for a fee, this self-report questionnaire assesses your personality type according to Holland's theory.

About Web Logs

http://weblogs.about.com/

As we discussed, your journal can take the form of a web log. This web site provides articles, tips, prompts, and resources for beginning and experienced web log writers.

Writing the Journey

http://www.writingthejourney.com/

Get the most out of your journal with these free articles designed to be a complete journal-writing workshop.

Career Key

http://www.careerkey.org/english/

The Career Key is a free web site with assessments to help you with career choices, career changes, career planning, job searches, and choosing a college major or training program.

JOURNAL EXERCISES

My Questions

This exercise helps you to identify unanswered questions and gives you prompts for future journal entries. Use your journal to formulate and record questions that you wonder about. What questions do you have about your schoolwork, personal life, and values, or about current events and items you've read about in newspapers, magazines, or books? As a college student, what do you need to know? Don't worry about the answers yet; just let your questions flow. Later on, weeks, months, or even years from now, when you're looking for something new to write about, look over your list. If any of the questions strike you as compelling, begin formulating answers in your journal.

Journal Reflection

Once you've amassed several weeks' or months' worth of journal entries, you might use your journal to reflect on how you're changing. Read over earlier journal entries. How have you changed? Do you have different ideas about a particular journal entry? Do you have new interpretations of events? Do you disagree with an earlier entry? Try to track how you think and how your thinking is changing. Can you draw conclusions about yourself from what you've written?

Life's Pleasures

What makes you happy? Record your favorite things and activities. What are you grateful for? This isn't just a corny exercise. Writing about the good things in your life is a form of celebration that makes you a happier person. Stop and feel the moment. Find something beautiful in your immediate surroundings.

Record all your senses. What does it look like? Listen to it. Can you smell it? What does it feel like?

Why College?

Why did you decide to attend college? What did you hope to gain? What have you learned since beginning college? Do you still have the same reasons for attending?

CHAPTER 3

Take an Active Role in Your Education

Chapter Guide

One of the biggest differences between high school and college is that college requires you to take an active role in your education. Whether you take anything of substance away from your college years—whether you learn anything—is up to you. Your own interest, motivation, and hard work will make or break your college years. Students are often surprised by this new level of autonomy, and they are often unsure of how to take control of their education. This chapter will help you to take advantage of the resources at your school so that you can get the most from your college years.

Consider Your Goal: What Are You *Really* Learning in College?

Taking an active role in your education involves mindfulness, being aware of the purpose of a college education and what you hope to gain during these years. Savvy students recognize that they are in college to learn two discrete sets of curricula: overt and covert (Appleby, 2001). The overt, observable curriculum refers to the one described in the course catalog and includes specific facts, concepts, and theories that college courses are designed to impart. However, in college, you learn more than the content of your major; college also entails a covert curriculum of which students often aren't aware. The covert curriculum refers to the broad sets of information acquisition and management skills and competencies that you will develop during your college years (Appleby, 2001). A college education consists of much more than facts and theories; you'll learn how to acquire information and how to learn. The thinking and information management skills you develop in college are more important than the content per se. In other words, college is all about learning how to think and problem-solve. Part of playing an active role in your education is being aware of the covert curriculum and how it will help you to develop lifelong learning skills such as the following competencies.

Communication Skills

Your college courses provide many opportunities to develop and strengthen your oral and written communication skills. The ability to communicate in a clear, organized, persuasive way is a skill that is useful in all careers and can be applied throughout life. Take advantage of courses to promote your oral and written communication skills such as English composition, public speaking, and writing-intensive courses. Don't just take writing and communications courses because they're requirements; don't take them to "get them out of the way." Instead, try to view English and other communications courses as important learning opportunities and seek additional experiences that will help you to polish your communication skills. Take extra courses in writing or public speaking because no matter your career and throughout your life, you will need to be able to make yourself understood in a clear, persuasive way. Remember that each course you take contributes something unique to your education; no course is "a waste" or just something to "get through."

Reading Skills

The ability to read with comprehension—to thoroughly understand what you've read—and to identify the major points of a body of work is a valuable skill that is useful regardless of what you choose to do after completing your undergraduate degree. For example, people employed in business, management, and advertising positions must keep abreast of the literature in their fields by reading books, magazines, and trade publications to help them perform their jobs more efficiently. The ability to read complex material quickly, understand it, extract the relevant material, and use the information to solve problems are skills that we hone in college (Appleby, 2001). In addition, savvy students quickly recognize that they must adapt their reading to the content at hand; for example, they approach scientific reading differently than fiction. Students who recognize the covert curriculum—the lifelong skills they will develop in college—read assignments to learn and sharpen their reading comprehension skills as well as to adapt their reading styles to the material being read.

Listening and Note-Taking Skills

Successful employees and graduate students have the ability to listen carefully and attentively and to understand and follow instructions. Lectures and class discussions offer valuable opportunities to develop active listening skills. Did you know that the abilities to take accurate notes and to identify the important points that emerge from a discussion are just as important to success after graduation as they are in college? The abilities to listen to others, recognize their arguments, summarize and organize large amounts of complex information, and write concise notes that you'll understand later are all vital skills that will serve you well throughout your career. Therefore, sitting in class offers learning opportunities that stretch beyond the content of the course.

Memory, Critical Thinking, and Problem-Solving Skills

Perhaps the most important skill that you will learn in college is how to think. Certainly, our heads aren't empty before we attend college—we *can* think, but our thinking can improve radically over the college years. It is during the college years that most students learn to think critically and analyze complex problems. As a psychology student, you have an advantage over other students because you've learned how the mind works. Apply that knowledge to improve your own problem-solving skills. For example, consider memory, the ability to select, store, and use information; it's vital throughout our lives. In your psychology classes you've learned about how our minds encode and retrieve information, as well as about factors that influence these processes. Sometimes students fail to make the connection that this material can be applied to improve their lives. Take an active role in your education by applying your knowledge about human cognition to improve your memory and thinking skills. Not only will your performance on tests improve, but you'll retain the material over a longer period of time, allowing you to apply what you've learned in class to real-world situations.

Successfully applying your content knowledge to solve problems requires critical thinking and analysis skills. The liberal arts and science background composing the psychology major provides many opportunities to develop and hone your critical thinking skills. Critical thinking refers to the ability to comprehend and analyze information to solve problems. It requires breaking complex problems or sources of information into smaller and more manageable units; understanding how these units fit together to form a larger whole; locating, gathering, and synthesizing information from a variety of sources; evaluating ideas and methods; and applying conclusions to solve problems. These thinking skills are critical to success no matter what your career.

Organizational and Time Management Skills

The demanding work environments of today require solid organizational skills. Your undergraduate years are an opportune time to develop and hone these skills. Learn how to set up a work space that is efficient for you, a place where you can think without distractions. Set up a system to organize your class materials. You might organize your notes and readings into binders with dividers and set up a filing cabinet to store old papers and the articles and references used to write them. Start small and become comfortable with your system, and you'll find that organization comes easily. Another important organizational skill that many students need help with is time management. We live in a fast-paced world where being able to manage your time is essential. Begin now. Learn how to maintain a date book and keep track of your classes and projects. Although your professor might accept late work and tardiness, your employer (or graduate advisor) certainly won't. See Chapter 4 for tips on organization and time management.

Self-Management Skills

During the college years we undergo dramatic changes in our abilities to understand and manage our emotions as well as to regulate our behavior. College is often the first time that we are truly independent and responsible for our own behavior. At first it is very difficult. You might find yourself late for class, forgetting about important assignments, or neglecting to do your laundry. With time, you'll become more independent and responsible for your actions and well-being. Part of the unwritten curriculum of college is learning to become more punctual, reliable, mature, and respectful—skills critical to a happy, healthy, productive adulthood.

Stress is probably a big part of your life as a college student. Learn how to deal with it now because all adults experience stress throughout their lives, in the workplace, at home, and in other settings. Take advantage of the resources on campus to learn how to manage stress. Similarly, obtain practice managing conflict now, because when you're an employee, you'll be exposed to stressful conditions and conflict and will have to learn how to work with difficult people. Take advantage of formal and informal opportunities to learn stress management and conflict resolution skills. Attend stress management seminars sponsored by the counseling center. Apply what you've learned from health or social psychology about stress and conflict to help you deal with your roommate. Remember that the content of psychology extends beyond the classroom; try to apply what you've learned to take an active role in shaping your environment and regulating your emotions. For example, we know that how we interpret situations determines how we respond to them. This is a basic psychological principle that is often difficult to practice and take to heart. Use this time in your life to learn how to interpret situations and stimuli in ways that will allow you to respond appropriately.

Technology Skills

Technology is a vital part of nearly every workplace. In college, you have a variety of opportunities to learn how to use computers to work with information. For example, you'll learn how to use databases and the Internet to find information and to use spreadsheets, statistical software, and databases to manage and analyze information. Learn how to utilize technology; you cannot avoid it, and your knowledge of technology will make you more employable and more efficient in the workplace.

As you can see, the college years entail more than learning facts and theories. The first step in taking an active role in your education is recognizing the covert, unwritten curriculum. Take note of the skill sets used to complete your class work, and you'll understand that writing a paper involves more than gathering facts; it's an opportunity to hone your skills and add to your body of knowledge. Become engaged in your education, and you'll develop thinking, analysis, and self-management abilities that will last a lifetime. Another important step in taking an active role in managing your education is getting to know faculty and developing professional relationships with them.

Develop Professional Relationships With Faculty

Many students don't take advantage of their school's most valuable resource: the faculty. Sure, they attend class, take notes, and learn the content of their discipline, but learning occurs in many places beyond the classroom. When students take an active role in their education, they soon realize that there is much to learn from professors, learning that can extend beyond mere content knowledge. Perhaps one of the most important pieces of advice offered in this book is to get to know your professors. Establish relationships with faculty.

Why?

Faculty help your professional development in more ways than by merely bestowing grades. Professors can also help you to enrich your college years through a variety of learning experiences within and outside the classroom. For example, professors can involve students in research activities—opportunities to assist in the generation of new knowledge. Faculty may play an important role in professional development by introducing students to others who can help them to meet their goals (e.g., a professor in a graduate department to which you might apply). Professors can also help students obtain special opportunities such as internships, summer positions, and teaching assistantships. They can also provide advice and emotional support. Finally, job and graduate applications often require several letters of recommendation from faculty. Recommendation letters discuss more than just grades; they discuss students' abilities and aptitudes from academic, motivational, and personal perspectives. Of course, obtaining persuasive recommendation letters should not be your only reason for developing relationships with faculty members.

Generally, professors want to work with students who are bright, motivated, committed, and enthusiastic. Your behavior both in and out of class can attract a professor toward developing a professional relationship with you or deter one from doing so. Do you display behaviors that faculty appreciate? Take Quiz 3.1 to assess your savviness about appropriate in-class and out-of-class behavior. Also, examine Checklist 3.1 for a list of behaviors that professors clearly do not want to see in class. Some of these items may appear humorous, but (believe it or not) they are regularly seen in class.

Quiz 3.1
Do You Display Appropriate In- and Out-of-Class Behavior?

Circle yes or no for each of the following items. Be honest!

1. Yes No I attend presentations and programs sponsored by the department.
2. Yes No During class, I often send e-mail with my cell phone or personal digital assistant (PDA).

3. Yes No I smile and say hello when I see a professor.
4. Yes No I take more than one makeup exam.
5. Yes No I stop by during professors' office hours to discuss something from class that sparked an interest or to seek assistance with class material.
6. Yes No I let my cell phone ring during class.
7. Yes No I help other students by sharing lecture notes and forming study groups.
8. Yes No I often leave class early without apparent reason.
9. Yes No I sit toward the front of class.
10. Yes No I often hand in assignments late.
11. Yes No I rarely miss class.
12. Yes No When the professor asks, "Are there any questions?" I often ask, "Is this going to be on the test?"
13. Yes No When my professor gives a particularly interesting lecture, I often offer a compliment and ask additional questions afterward.
14. Yes No After each exam I often nit-pick over answers to test questions, trying to get additional points.
15. Yes No I participate in departmental events, clubs, and activities such as Psi Chi or the psychology club.
16. Yes No I often read other books or newspapers in class.
17. Yes No I prepare before class.
18. Yes No I often leave class at the break.
19. Yes No I try to offer good answers to professors' questions during class discussions.
20. Yes No I turn off my cell phone or turn the sound off and don't answer it in class.
21. Yes No I participate in class but try not to dominate class discussions (i.e., I let others speak too).
22. Yes No I often interrupt my professor's lecture with, "But I thought you said . . ."
23. Yes No I try to show interest in the course and remain attentive during class.
24. Yes No I often arrive late to class.
25. Yes No I try to ask well-reasoned, well-formulated questions during class.
26. Yes No After missing class or arriving late, I often e-mail my professor requesting that he or she e-mail me the lecture or an explanation of what I missed.

Scoring:

Add up the number of times you responded yes to even-numbered items and no to odd-numbered items. The higher your score, the greater number of appropriate behaviors you display and the more likely professors are to view you favorably.

Reflection:

1. Given your score, how favorably are professors likely to view you? Why?
2. How might your in- and out-of-class behavior influence your ability to develop professional relationships with faculty?
3. How can you improve your in- and out-of-class behavior? Discuss at least three ways in which you can improve your behavior.

CHECKLIST 3.1

What Not to Do: Behaviors That Most Faculty Abhor

- ❑ Pass notes in class
- ❑ Chat in class
- ❑ Pack up books and notes before class is over.
- ❑ Ask, "How many cuts are allowed?"
- ❑ Do homework in class.
- ❑ Ask, "I missed last class, did I miss anything important?"
- ❑ Near the end of class, close your books firmly and jingle your car keys to help remind your professor that time is just about up
- ❑ Attempt to make term papers look longer by adding blank pages after the front and back pages and using a large font and huge margins
- ❑ Sit in the back of class when there are empty seats in the front
- ❑ Visit a professor's office for the first time at the end of the semester, after receiving a poor mark, to ask for extra credit
- ❑ Roll your eyes at a professor's lame jokes
- ❑ Be more interested in grades than in learning
- ❑ Sleep in class
- ❑ Sneer when you don't agree
- ❑ Read a book in class
- ❑ Balance your checkbook in class
- ❑ After an hour-long presentation on a topic not included in the required reading, ask, "Is this going to be on the test?"
- ❑ Keep your phone or pager on high volume and let it ring several times during class
- ❑ Leave at a break
- ❑ Repeatedly interrupt your professor with, "But I thought you said . . ."
- ❑ Leave class early without apparent reason
- ❑ Take more than one makeup exam
- ❑ Hand in assignments late without explanation
- ❑ When the professor asks, "Are there any questions?" ask "Is this going to be on the test?"
- ❑ Miss classes repeatedly
- ❑ Arrive late to class repeatedly
- ❑ After coming to class late, ask the professor to go over what you missed
- ❑ Repeatedly dominate office time with personal needs and problems
- ❑ Nit-pick over answers to test questions after each exam
- ❑ During class, send e-mail with your handheld pager or device

Source: Keith-Spiegel & Wiederman, 2000.

Your Academic Advisor

Typically when students select a major, they are assigned an academic advisor. An academic advisor is a faculty member whose role is to help you select courses and other learning opportunities to provide you with a well-rounded education and prepare you for your chosen career. Your advisor may assist you with academic advising, which focuses on issues such as course scheduling and availability, meeting prerequisites, fostering academic success, and graduation requirements. He or she may also assist you with career advising, which emphasizes your short- and long-term career goals and occurs during multiple discussions over your years in college. The advisor-student relationship is a two-way street; you should come prepared to discuss your interests, needs, and goals. Your advisor may have as many as 60 other students to advise, so use your scheduled time with him or her wisely. Help your advisor to help you by following the tips in Checklist 3.2.

CHECKLIST 3.2

Advising Checklist

- ❑ Know who your advisor is:
  Advisor name: ______________________________
  Location: ______________________________
  Phone number: ______________________________
  E-mail: ______________________________
  Office hours: ______________________________
- ❑ Schedule an appointment at least 1 week prior to your registration date.
- ❑ Study the university handbook to determine what courses are required for your major.
- ❑ Write down questions as they arise.
- ❑ List the courses that you have taken. Most departments have a worksheet for majors to complete that lists all general education and major requirements. Complete this sheet and keep an up-to-date copy filed away in some place safe.
- ❑ Examine the registration booklet to choose potential courses.
- ❑ Prepare a tentative schedule with several course alternatives.
- ❑ Be prepared to explain how the courses you have selected fulfill the curricular requirements of your major.
- ❑ Consider your ultimate career goals and write down any questions that you have about your plans for after graduation.
- ❑ Actively discuss your career goals with your advisor and seek advice on how to plan to meet them.

Although your academic advisor may seem busy (and probably is!), he or she has time for you. Consult with your advisor when you are having academic difficulties, as well as when you are considering adding or dropping a course, changing your major, withdrawing from school, or transferring to another college. Schedule an appointment and openly discuss your concerns. Your advisor has your best interests in mind and will provide you with the advice that you need to make sound decisions. When making big decisions such as whether to change your major, drop out of school, or go to graduate school, your advisor may suggest that you seek additional input and feedback from other sources such as other faculty, family, friends, and the counseling center. Your academic advisor is an important source of feedback and advice; take advantage of this important resource. But always remember that your academic and career decisions are your own. Seek advice and assistance in order to make informed decisions but accept ultimate responsibility for the decisions that you make.

The Importance of a Mentor

Seek to develop a special relationship with a faculty mentor. A mentor is a person with expertise who takes a special interest in you; he or she may be a college professor, an advisor, or a job, research, or practicum supervisor. Mentors provide their protégés with opportunities to learn, be advised, and obtain moral support (Keith-Spiegel & Wiederman, 2000). Seek a faculty mentor, and you'll have opportunities for intellectual engagement that will enhance your college career. Note that mentors are more than academic advisors; your academic advisor may or may not also become your mentor. A mentor facilitates your undergraduate accomplishments, provides intellectual and emotional support, and helps you on the path toward your career.

How Do You Find a Mentor? Students who are motivated and visible in their departments and who seek to become involved in faculty research usually find it easier to meet professors who are interested in developing professional working relationships. Seek opportunities and approach professors. This may seem scary and require initiative, but the rewards are immense. Tell professors that you're planning to become involved in research. Explain that you hope to work closely with someone on their research and ask questions about their work. Demonstrate honest intellectual curiosity and motivation. If you are perceived well, word will get around that you're an excellent student looking for research experience (that's why classroom behavior is so important). It can be intimidating to approach a professor, but try bringing in an interesting article or cartoon that relates to course content, ask a question after class, or visit during office hours.

If you do well in your courses and present yourself as competent, motivated, wanting to get involved, and committed, you may even be approached by a faculty member who wants to mentor you. Students with excellent literature-searching, critical analysis, and writing abilities are helpful assistants. Students with expertise and interest in research and statistical analysis are often especially appealing to faculty because they require less instruction—and therefore can become deeply immersed in research at a faster pace.

As you look for a mentor, remember that the most popular professors may have more students coming to them than they can mentor. Working closely with a student in a mentoring relationship requires a great deal of time, attention, and intellectual focus; faculty can mentor only so many students at once. Some faculty may not be able to take on additional students. Remember that popularity, whether a particular professor is liked by the majority of students, should not be your main criterion for selecting a mentor. Consider faculty who are actively involved in research and whose interests parallel yours as much as possible. Visit during office hours to ask a question or two about graduate school or about your career interests; get a feel for the professor's approachability. If he or she seems interested in discussing these questions, express your desire to gain some experience in research. In the vast majority of cases, there is no pay involved for assisting professors with their research. Instead, you'll get a free learning experience that will improve your skills and abilities as well as make you more appealing to graduate schools and employers. Sometimes you can earn course credit for your work. Finally, volunteer to work closely with a professor only if you have the time to commit. Remember that falling behind or dropping out will reflect negatively on you—more so than if you hadn't become involved at all.

What to Look For in a Mentor The role of a mentor is to provide guidance so that students are aware of resources and opportunities and understand their options. Successful mentoring relationships are not an accident. Mentoring relationships are most successful when students make careful and conscientious efforts to find mentors who possess certain characteristics and who complement their needs. A successful mentoring relationship requires chemistry, the ability to work together.

In order to find a helpful mentor, be aware of your needs and career goals. Where are you now in terms of skills? Who do you want to become? How must you grow and what skills and experiences must you obtain to do so? A well-chosen mentor can help you to find the answers to these questions, whereas a poorly chosen mentor might leave you hanging, frustrating you with more questions than answers. Chose a mentor whom you admire, with whom you can communicate, and whose interpersonal skills and interactional patterns work well with your own. Some desirable characteristics to look for in mentors are listed in Checklist 3.3.

CHECKLIST 3.3

Choosing an Effective Mentor

Check off the characteristics that match the attributes of a faculty member from whom you are considering seeking mentorship.

Effective mentors are interpersonally skilled. They are

- ❑ Responsive, warm, and encouraging
- ❑ Empathetic and nonjudgmental
- ❑ Helpful in promoting students' positive self-concepts
- ❑ Promoting and sponsoring in that they help open doors to career and graduate school opportunities by telling others of the positive aspects of protégés
- ❑ A source of emotional support
- ❑ Challenging and demanding to motivate students to attempt new tasks that stretch their abilities
- ❑ Unwilling to accept less than optimal performance

Effective mentors have positive personal attributes. They are

- ❑ Mature and wise
- ❑ Providers of accurate and useful advice
- ❑ Friendly and optimistic in that they appear to enjoy mentoring
- ❑ Positive in their life outlook
- ❑ Admired and respected in that they possess characteristics that students aspire to attain
- ❑ Held in high regard by their peers
- ❑ Trustworthy and dependable
- ❑ Ethical and have high moral standards
- ❑ Willing to provide assistance even under difficult circumstances

Effective mentors have attained professional competency. They are

- ❑ Qualified and competent
- ❑ Experienced and willing to provide advice
- ❑ Knowledgeable and well-informed (with up-to-date information)
- ❑ Able to communicate well
- ❑ Actively involved in professional or academic organizations
- ❑ Involved in research
- ❑ Interested in lifelong learning

Source: Appleby, 1999.

No one person will have all these characteristics; you must decide which are the most important to you and find someone who approximates them.

As you consider potential mentors, ask yourself the following questions, or respond to them in your journal:

- Is the professor in a position to share his or her time and advice?
- Does he or she have a reputation for producing high-quality and timely research? Is the professor interested in mentoring you?
- Are you comfortable with the professor's demeanor and personality? Does he or she fit your academic style and needs?
- From your perspective, does the professor exhibit the ability to communicate openly and clearly?

Active Learning Outside the Classroom

Research Experience

Taking an active role in your education entails looking for opportunities to learn and develop useful skills. Engaging in research promotes a host of abilities and skills that employers and graduate programs seek. Make yourself more competitive by seeking opportunities to assist professors in their research and perhaps even carry out your own research studies under the guidance of a faculty mentor. A research assistantship is an opportunity for an undergraduate student to assist a faculty member in his or her program of research. Assisting a faculty member in research is an exciting opportunity to do research rather than just read about it.

Why Become a Research Assistant? Research generates new knowledge. When we engage in research, we make new discoveries and learn new things. Sure, you read about psychology research, but carrying it out is an altogether different animal that will help you learn more than you have in any class. It's an opportunity to be on the cutting edge of psychology. Aside from the thrill of generating new knowledge, assisting a professor with research provides many other valuable opportunities, including the following.

- Gaining skills and knowledge that aren't easily attained in the classroom by working one-on-one with a faculty member
- Exposure to methodological techniques that will be helpful in completing your senior thesis or later graduate work
- Practicing written and oral communication skills by learning how to express research findings and preparing papers for submission to professional conferences and journals
- Developing a mentoring relationship with a faculty member
- Obtaining experiences that will enhance your applications to employers and graduate programs
- Acquiring outstanding letters of recommendation, as faculty who work closely with you can write more detailed letters that fully demonstrate your capacities and strengths.

Engaging in research is a worthwhile experience for all students, those who wish to enter the workplace after graduation as well as those who wish to attend graduate school, because it gives you an opportunity to think, organize information, and solve problems, as well as to demonstrate commitment to a project.

What Does a Research Assistant Do? What will be expected of you as a research assistant? We cannot predict the specific tasks that you will be assigned, because a research assistant's tasks vary by faculty member, project, and area of psychology. Some might be involved in data collection through the administration of surveys or in maintaining and operating lab equipment. Others might code and enter data, make photocopies, or write literature reviews. Here are some general tasks that research assistants perform (Landrum, Davis, & Landrum, 2000):

- Collect data by administering surveys, conducting interviews, or running research protocols.
- Score, code, and enter data into a spreadsheet or statistical analysis program.
- Conduct library research including literature searches using databases (e.g, PsycINFO, Social Sciences Citation Index, PsycARTICLES), making copies of articles, and ordering unavailable articles and books through interlibrary loans.
- Assist the faculty member in developing new research ideas.
- Use computer skills such as word processing, spreadsheet, scheduling, and statistical analysis programs.
- Assist in preparing submissions for local or regional conferences and, if accepted, work on poster or oral presentations for professional conferences.
- Assist faculty in preparing a manuscript to submit the results of your collaborative research to a scientific journal.

Frequently students who work with faculty members as research assistants develop their own ideas for research projects that stem from the faculty members' work. For example, one of my students worked with me on several related projects and developed her own hypothesis to extend my work by adding additional variables. She carried out her project under my supervision as her senior thesis, presented it at a regional psychology conference, and together we are preparing an article for submission to a scholarly journal. Research assistantships provide substantial educational and professional development opportunities.

How Do You Get Involved as a Research Assistant? First and foremost, you should perform well in class and be motivated and visible in your department. Let faculty know that you're interested in becoming involved in research. Approach faculty during office hours and ask for leads on who might be looking for research assistants. When you find a faculty member who is in need of an assistant, carefully and honestly describe what you can offer (computer skills, Internet skills, and statistical skills, as well as the number of hours per week you're available). Let the faculty member know that you're willing to work hard (be honest). Ask about specific requirements such as the duration of the project, what your responsibilities will be, and the length of commitment (a semester or a year?). Remember that although you might not find anyone working on a project that you find fascinating, you will obtain excellent experience; besides, your interests will most likely change as you gain more experience and education.

Benefits for Faculty You're now aware that there are many benefits of becoming involved in research. Did you know that there are benefits for faculty too? They get a hardworking student to perform some labor-intensive aspects of their research. Faculty, especially those at undergraduate institutions without graduate programs, often depend on undergraduates to further their research programs (Landrum et al., 2000). Many faculty members have ideas for studies that they don't have time to conduct. Motivated students can help them to carry out these studies. If you develop a relationship with a faculty member, you might be able to help him or her conduct a project that may otherwise remain shelved for lack of time.

Involving undergraduates in research also offers an opportunity for faculty to witness a student's professional growth, which can be quite rewarding. There are other benefits for faculty who involve undergraduates in their research (Davis, 1995) including the following:

- remaining current by conducting reviews of the current literature in a particular research area;
- keeping analytic skills active through the design and completion of research;
- maintaining and expanding professional networks through attending conventions to present research completed with the help of students;
- bringing research into the classroom and enhancing teaching effectiveness through active involvement in research.

As you can see, student-professor research relationships offer benefits to all involved; however, the commitment to become a research assistant is a big one. You will be given responsibility to ensure that certain aspects of the project get done. The faculty member will count on you to be responsible and complete your assignments correctly. This includes asking questions and seeking assistance if you don't understand the task. Your performance as a research assistant can give faculty members many good things to write about in letters of recommendation, including specific examples of your skills, competencies, and personal characteristics. If you complete tasks competently, you might be asked to take on more responsibility, and you will learn more as well as earn a reputation as an excellent student and a potential future colleague (and thereby earn excellent letters of recommendation). However, there is a positive payoff from conducting research with faculty only if you consistently perform competent work. If you don't take the commitment seriously, are unreliable, or make repeated mistakes, your relationship with the faculty member will suffer (as will your recommendations and your general standing in the eyes of the faculty). If you decide to work with a faculty member on his or her research, treat it as a primary responsibility.

Disseminating Results of Research: Presentations and Publications

If you conduct research with a faculty member and the results of the research project turn out favorably, the next step in the project is to disseminate the results and tell the scholarly community about your findings. Most commonly, research results are disseminated through presentations at professional conferences or through articles in scholarly journals.

Most students obtain their first experiences with research dissemination through presentations at local or regional professional conferences. Most professional organizations for psychologists host annual or biennial meetings where psychologists meet, present current research findings, and network. Presenting research results at a conference is a wonderful learning opportunity that is an impressive addition to a résumé or graduate school application.

Typically, conference presentations take two forms—papers and posters. A paper is a 12- to 15-minute presentation made to an audience in which you describe your research concisely with the aid of handouts, overheads, or slides. Checklist 3.4 offers suggestions for paper presentations. Posters are more common formats for student presentations. A poster presents your research concisely on a 3-by-5- or 4-by-6-foot free-standing bulletin board. All posters are displayed in a large room for a period of time (usually 1½ to 2 hours), and the audience wanders through, browsing posters of interest. A poster presentation offers opportunities for lots of one-on-one interaction as audience members stop at posters of interest to them and ask questions about the project. Designing an effective poster isn't easy; Checklist 3.5 offers some advice on how to create an informative poster.

CHECKLIST 3.4

Checklist for Preparing Effective Paper Presentations

Preparation: Before Your Talk

- ❑ Carefully plan your talk. Realize that you can make a limited number of points within your 10- to 12-minute time frame.
- ❑ Be aware of your audience's attention and comprehension limits; don't overwhelm them.
- ❑ Consider the "big picture." What are the main ideas and findings of your project?

- ❑ Minimize the extraneous details.
- ❑ First, write out your presentation. Then look over your write-up and decide whether any details can be eliminated.
- ❑ Using the write-up that you've prepared, create a detailed outline as a guide to your talk.
- ❑ Remember that your goal is to tell a coherent story about your data. State the point of your research, what you found, and why it matters.
- ❑ Practice giving your talk in front of a mirror, or videotape your practice sessions.
- ❑ Practice giving your talk to an audience and accept their constructive feedback.
- ❑ Prepare overheads, slides, or handouts to enhance the informational value of your presentation.
- ❑ Be sure to include identification information on your handouts—your name, the conference source reference, and whether the paper can be quoted.
- ❑ Try to visit the room that you will be speaking in beforehand to familiarize yourself with its layout.

During Your Talk

- ❑ Do not read your talk; use your outline as a guide.
- ❑ Speak loudly and clearly.
- ❑ Look out at the audience.
- ❑ Understand that there will be distractions, such as people getting up and leaving or reading—don't take it personally.
- ❑ Try to be enthusiastic and focused; look away from distracting stimuli.
- ❑ End on time and be prepared for questions if time permits.
- ❑ Bring copies of your paper and a sign-up sheet in case you run out of copies.

Source: Karlin, 2000; Psi Chi, 2001.

CHECKLIST 3.5

Tips for Preparing Effective Poster Presentations

Consider the big picture. What are the main ideas and findings of your project?

- ❑ Remember that your goal is to tell a coherent story about your data within a very limited space.
- ❑ Your poster should reveal the point of your research, what you found, and why it matters.
- ❑ Don't overwhelm readers with too much information. Include only essential details. Present only what is necessary to tell your story.
- ❑ Remember that you are there to answer readers' questions. Your goal is to engage the reader and have a conversation about the study.

- ❑ The components of your poster should be clearly visible from 3 feet away.
- ❑ Include the title, the authors, their affiliation, and an abstract of the research.
- ❑ Use a large font (at least 18 point and preferably 24 point).
- ❑ Pictures, tables, and figures are helpful.
- ❑ If possible, use color in your figures and pictures.
- ❑ Bring thumbtacks and tape.
- ❑ Bring at least 50 copies of a handout to provide additional information about the study and contact information.
- ❑ Be sure to include identification information on your handouts: your name, the conference source reference, and whether the paper can be quoted.
- ❑ Be on time. Poster sessions are often scheduled back-to-back, so it is important that you end on time and take your poster down because someone else will be waiting.
- ❑ Never take your poster down early.
- ❑ Have your name badge prominently displayed and be ready to answer questions.

Source: Karlin, 2000.

If the research you are conducting with a faculty member turns out especially favorably, you might prepare the results for submission to a scholarly journal. Although professional journals in psychology abound, there are a handful that specialize in publishing the work of undergraduates. The most prestigious of these is the *Psi Chi Journal of Undergraduate Research*, which is sponsored by Psi Chi and published quarterly. Submissions to this journal are reviewed by three psychology professionals. Other undergraduate journals and criteria appear in Table 3.1.

If you decide to submit your results to a journal, realize that it will take a great deal of time and effort. The time it takes to prepare a paper for submission is always longer than anticipated. Once the paper is submitted, there will be a long wait (typically several months) to hear from the publisher. Even if a paper is accepted, it is usually under the condition that further revisions will be made. It is important to understand that not every paper submitted to a journal is published. The standards for publication are much higher than those for getting an A in a course. Journal editors expect articles to make a contribution to the literature, and "nonsignificant results are typically not a big contribution in their eyes" (Powell, 2000, p. 28). Despite these cautions, the rewards of publishing are great. Publishing in a scholarly journal is a major achievement that employers and graduate schools look on favorably.

TABLE 3.1 **UNDERGRADUATE PSYCHOLOGY JOURNALS**

Journal Title	Publication Schedule	Requirements	Contact Information
Caltech Undergraduate Research Journal	Two issues a year: fall and spring	Use the online submission form. Submissions must be accompanied by a submission approval form attesting that the document has not been published elsewhere.	Editor-in-chief: Tim Tirrell. E-mail: ttirrell@caltech.edu. http://www.curj.caltech.edu/front/index4.1.php
Canadian Undergraduate Journal of Cognitive Science	Two issues a year: fall and spring	An electronic journal published by the Cognitive Science Student Association at Simon Fraser University in Vancouver, Canada. "The journal is a unique reference for students, showcasing quality research by other undergraduate students, improving the contact and exchange of ideas between students and cognitive scientists alike, and illustrating the interdisciplinary work that is the hallmark of the field."	E-mail: cogs-journal@sfu.ca. http://www.sfu.ca/ cognitive-science/journal/
Journal of Psychological Inquiry	One issue a year	Primary author must be an undergraduate student (a) from an institution sponsoring a Great Plains Students in Psychology Convention and the *Journal of Psychological Inquiry* or (b) whose manuscript has been accepted for or presented at a meeting of the Great Plains Students in Psychology Convention, the Association for Psychological and Educational Research in Kansas, or the Nebraska Psychological Society. Publishes empirical and theoretical papers.	Mark Ware, Managing Editor, Department of Psychology, Creighton University, Omaha, NE 68178. Phone: (402) 280-3193; E-mail: meware@creighton.edu. http://puffin.creighton.edu/psy/journal/JPIhome.html

(continued)

TABLE 3.1 **UNDERGRADUATE PSYCHOLOGY JOURNALS (CONTINUED)**

Journal of Psychology and Behavioral Sciences	One issue a year	Authors can be undergraduate students. Submission deadline is February 1. Publishes empirical and theoretical papers.	Donalee Brown, JPBS Faculty Editor, Department of Psychology M-AB1-01, Fairleigh Dickinson University, 285 Madison Avenue, Madison, NJ 07940. Phone: (973) 443-8974; e-mail; donalee@fdu.edu. http://alpha.fdu.edu/psychweb/JPBS.htm
Journal of Undergraduate Research in Psychology	Two issues a year	Publishes abstracts of papers and posters presented by undergraduates at local, regional, and national conferences. Papers from award-winning presentations are published in their entirety.	http://www.georgefox.edu/academics/undergrad/departments/psychology/JURP/index.html
Modern Psychological Studies	Two issues a year: September and March	Primary author must be an undergraduate student. Submissions deadlines are April and October. Publishes empirical papers but will consider theoretical papers.	Modern Psychological Studies, Department of Psychology, 350 Holt Hall, University of Tennessee at Chattanooga, 615 McCallie Avenue, Chattanooga, TN 37403-2598, or e-mail submission to David-Ross@utc.edu.
Psi Chi Journal of Undergraduate Research	Four issues a year	First author must be an undergraduate Psi Chi student. Submissions accepted on an ongoing basis. Publishes only empirical research.	Warren H. Jones, PhD, Managing Editor, Department of Psychology, University of Tennessee, 307 Austin Peay Building, Knoxville, TN 37996-0900. Phone: (865) 974-0514; e-mail: psichijournal@utk.edu. http://www.psichi.org/pubs/journal/submissions.asp

Undergraduate Research Journal for the Human Sciences	One issue a year	Primary author of a submitted paper must be an undergraduate student. "Papers may represent a full range of research design, including experiments, surveys, case studies, and documentary research."	URC/URJ Call for Papers, 4990 Northwind Drive, Suite 140, East Lansing, MI 48823-5031. Phone: (517)-351-8335; fax:(517)-351-8336; e-mail: dmitstifer@kon.org http:// www.kon.org/CFP/cfp_urjhs.html
University of California Los Angeles Undergraduate Psychology Journal	Two issues a year: fall and spring	"We are looking for research that draws upon the varied areas of psychology and related fields. Research should emphasize possible behavioral, psychobiological, cognitive, neurological, physiological, social, developmental, and/or emotional mechanisms behind psychological functioning." See web site for submission requirements.	A floppy disk containing your manuscript should be submitted to the *Undergraduate Psychology Journal,* UCLA Department of Psychology, 1285 Franz Hall, Box 951563, Los Angeles, CA 90095-1563. In addition, we request that an electronic copy be sent to upj@ucla.edu. http://www.studentgroups.ucla.edu/upj/upj/inde
Undergraduate Journal of Psychology		All manuscripts are to be double-spaced, must follow American Psychological Association (APA) guidelines, and should be produced on a computer. Submit two copies.	The University of North Carolina at Charlotte, Department of Psychology, 9201 University City Blvd., Charlotte, NC 28223-0001. http://www.psych.uncc.edu/Journal.htm

Source: Jalbert, 1998.

Field Experience: Internships and Practica

Taking an active role in your education entails seeking opportunities for personal and professional development. Field experiences in the form of internships or practica involve students in relevant academic experiences and provide a useful service to agencies and communities (Jessen, 1988). Through their participation in field experiences, students begin to recognize that they have skills to contribute to practical settings (Jessen, 1988). Field experiences give students opportunities to apply what they've learned outside the classroom and to explore potential careers.

What to Expect Most field experiences are with agencies that relate to human behavior. Examples of field placements include being an intern at a social service agency (where you might assist with intake of clients, psychological testing, report writing, and behavior modification) and working in the human services department of a company or business (where you might learn to administer structured interviews, write performance appraisals, and coordinate special projects or programs). As an intern, you have a chance to get an idea of what it is like to work in a particular setting. You may learn new skills and hone others. For example, you might sit in on a group therapy session or help personnel run it.

The organization of field experiences varies by institution and department. Many departments have a faculty member who serves as a campus coordinator for field experience and internship programs. He or she makes sure that internship sites are appropriate, develops working relationship with them, and evaluates student performance. Other departments may not have one coordinator; in some cases different faculty are responsible for each internship site depending on their relationship with that site.

Benefits of Field Experience There are many benefits to participating in field experience. If you hope to become a mental health professional and provide services to others, it is important to seek practice opportunities as an undergraduate. It is not uncommon for students to believe that clinical or counseling psychology is for them until they gain some experience and realize that they don't like working with people. Therefore, one of the most important reasons for seeking field experience is to become more certain of your career choice. Working in the field helps you to identify not only what work-related outcomes you value (e.g., pay, autonomy, responsibility) but also what interests and abilities you need to be satisfied in that work (Taylor, 1988; LoCicero & Hancock, 2000). It is a sort of job tryout. You'll learn about a particular job environment, duties, and support. You'll learn about typical clientele you might work with and what you can expect in terms of resources.

Other benefits of field experience include the opportunity to apply what is learned in class in a real-world setting, acquire knowledge and new skills, and learn about the practice of psychology (Jessen, 1988; LoCicero & Hancock, 2000). Through an internship—depending on the placement—you might learn more about psychological problems, ways of helping, agency functioning, professional relationships, interviewing techniques, psychological testing, report writing, consultation, behavior modification, and group therapy (Jessen, 1988). Field experience gives you a chance to develop useful skills that may be hard to practice and develop in class, and it helps you to integrate what you've learned. Personal benefits include developing responsibility, maturity, and confidence (LoCicero & Hancock, 2000).

Aside from educational and personal benefits, field experience offers professional benefits. These include gaining a realistic understanding of working environments, developing professional contacts, and enhancing your résumé (Jessen, 1988; Landrum et al., 2000). Research has shown that interns obtain access to informal job sources and contacts, positive evaluations from recruiters, higher salaries in the workplace, and greater job satisfaction (Taylor, 1988). Students who work as interns are more likely to be satisfied with their jobs after graduation. They also remain in their jobs longer than students who do not obtain field experience. By seeking opportunities to work in the field as an undergraduate, you will have a chance to experience the conflict between your academic preparation and real-world work requirements (e.g., students are often poorly equipped for the stresses of work, including the realities of politics, difficult clients, and the conflict between theory and application) while you're still in school. This preparation will give you time to learn more and to resolve the conflicts early. Therefore it may not be surprising that after graduation, students who have obtained field experience often have a smoother, easier transition to work without the "reality shock" that other graduates often experience (Taylor, 1988).

Involvement in Organizations

Psi Chi, the National Honor Society in Psychology, is an organization designed for students and founded in 1929. Its purpose is to encourage, stimulate, and maintain excellence in scholarship and to advance psychology as a science. Students enrolled at institutions that have a chapter must meet minimum qualifications to apply for membership in Psi Chi. Students at community colleges are eligible to apply to Psi Beta, the sister organization of Psi Chi.

Become involved in your institution's chapter of Psi Chi, and you'll have an opportunity to get to know other psychology students, develop leadership skills, and be involved in departmental activities. Psi Chi also offers opportunities for students at the regional and national levels. It sponsors sessions at most regional and national conferences that promote the research and scholarly achievements of undergraduate psychology students. Psi Chi offers programming relevant to psychology students at these conferences, such as presentations on careers in psychology and how to apply to graduate school. Another important benefit of membership in Psi Chi is its quarterly magazine *Eye on Psi Chi*. Each issue includes articles on psychology as well as practical advice on how to pursue a career in psychology. The *Psi Chi Journal of Undergraduate Research* is also published by Psi Chi; it's a national peer-reviewed scholarly journal dedicated to research conducted by undergraduate students. Because there are so many benefits to becoming a member of Psi Chi, if your institution does not have a chapter, discuss the possibility of starting one with a faculty member.

Another opportunity to become involved in psychology and promote a campus culture oriented toward psychology is to join (or start) a psychology club. Most psychology clubs are open to anyone with an interest in psychology regardless of their major. Many students who are unable to join Psi Chi because of low grades get involved in a school's psychology club. Frequently, the psychology club and Psi Chi work together to organize psychology-related activities for students.

When considering ways of becoming involved in psychology-related activities, don't forget to pay attention to what's happening in your department. Departments often invite guest speakers to the campus, or faculty members give presentations on their research interests. Attend these activities to support the department's efforts and to demonstrate your interest in and commitment to learning more about psychology.

Finally, two professional organizations for psychologists offer resources that are helpful to students: the American Psychological Association (APA) and the American Psychological Society (APS). Both offer advice on entering the field of psychology, and APA offers a student affiliate membership that permits you to join for a reduced fee and to obtain discounts on psychology journals and books.

There are a variety of ways to take an active role in your education, but all involve stepping back and recognizing the covert, unstated college curriculum (Appleby, 2001); you can learn much more in college than just theories and facts. Taking an active role in your education means that you must seek out opportunities to learn and enhance your skills. It means that you must develop relationships with faculty and do more than just attend class. Although taking an active role in your education takes effort—it's much easier to just sit back and attend class—the benefits are immense.

Suggested Readings

LaRoche, K. (2004). Advantages of undergraduate research: A student's perspective. *Eye on Psi Chi, 8*(2), 20–21.

Powell, J. L. (2000). Creative outlets for student research or what do I do now that my study is completed? *Eye on Psi Chi, 4*(2), 28–29.

Sadowski, G., Glagler, D., Dowd, K., Ball, J., & Collins, L. H. (2002). Finding opportunities to get involved in research: Some advice from the students' perspective. *Eye on Psi Chi, 6*(2), 28–29.

Santrock, J. W., & Halonen, J. S. (2005). *Your guide to college success: Strategies for achieving your goals.* Belmont, CA: Wadsworth.

Van Blerkom, D. L., & Mulcahy-Ernt, P. I. (2005). *College reading and study strategies.* Belmont, CA: Wadsworth.

Wahlstrom, C. M., & Williams, B. K. (1997). *Commuter student: Being your best at college and life.* Belmont, CA: Wadsworth.

Watson, D. (2001). *Learning skills for college and life.* Belmont, CA: Wadsworth.

WEB RESOURCES

The following web sites are hot-linked at *The Psychology Major's Handbook* web site at *http://info.wadsworth.com/kuther*

Academic Skills Center

http://www.dartmouth.edu/~acskills/success/

At this web site, you'll find everything you need to succeed in college. There are links to study tips and other information to get you motivated.

Psi Chi

http://www.psichi.org

The Psi Chi web page provides links to articles on all aspects of student development (research, field experiences, graduate school, and other topics).

Becoming an Active Learner

http://www.lafayettehigh.org/Course%20Guide/becoming_an_active_learner.htm

This article describes the benefits of active learning and presents concrete strategies for changing your learning style and becoming a more engaged learner, increasing your effectiveness as a learner.

JOURNAL EXERCISES

My Advisor

Who is your advisor? Write down the contact information for your advisor. Now reflect on your meetings with him or her. Do you set up an appointment or just visit during office hours? What kind of advice does he or she give you? Do you feel comfortable interacting with your advisor? Identify questions to ask during your next meeting.

Relationships With Faculty

Explore your feelings about interacting with faculty. How often do you interact with professors? List the professors you interact with. Explore the context of your discussions. For example, is it after class or in the professor's office? Are your discussions focused on the course material or do you talk about other things, like life and career goals? What, if anything, is holding you back from interacting with professors? Explore your feelings. How can you overcome these obstacles?

Finding a Mentor

This exercise helps you to gather information about faculty and use it to make decisions. First, write down the name of each faculty member in the department. After you have listed everyone, begin gathering information on their research activities. Look at department bulletin boards, explore the department and faculty web sites, and use databases to find information about each faculty member's research interests and activities. Take a few minutes to speak with the faculty member about his or her research. In your journal, write your overall impressions: What type of work does he or she do? Do you find it interesting? Why or why not? How comfortable do you feel speaking with this faculty member? If you're uncomfortable, try to identify why. Complete this process for each faculty member, and you'll begin to get ideas about which faculty you're more interested in working with.

My College Career

An important part of taking an active role in your education is planning your course work. Look through your college handbook and write down the requirements for your major. What courses are required? Are any other experiences required? Now list all the courses that you have taken. Make a list of all the courses that you need to take. In what ways have you been active in shaping your education to match your goals? What steps can you take to become more active?

CHAPTER 4

Study Tips: Tools for Academic Success

Chapter Guide

Have you ever spent hours studying for a test only to get a mediocre grade? Meanwhile, your friend says he studied for only an hour and got an A. What's the deal? Consider this scenario:

Tom gets home from his part-time job and fixes himself a snack. It's been a long day. It's almost 6 p.m., and he knows that he has to start studying for that test tomorrow. It's been a rough semester, and he's attended all the classes but has had a hard time taking notes. Tom finds that his mind wanders and that it's difficult to understand the point of the professor's lectures. He knows that he should have read the assignment before each class, but it's hard to keep up when you're taking five classes and working 20 hours a week. How do you find time for it all and have a life too? Tom decides that he'll complete the reading tonight, hoping that some of it will stick for the test tomorrow. It will be a long night. He brings his snack to the kitchen table and clears a space among the breakfast dishes piled on the table. He begins reading but finds it difficult to concentrate. He tries to read while eating his snack.

"Those dishes!" Tom exclaims. "That's why I can't focus." He takes a break to wash them. Twenty minutes later, after washing the dishes and clearing off the counters and stove, Tom sits down to read. Thirty minutes into his reading, his roommate comes home and begins a long story about his horrendous day. Nearly an hour later, Tom realizes that his studying isn't working, but he's hungry, and so he and his roommate order a pizza. He vows to study after dinner. "This is gonna be an all-nighter," he thinks to himself.

Sound familiar? Tom has good intentions and is motivated to study, but he's developed poor study habits—like cramming. He's having trouble keeping up with his classes and is simply studying in the wrong place at the wrong time. Tom's predicament isn't unusual, but *you* don't have to fall prey to it. This chapter describes simple techniques to help you manage your time, get organized, and improve your study habits so that you don't find yourself in Tom' shoes.

An important theme of this chapter is somewhat counterintuitive: Spending lots of time studying will not guarantee you good grades. Instead, it's the *quality* of your studying that counts. It doesn't do you much good to spend countless hours poring over your books if you aren't retaining anything. It is essential for you to realize that improving your study habits is going to take time and effort on your part. The work that you put in now will help you save time later. Learn to make the most constructive use of your time, and you will accomplish more in less time. With effort and consistent practice, you'll find that you can study more efficiently and effectively. Believe it or not, studying is more enjoyable when you are successful and productive.

SELF-AWARENESS: THE KEY TO SUCCESS

How can you improve your academic and study skills? You might be surprised to hear this, but one of the best ways to improve your academic performance is through self-awareness. What does self-awareness have to do with studying? By becoming aware of yourself, you'll be able to tailor your study strategies to suit your needs, preferences, and abilities. There is no right way to study; do what works for you, which means you must be self-aware.

How do your study skills rate? If you're like most students, they can use improvement. Complete the study skills assessment in Exercise 4.1 to learn more about your own study needs. What did you learn about yourself? Let's continue our discussion of learning by writing. As we've seen in the past few chapters, writing is an excellent way of becoming more self-aware. Freewriting is a technique that can help you identify your ideas and feelings. It is a way of using writing for thinking by writing without censoring or editing as you go. Just write what's on your mind. When you're done, read through what you've written.

EXERCISE 4.1
Study Skills Assessment

Use the following scale to respond to the study skills assessment below.
Be honest!

1 = none of the time
2 = some of the time
3 = most of the time
4 = all of the time

How often do you

_____ 1. Manage your time to meet school and job responsibilities, as well as to relax?
_____ 2. Set and monitor academic and personal goals?
_____ 3. Read your textbooks before class?
_____ 4. Understand how you learn?

_____ 5. Maintain attention during classes?
_____ 6. Use active listening strategies to get the most out of classes?
_____ 7. Take effective notes that are useful for later studying?
_____ 8. Study early and often for exams rather than cramming?
_____ 9. Use a variety of strategies for recalling information?
_____ 10. Test yourself to determine whether you understand the material?
_____ 11. Have a well-defined study space?
_____ 12. Differentiate between essential and nonessential information in lectures?
_____ 13. Differentiate between essential and nonessential information in readings?
_____ 14. Take notes on readings?
_____ 15. Vary your learning and study strategies according to the material at hand?

Scoring:

Add the points for each item. Higher scores indicate more effective use of study skills.

Reflection:

1. Consider your score. Identify the areas in which you can improve.
2. Identify one area of strength. How can you further strengthen this study skill?
3. Identify one area of weakness. How can you improve your skills in this area?

You might gain some new insights into yourself. Pull out your journal or some paper and freewrite about each of the following questions:

- Think back to a course in which you excelled. Describe the circumstances surrounding the course. What kinds of assignments were required? Why do you think you did well?
- How do you learn best?
- Under what conditions can you best concentrate? Do you need absolute silence to concentrate or do you need some background noise?
- What are your academic strengths and weaknesses? Consider each of these areas: listening, speaking in class, memory, taking notes, and taking tests.
- Describe your study environment. Where, when, and how do you study?
- Do you know where your notes from last week are? How about those from last semester? Do you feel organized? Where can you improve?
- Do you know what assignments are due next week? Are any major term papers due for any of your classes? Have you begun working on them? Why or why not?
- Do you have a calendar or planner? How often do you use it?
- Have you forgotten an appointment or assignment recently?

- Do you feel overwhelmed with work? List all the tasks that you must keep track of.

Carefully consider your answers in order to glean clues about where to focus your efforts to improve your studying. You need to develop your own formula for academic success based on your understanding of yourself. Once you've created a formula for studying with the tips described in this chapter, you'll understand how to focus your attention and concentration, allowing you to increase your academic efficiency and get more work done in less time.

TIME MANAGEMENT

At one time or another, most of us complain about feeling overwhelmed—as if there is not enough time in the day to get everything done. Answer the time management questions in Quiz 4.1 and see how you rate.

QUIZ 4.1
Time Management Quiz

Check off the items that you find are true for you.

- ❑ Do you ever feel that you can't control your time?
- ❑ Do you find yourself doing your course work at the last minute?
- ❑ At this very moment, do you know what your priorities are?
- ❑ Do you ever struggle to begin unpleasant tasks?
- ❑ Is your workspace neat and tidy?
- ❑ Do you have a to-do list for today?
- ❑ Do you often find yourself daydreaming when you should be working?
- ❑ Do you feel that your friends are better organized than you are?
- ❑ Do you tend to hand in course work and papers late?
- ❑ Are you easily distracted?
- ❑ Do you put off things that require big blocks of time?
- ❑ Do you have a to-do list for this week?
- ❑ Do you know what time of day you work best?
- ❑ Do you check your e-mail more than four times a day?
- ❑ Do you often feel overwhelmed by work?
- ❑ Do you know how long it takes for you to write a 20-page paper for a course?
- ❑ Do you ever attend classes, seminars, or workshops unprepared or wishing that you had done the reading?
- ❑ Do you find yourself surfing the web when you should be working?
- ❑ Do you have a wall chart showing the important deadlines for the semester and for the year?
- ❑ Do you prioritize your tasks and activities?
- ❑ Do you set aside time for relaxation and socializing?
- ❑ Do you put off things that are unpleasant?
- ❑ Are you usually in a panic to complete course, research, and lab assignments? Do you often lose important papers or articles?
- ❑ Do you often forget to complete important tasks?

- ❑ Do you feel in control of your time?
- ❑ Have you ever gone on a cleaning frenzy (i.e., cleaning your room or home) instead of working?
- ❑ Do friends often just drop by your office or home, interrupting your work?
- ❑ Do you write down what you need to get done?
- ❑ Do you know any useful time management techniques that you are not using right now?

Scoring:

Count your checkmarks. The closer your score is to 30, the more help you need in managing your time.

Reflection:

1. Consider your score. Consider each checkmark. Why did you check it?
2. Given your response to the first item, what aspects of time management are challenging for you?
3. How can you improve your time management skills? Discuss three strategies for improving these skills.

Before you can begin studying, you must gain control over your time: "Be the master of it instead of its slave" (Pauk & Fiore, 2000, p. 2). Most students could use some help in managing their time. The first step toward gaining control over time is to understand how you use time. There is more time available in the day than you realize. Assess your use of time; keep a diary of how you spend your time for a few days or a week. Each day, carry your journal, a notebook, or a chart where you can record all your activities and the time spent on each one. Be honest. After a day or two, or even a week, analyze your patterns of time use. Are you using your time most efficiently? Where can you cut back? Are you spending enough time to complete your studying? Does your time use reflect your priorities? You might be surprised where all the time goes. That 10-minute coffee break might really be closer to 40 minutes! You may find that there's lots of "lost" time—time that you can find and use if you manage it better. Once you understand your time-use patterns, create a plan to use some of that lost time. In other words, create a schedule so that you can use the time that you usually waste.

Benefits of Time Management

Many students and professors avoid time management, fearing that it will deprive them of flexibility or creativity (Fry, 1991). This is a myth. A schedule permits freedom because controlling or planning part of your day allows you to be more flexible with the rest of the day. Some students might choose to schedule the morning and afternoon but keep their evenings free, for example. Your time management system can be as flexible as you choose. The best time management systems are simple guides (Fry, 1991). Many students (and professors) dislike schedules, but there are many benefits to managing your time.

Gets You Started Have you ever had one of those days when you can't decide what to do next? Perhaps you're so overwhelmed with tasks that you can't decide where to begin and don't feel motivated to begin. After all, with so much to do, you'll never finish it all anyway. One of the primary benefits of a schedule is that you won't need to waste time deciding what to do. A schedule can act as an external force that can give you a jumpstart (which might be particularly effective in the morning).

Keeps You From Forgetting to Study for Subjects That You Dislike It's not intentional, but it's easy to get off track and let time slip away while studying. Many students put other tasks first and find that they've run out of time to study subjects that they dislike. A schedule prevents this type of forgetfulness. In fact, consider studying for classes that you dislike first, when you have the most energy and interest.

Can Make Studying More Interesting Sound unbelievable? Without the pressure of cramming for an exam, you will have time to think about what you're studying. When you have a chance to think about a subject and how it fits in with your experience and perspective, learning can become more interesting and enjoyable. You're also more likely to learn the material and remember it longer.

Promotes Cumulative Review and Eliminates Cramming Contrary to popular belief, long study periods (e.g., 4 to 6 hours) aren't effective. The best way to retain knowledge and prepare for exams is to squeeze in short review periods throughout your day. Distributing four 30-minute sessions throughout the day is less fatiguing and more effective than a single 2-hour session (Pauk & Fiore, 2000). Why? The more often you encounter material, the more likely you are to remember it. By distributing your learning sessions over the semester, you'll find that you'll learn more and won't need to cram.

Frees the Mind Putting things to do on paper relieves you from thinking about them. Once you've written an item down, there's no need to worry about forgetting it, so you're free to focus on other things. Seeing everything that you have to do on paper, with time allotted for each item, can help to alleviate anxiety and pressure because you have a concrete plan to get it all done.

Helps You to Put Your Priorities First It's easy to spend lots of time doing busy work for an easy class only to find that you haven't spent enough time studying for a test or preparing a major paper for a more difficult class. A schedule forces you to list all the tasks that must be done and prioritize them to ensure that the most important tasks are completed—even if that means that you don't get everything done.

Lets You Avoid Time Traps and Control Study Breaks A schedule makes you conscious of your time so that you're less likely to find that your 10-minute coffee break has turned into a 45-minute break. Schedules help you to avoid time traps like wasting 2 hours to go back home to get a book or assignment that you've forgotten. If it's all written down, you're less likely to forget it.

Keeps You From Overlooking Fun We need balanced lives to stay healthy. As the semester progresses and you become busier, it's easy to forget to take care of your nonacademic needs. It's important to have fun. You need to engage in physical and social recreation so that you maintain a balanced and less chaotic life. A schedule also can help you enjoy leisure without feeling guilty because you're not studying. When you schedule time to do your work, you know that it will get done. Then you can enjoy "play time" without worrying or thinking about studying.

Helps You Learn How to Study Smarter, Not Harder By getting organized and taking control of your time and tasks, you'll find that you can concentrate more effectively and get more done in less time. A schedule can keep you on track and prevent end-of-the-semester slacking off because it's easier to finish all your work (and stay motivated) when you've scheduled enough time to complete it. A schedule also helps you stay aware of deadlines and keep the big picture in focus, allowing you to plan ahead so that busy weeks are in control and papers are done ahead of time.

Take Control of Your Time

Many of us let too much time slip through our fingers because we haven't been taught how to manage it. Some use a "natural" approach to time management, taking things as they come without a schedule or plan (Fry, 1991). Juggling school, a job, extracurricular activities, and a social life is difficult and nearly impossible to manage successfully without a plan. I often hear students say that if they just tried harder they'd be able to do it all. They resign themselves to all-nighters and walk around campus like zombies. This approach, trying to do everything without acquiring the skills to manage your time, will lead to burnout. Life may seem busy now, but it won't suddenly get easier after graduation. In fact, demands on your time often increase with career and family responsibilities. How do you take control of your time? Follow these principles.

Make a List If you've decided that you're ready to get a handle on your time, the first thing you must do is to write down all the demands on your time. Then, evaluate your list. Are you committing yourself to too many activities? Are you trying to do too much? You might love music, but can you juggle a jazz band, a guitar trio, and an off-campus rock band? Can you write for the school paper and maintain six different web pages at once? Recognize that sometimes you can't do it all. Decide what is important and what isn't. Difficult as it might be, you must remove activities that aren't meaningful to you in order to devote time to those that are. Make conscious choices of how to spend your time so that you have more control over your days and your life rather than running late on everything and constantly feeling harried and behind.

Now that you've listed all your activities, you might realize that you are quite busy—and perhaps overextended. A schedule will help you to feel more in control. Where should you begin? Decide how you will record your schedule. You can use a notebook or a calendar. Browse the office supply store, and you'll find a myriad of calendars and time management tools. Whatever format you choose, make sure that it works for you and is easy to use so that you will be motivated to use it.

Create a Schedule As early as possible in the semester, preferably before school begins, prepare a schedule. Create a plan for the whole semester so that you can see all that needs to be done. As you receive each syllabus, write in all your class assignments for the semester. This will permit you to consider the entire semester at once and will help keep you from spending too much time on a low-priority class that has regular assignments while falling behind in an important class with a major term paper. Write in all your classes and regular commitments (e.g., a part-time job). Include appointments, extracurricular activities, and other personal commitments. Enter time to study.

Examine each assignment and record reminders to yourself beforehand, listing personal due dates for portions of each assignment. For example, suppose you have a major term paper due at the end of the semester. During the second week of class, schedule time to search for topics. In later weeks, set aside time to go to the library, read articles, compose an outline, and write a first draft. If each step for each assignment is recorded in your schedule, you'll be more likely to stay on track and finish your assignments on time (or early).

Write It Down The cardinal rule of time management is that you must write everything down—all your plans. It's difficult to make detailed plans far in advance if you don't have a record of your activities and commitments. Keep a record of all your assignments and obligations in one place, including class times, study times, project due dates, assignments, appointments, and social events.

Consistently write everything down so that you don't forget anything—and more important, so that you'll be free to think without worrying that you've forgotten something. Always carry your schedule and to-do list with you so that you can bring order to your life and have peace of mind. Make no mistake about it; this will take some time and practice, but creating a schedule produces important returns. You'll feel like you have extra time. You'll feel more in control.

Use To-Do Lists Each week, create a to-do list of tasks that must be accomplished. Then rank their priorities. If you don't have time for everything, you can at least finish the most important ones. Each evening, plan your next day by listing what needs to be done and when you'll do it. List the subjects you plan to study; errands, appointments, and activities to be completed; and the time allotted for each. Schedule enough time for each task, including time to warm up and time to finish. Don't overdo it, but plan for rest breaks and fun. Use your schedule each day. The advantage of a daily schedule is that it forces you to break large tasks into small bites of time, making them seem easier and more manageable.

It's important to make a to-do list each night so that you have a plan for the morning and so that you unclutter your mind. Believe it or not, it just takes 5 or 10 minutes but is especially valuable. The act of thinking through your day puts together a sort of psychological clock that helps to prepare you for the day. Each evening, write your next day's schedule on a 3-by-5-inch card so that it's handy and fits in your pocket.

Work With It The time management system that is best for you will be one that is tailor-made for you. Make it work for you by altering and modifying it as needed. Give your time management system a trial run and time to work. It will be hard at first, but once you get the hang of it, you'll find that you don't have to think about it. And it gets easier. Don't be surprised at the initial effort that is required. It takes practice, but it is worth it. Here are some more tips for making the most of your time (Pauk & Fiore, 2000).

- Plan blocks of time, preferably hour or half-hour blocks. Even 20 minutes can be productive.
- Schedule the most difficult tasks during daylight hours, when people tend to be most alert and awake.
- Avoid too much detail in your schedule. You don't want to spend too much time writing it, and you also should leave some flexibility. Allow time for play; leave room for last-minute problems.
- Allow time for sleep. You need at least 8 hours of sleep each night (this is supported by medical evidence). Without sleep you are less likely to remember material, which means that you'll be less likely to learn.
- Start big projects early. Most people tend to underestimate the time needed to complete a hefty project. To avoid finding out that you can't

write a 10-page paper the night before it's due, start early—even if it seems ridiculously early. For example, begin considering topics for a 10-page term paper during the second week of the semester so that you have enough time to obtain the needed articles and books, read and comprehend them, and write the paper without feeling pressured.

- Use your spare time to think. For example, while walking from class, try to think of the main points of the lecture and how they apply to what you know. While exercising, think up titles for papers or think about how to organize papers.
- Carry pocket work (reading, an article, flash cards) that you can do while waiting in lines, at the bus stop, sitting, and so on. Ten minutes here, 15 minutes there, and it all adds up. In addition, cognitive psychology and memory research has shown that we can recall more information if we study in short periods rather than long ones, and so you just might learn more.
- Know your sleep pattern and work with it. We all have a natural rhythm of times when we are alert and awake and times when we are less alert. Arrange your study times around your natural rhythm. Study when you're alert and sleep when you're sleepy.

READING: TIPS FOR IMPROVING COMPREHENSION AND EFFICIENCY

Have you ever read a chapter, yet were unable to remember much about it? Many students have difficulty retaining what they read. Reading a textbook is very different from leisure reading (e.g., novels or magazines), but students often attempt to read a textbook as if it were a novel. Reading a textbook requires a different set of strategies.

Preview the Text

Read the preface. Most students skip the preface; however, the preface contains essential information for understanding the author's perspective. The preface usually provides information about the author's objective, the organizational plan of the book, how the book is different from others on the market, and the author's background and qualifications (Pauk & Fiore, 2000). Once you know the author's objective or goal, it's easier to see relationships among the facts presented. The organizational plan is like a road map explaining where the author will take you. Reading the author's view of how the book is different from others on the market and learning about his or her background and qualifications gives you more insight into his or her perspective, perhaps making it easier to comprehend the ideas that appear in the text.

Read the introduction; it is a window into the book. It is often packed with facts and ideas, laying the foundation for the main text (Pauk & Fiore, 2000). The introduction provides an overview of a text, making it easier to digest information in the subsequent chapters.

SQ3R Method

The SQ3R method (Robinson, 1970) is designed to help students read faster and retain more. The name stands for the steps in reading: survey, question, read, recite, review. Let's examine each step of this technique.

Survey Before reading a book chapter, for example, survey it. Glance through the topic headings for an overview of the chapter. Skim the sections and read the final summary paragraph to get an idea of where the chapter is going. This survey should take only a few minutes; it will highlight the main ideas of the chapter, providing an initial orientation that will help you organize the material as you read it. Surveying a chapter gives you background knowledge—something to link with what you're learning. Pauk and Fiore (2000) warn, "If you skip this step, you will lose time, not save time. If you burrow directly into one paragraph after another, you'll be unearthing one compartmentalized fact after another, but you won't see how the facts relate to each other" (p. 71). Instead, you'll develop tunnel vision and won't be able to see the big picture. Surveying holds other benefits, such as warming up or limbering up the mind, and eases you into studying (Pauk & Fiore, 2000).

Question Look at the first heading in the chapter. Turn it into a question. This will help you remember information that you already know and arouse curiosity, which will increase comprehension. This step requires a conscious effort but is worth it because active reading is the best way to retain written material. For example, if the heading is "Prevalence of Substance Use and Abuse in Adolescence," you might ask, "How many adolescents use illegal drugs?" If the heading is "Multiple Personality Disorder," you might ask, "What are the characteristics of multiple personality disorder?" Asking questions focuses your concentration. Take an active role in your reading and interrogate the author; don't just passively read.

Read Read the first section to answer your question. Actively search for the answer to your question. If you finish the section and haven't answered the question, reread it. Read reflectively. Consider what the author is trying to say and think about how you can use that information.

Recite Now that you've read the first section, look away and try to recite the answer to your question. Use your own words and examples. If you can do this, it means that you understand the material. If you can't, glance over the section again. Once you've said each answer, write it down. You might also reconsider your initial question, fine-tune it, write it in the margin of the text, and underline the key words that provide an answer (Pauk & Fiore, 2000).

Review Once you have read the entire chapter in this manner, test your memory by asking yourself the questions that you've identified. Review your notes and get a bird's-eye view of the chapter. Consider how it fits with what you know from the course, experience, and other classes. What is the material's significance? What are the implications or applications of this material? What questions are you left with?

Additional Tips

By now you probably realize that reading articles and textbooks often requires more than one pass. It usually takes two, three, or even more readings to grasp difficult concepts. Whether or not you decide to employ the SQ3R method, you should always preview the material to be read. Skim the table of contents, preface, headings, and conclusions. Stop and think about the instructor's purpose in making the assignment as well as your additional purposes for reading it. Take the briefest of notes while reading by adding brackets in margins or underlining minimally. Note pages where you might want to take formal notes. After reading, take more extensive notes. When your reading and note taking are complete, reread all your notes, think about what you've read, and add more notes based on your reflections (Kahn, 1992). Here are some additional pointers:

- As you read, keep a dictionary nearby to look up unfamiliar words. If you don't understand a word, stop and look it up in the dictionary. After looking up an unknown word, consider its meaning in the sentence.
- Pace yourself. Note that difficult readings will require more than one pass. Permit yourself the time to read such assignments over more than one session.
- Read the chapter before attending the lecture so that you'll be familiar with the material beforehand. Note unanswered questions or particularly difficult material and seek answers during the lecture.
- If you underline text, do so minimally and stay focused on the important details. Avoid the temptation to highlight every line. Heavy highlighting is a procrastination technique because you're usually just marking what you should learn instead of focusing on learning it.
- Instead of underlining or highlighting, take notes. As you read, write the main points in your own words. As you finish each section, or even each paragraph, take a moment to write down what you've learned. Be sure to use your own words and not those of the author (to lift an author's words

is plagiarism, as we will see in Chapter 5). Your notes will be a valuable resource when it comes time to study.

- Don't write down concepts that you don't understand. Reread the section until you understand the concept, or explain as much of it as you can and indicate your questions so that you can ask your instructor for assistance.

Getting the Most Out of Lectures: Note-Taking Tips

If you expect to learn and retain information from lectures, you must take notes. Without taking notes, even professors find it difficult to remember the main points of lectures. Your class notes are an important study resource, a sort of handwritten textbook that may contain information not available anywhere else. When you take notes, you listen more actively and are more involved in the subject, promoting learning, improving memory, and reducing boredom. Note taking is a lifelong skill; most careers require at least some note taking (how else can you remember what happened at that staff meeting, for example?). How can you improve your note-taking skills?

Be Selective

Don't write down everything the instructor says; just record the main points. Identifying the main points requires active listening. Beginning note takers often make the mistake of trying to write down every word and become frustrated when they find that it's impossible. Instead, take notes in your own words. Listen actively; that is, listen while thinking about what you are hearing, make connections with what you already know, and evaluate it. Your notes should include not only what the speaker says but also a critical response to what is being said (clearly marked as *your* response; Kahn, 1992).

Determine the Main Points

"Easier said than done," you're probably thinking. How do you determine the main points? Remember that the instructor usually provides clues to what is important. One clue is repetition; material the instructor repeats is more important. Notes written on the board or presented in overheads offer other clues. Remember that when you copy notes from the board or overhead, you will need to write more than the phrase or words indicated; you'll probably need to write an explanation too. The instructor's tone of voice might signify important information. Finally, instructors often highlight essential information by using specific phrases. Table 4.1 lists signal phrases that instructors might use to draw attention to critical information.

TABLE 4.1 **SIGNAL WORDS AND PHRASES**

Listen For	Type of Phrase
To illustrate, for example, for instance	Examples to make a point more clear
Before, after, formerly, subsequently, prior, meanwhile, first, second, last	Time words to note the time relationships among ideas or to enumerate them
Furthermore, in addition, moreover, also	Additional information to add to a list
Therefore, as a result, if . . . then, accordingly, thus, so	Suggesting cause and effect
On the other hand, in contrast, conversely, pros and cons	Contrast words to discuss both sides of a controversy
More important, above all, remember	Emphasizing important information
In other words, in the vernacular, it simply means, that is, briefly, in essence	Repeating the information presented in a simpler form

Prepare for Listening and Learning

Another way to become aware of main ideas and major points is to preview the material before coming to class. Read before class so that the lecture material isn't completely new. Reading beforehand will also help you to see how closely the instructor follows the textbook. The main benefit of previewing the lecture material is that you will be on the same wavelength as the instructor and can participate in discussions as well as answer questions. You'll be able to recognize and organize the main ideas and terms more easily (Kahn, 1992).

Mechanics of Note Taking

When taking class notes, use a telegraphic style that includes only the essential elements and leaves out unnecessary words. Forget grammar; grammatical sentences require more time than you have while taking notes. Instead, record a streamlined version of the instructor's lecture. Here are some other note-taking tips:

- Create your own abbreviations for common words used in class (just be sure to record what each abbreviation stands for). For example, as a student of developmental psychology, many of my lecture notes referred to "dev" instead of *development* and "Ψ" for *psychology*.
- Don't write in script. Instead, print your notes so that they are legible. Many students plan on typing their notes after class, but I don't suggest this because it's a waste of time. The typing itself takes too much concentration, slowing down your learning and distracting you from comprehending the facts and organizing your notes.

- Use a loose-leaf binder so that you can rearrange the pages as needed, add handouts from class, and remove pages neatly. Write notes on only one side of each loose-leaf page so that you can see all the information at once.
- As you take notes, use deep indentations to help you understand the organization of the lecture (such as an informal outline) and to provide room for later notes and comments.
- If you find note taking particularly difficult in a class, leave extra blank space at the end of each section or paragraph so that you can add more later (e.g., after asking a question or reading the text).
- Note the examples the instructor uses, or points from the discussion.
- Review your notes soon after class, making corrections or adding information as needed.

STUDY TIPS

Improving your skills in time management, reading, and note taking is key to enhancing your academic performance, but doing so is not enough to excel in college. You must also set aside a time and place to study.

Study Environment

Become aware of your study environment. Paying attention to where and when you study might seem overly conscientious, but this can help you to study more efficiently. Create a place just for studying. Why? We're conditioned by our environment to behave in certain ways. The more we behave a certain way in a given environment, the stronger the tendency gets. This is a powerful principle of psychology that you can use to your advantage. Create a habit for yourself. Designate an area to be used only for studying.

Choose a quiet place with adequate light. Make your study area pleasant and motivating. Avoid distractions; don't set up a study area in a high-traffic place (like the kitchen). If you are prone to distraction and procrastination, be sure your study area is away from the television set or anything else that might distract you (e.g., a big window). Create a barrier between you and the world. If possible, shut the door or at least create an invisible barrier by facing the wall.

Your study area should be convenient—a place that's easy to use—so you'll use it often. Don't underestimate the importance of a sturdy, comfortable chair. You'll spend a great deal of time in this chair, so you want to be comfortable (though not so comfortable that you fall asleep). An uncomfortable chair might make studying even less appealing and dampen any motivation that you muster up. Some students need light background noise to study—but be careful that it's not distracting. Before you decide that you "need" background noise, such as your television set or radio, try spending some time without any noise to see how it feels. If it's tough, then try studying with a little background noise as a comparison. Depending on your schedule, you might consider studying in more than one place (e.g., at home and at school). Find other places, such as a corner of the library, where you can study regularly. Is your study space conducive to learning? Quiz 4.2 will help you to evaluate your study area and determine if it is conducive to work.

QUIZ 4.2

Study Environment Quiz

Check off the items that you find are true for your study environment.

- ❑ Your desk is free of clutter, with space to spread out books and papers.
- ❑ The lighting is good.
- ❑ Your desk is in a quiet area.
- ❑ There is no television set nearby.
- ❑ Your chair is sturdy and comfortable.
- ❑ Pencils, pens, paper, a sharpener, and an eraser are handy.
- ❑ Tape, scissors, a stapler, a calculator, and a wastebasket are handy.
- ❑ Your desk is in a low-traffic area.
- ❑ Your desk faces the wall.
- ❑ Your calendar and schedule are handy.
- ❑ Your to-do lists are handy.
- ❑ Books, binders, and files are handy.
- ❑ The telephone answering machine is on, and the phone's ringer is off.
- ❑ The area is clutter-free.
- ❑ The e-mail announcement is turned off.
- ❑ There are few distractions.
- ❑ There are few things nearby that have nothing to do with school work.
- ❑ You work well in this workspace and feel that your studying is effective there.

Scoring:

Count your checkmarks. The closer your score is to 18, the better your study environment.

Reflection:

1. How does your study space rate? Reflect on your score.
2. In what ways might the quality of your workspace influence your learning and academic achievement?
3. In what ways can you improve your study space to make it a place more conducive to working? Identify three strategies for improving your workspace.

We've discussed the importance of developing the habit of studying by monitoring your study place and atmosphere, but you should also pay attention to the time of day. Decide on a routine time to study—ideally when you're at your best, when you're awake and alert. Try to study at the same time each day. When you set a discrete period of time aside for studying each day, your mind gets used to the pattern. It becomes easier to work during that time. Psychological research suggests that if you stick to a routine study time and place, you'll spend less time warming up and more time studying effectively.

Get Organized

Studying is easier if you're organized. Have you ever sat down to study only to realize that you need materials from another room? Not having your materials together is a time trap because you'll need to spend extra time gathering them and risk being sidetracked and wasting time. Save time by keeping all your study materials in one place, near your desk.

Do you have a filing system? If you wanted to look at your notes from last month or from last year, would you know where to look? One of the best ways to get organized is simple: Use a three-ring binder for your schoolwork. Keep lecture notes and handouts from each class together, marked by a tab. Use one large binder for all your classes, separating each class with tabbed dividers. You can also add a section for other necessities such as calendars, weekly schedules, lists, and phone numbers. All that you have to carry around is a single binder—not five notebooks, folders, and many scraps of paper. You will also be less prone to losing handouts if they're kept in a binder.

If your binder is full or gets too bulky, empty the contents into file folders labeled for each class. Keep a small file holder near your desk to hold the semester's work or consider using a filing cabinet to keep all your college work. This, of course, isn't the only way to get organized. There are many ways to arrange your study space and materials. The important thing is to always have everything handy when you study.

Organization is especially important if you plan to study in more than one place (e.g., at home and at school). Each morning, be sure to look over your schedule and determine what you'll need for the day. It might be easier to pack your book bag the night before to avoid wasting time during the hectic morning and possibly forgetting something important.

Prepare for Tests

We've discussed habits of studying, reading, and note taking that should keep you immersed in the subject matter of your courses. A test is on the horizon; how do you prepare? Well ahead of time, conduct an overview of all the work that needs to be done. Make a list of tasks and allocate time to complete them. If you're behind on your reading, approach the unread material with a plan.

What do you need to get from the readings? Decide how much time you have to catch up. Preview the reading, deciding which parts are most important to focus on and which can be omitted. Use the reading techniques described earlier in this chapter.

Create Study Sheets As you conduct your overview, list all the major topics covered in the course. Create a series of study sheets that summarize important information for each major topic. Each study sheet should list relevant factual information, vocabulary, and theories relating to the topic. Note the similarities and differences among the ideas, facts, theories, and other observations presented in the course.

Anticipate Test Questions Ask yourself, "If I were making up this test, given what we've focused on in class and the readings, I would probably ask my students . . . ," and then answer the questions. How do you anticipate questions? Think about how the various course topics relate to one another. Are there any repeated themes? Examine your notes and readings to determine how the course content supports the major themes of the course (you can often find these in the syllabus, first few lectures, and first chapter of the text). Note that in class, instructors often use cues to communicate content that is important and that may appear on a test. What kinds of cues do you look for?

- Repetition
- Repeated use of examples
- Changes in the tone of the voice
- Pauses in speaking to permit students to take notes
- Writing on the board or emphasizing a point on an overhead
- A pause in pacing when the lecturer makes eye contact with the class.

You have more power than you think when it comes to test taking. The trick is to determine the importance of material as it is presented in class and in reading assignments.

Rehearse Practice the activities involved in the test. If you will be solving problems, then solve problems while you study. If you will be conjugating French verbs, then write (and say) them. If you will be writing essays, then anticipate potential questions and write out answers. Rehearsal will make you more comfortable with the test-taking situation, reduce anxiety, and improve your performance.

Use Your Memory How do you ensure that you'll remember what you study? Become personally invested in the material. Care about and be interested in what you're studying. In other words, find something interesting about the material. Identify how it is relevant to your life. How does it fit with what you already know? Associate what you want to learn with something that you already know and intend to remember it. Tell yourself, "I will remember this because . . ." (Kahn, 1992).

Review and recite the information to be remembered by recalling it often. Use short 15- to 20-minute review sessions spaced out over several days (Kahn, 1992). In addition, try to recite the information at odd moments (say them in the shower or while walking to your car). By verbalizing the material you'll get an idea of how well you know it and where your weaknesses lie.

Test-Taking Tips

An essential element to performing well on tests is preparation; however, preparation is not always enough to perform at your best. Test-taking skills also count. Students who excel understand *how* to take tests. They tailor their strategies to the type of test (e.g., multiple choice or essay) and know how to prepare themselves emotionally. Let's examine test taking in detail.

Preview Your Test: Read Everything

The first step after receiving any test is to read the directions carefully. This is true even if it is a multiple-choice test. For example, some instructors might require that you choose the *best* answer, whereas others might require you to mark *all* correct answers. If you are asked to choose the best answer and you mark more than one response, you'll lose credit. On the other hand, if you are asked to mark all correct answers, you may lose credit if you don't chose more than one answer. So read the directions carefully; if they are not clear, ask your instructor to explain them.

Once you have carefully read the directions, preview the entire test. Check to be sure that your test has no missing or duplicate pages. Read through the test and decide how to allocate your time. If your head is swimming with information that you're afraid you'll forget, jot it down quickly. The following sections present strategies for taking multiple-choice tests and essay tests, as well as for test preparation in general.

Multiple-Choice Tests

When taking a multiple-choice test, begin each item by reading the question. Then read all the options. Don't rush, but take your time to read the question and each option completely. If the question is difficult, cross out any options that don't fit. In other words, eliminate distracters. If you can eliminate all the distracters, you'll have the correct answer. How do you identify distracters? Combine the question and each option into a complete statement. If the resulting statement is false, you've found a distracter. Stick with the subject matter of the course. If an option includes terms that seem out of place or that you don't recognize, it's probably a distracter (Pauk & Fiore, 2000). Here are some other tips:

- If one of the options is "all of the above," all that you need to do is determine whether two of the other options are correct. If so, then "all of the above" is the answer.
- Multiple-choice tests often include options that look alike; two options might be identical except for one or two words. It's logical to assume that one of the pair is correct (Pauk & Fiore, 2000).
- Note that correct answers are often longer and more inclusive than distracters.
- Tests often give away information relevant to one question in another question.
- After you have selected your answer, read the entire statement to be sure that it makes sense.
- Don't waste time on difficult questions. Eliminate as many distracters as possible. If you still don't know the answer, guess, mark the question, and return to it later.
- Don't leave any items blank.
- Sometimes questions are simple. Don't read into questions. Don't make the question more complex than it is intended to be.
- Because your first choice is usually correct, change your answer only if you are certain of the correction.

Essay Tests

Your first step in taking an essay test is to read all the questions thoroughly. Jot down any ideas and examples that come to you so that they don't clutter your mind. Consider the difficulty of each of the questions and answer them in a strategic order. Complete the easy questions first to reduce anxiety and facilitate clear thinking. Then move on to the questions with the highest point value. The last questions you answer should be the most difficult, require the greatest amount of writing, or have the least point value.

As you consider each essay question, determine what is being asked. What do you know that is related to the question? Take a moment and organize your essay. Jot down some notes or an outline of points that you want to make. Once you have a list of points or a basic structure, start writing. Don't meander, but get right to the point. Use your first paragraph to provide an overview of your essay. Be sure to state your main point within the first paragraph. Use the rest of your essay to discuss your points in more detail. Back up each point with specific information, examples, or quotations from the class readings and notes. Leave space at the end of each paragraph to allow you to add further information, if needed, as you proofread. Write on every other line and on just one side of the page, not only to allow space for adding information but also to make the answers easier for your instructor to read.

Budget your time for each essay question. When you reach the end of the time allotted for a given question, list your remaining points, leave extra space, and move on to the next item. Partially answering all the questions (especially by listing all the points that you want to make) is better than fully answering only a few questions and skipping others. You won't earn credit for the questions that you skip. After you've completed the rest of the test, return to the items that are incomplete.

Once you're finished with the test, proofread your answers. Modify them for clarity, adding details, if needed, to make them complete. Check for spelling, grammar, and punctuation errors. Remember that students tend to lose points on essay tests because they fail to answer the question asked, don't provide examples or evidence to support their statements, don't write enough, are disorganized, or don't follow directions. Finally, avoid the "kitchen sink" method of answering essays—writing all that you know about a subject and hoping that the answer is somewhere in your essay (Landrum, Davis, & Landrum, 2000).

General Suggestions

Test-taking skills are important, but they may not be enough for you to perform at your best. Take care of your physical and emotional needs too. Get a good night's sleep. Set your alarm a little early and take the time to have breakfast. Arrive early for your test, allowing time to acclimate yourself, relax, and prepare. Bring all the materials you will need for the test, including pencils and pens, a calculator, and a watch. Having all the materials necessary and arriving early will help you focus on the task at hand. Choose a seat that is well lit, located where you can't see many other students (and can't be easily distracted).

Don't let yourself become anxious. Try not to talk to other students before a test because their anxiety can be highly contagious. If you feel anxious, take some slow, deep breaths to relax, and use positive self-talk to raise your confidence. Research shows that students who are anxious tend to engage in negative self-talk (e.g., "Everyone in this class is smarter than I am," "I always screw up on tests," and "If I don't do well on this exam, I'll flunk the course."). Negative self-talk just brings you down and increases your stress level. When you find yourself engaging in negative self-talk, catch it and stop. Try to encourage yourself as you would a friend. Repeat positive statements to yourself in place of negative ones. Remind yourself that you are well prepared for the test and believe that you are going to do well.

If you feel rising tension, try using progressive relaxation techniques to help reduce your muscle tension. Breathe in deeply and flex your toes. Release and breathe out. Do the same for your calves, then your thighs, buttocks, stomach, chest, arms, shoulders, and neck. Repeatedly tense and release your major muscle groups; it takes only a moment and produces big results. You'll feel more relaxed and able to concentrate.

Learn From Returned Tests

Think that your learning is over once the test is? No! There's a lot you can learn from returned tests, so don't fall into the trap of checking your grade and not reviewing the test. When you get a test back, you should examine it carefully.

Examine Your Errors Revisit your errors. Why was the correct answer correct? Identify why you missed a question. Did you read it correctly?

Get Clues About the Next Test Look for the origin of each question (test, lectures, labs, supplementary readings, discussions). Check the level of detail and skill of the test. Were most of the questions about vocabulary or did they ask for precise details and facts? Were the questions about main ideas, principles, applications, or all of these?

Strategize Decide which strategies worked and which didn't. Were you prepared for the test? Did you run out of time? How might you have better allocated your time? Identify the strategies that didn't work well and replace them. Use your tests to review when studying for final exams. Did you have any problems with anxiety or blocking during the test? Did you really know the answer to a question but failed to read the question carefully enough to recognize it?

Academic success requires work; it's an active process. Practice the tips presented in this chapter and refine them based on your own needs. Not everyone studies in the same way. Be flexible in your study habits and do what works for you. Above all, remember that a little work on getting organized, creating a schedule, and staying on top of your reading can save you from cramming later. Perhaps even better is knowing that you'll retain what you've learned well beyond the test, the course, and college.

Suggested Readings

Gardner, J. N., & Jewler, A. J. (2005). *Your college experience: Strategies for success.* Belmont, CA: Wadsworth.

Hallberg, E., & Hallberg, K. (2004). *Making the dean's list.* Belmont, CA: Wadsworth.

Longman, D. G., & Atkinson, R. H. (2005). *CLASS: College learning and study skills.* Belmont, CA: Wadsworth.

Tyler, S. (2001). *Been there, should've done that II: More tips for making the most of college*. Lansing, MI: Front Porch Press.

WEB RESOURCES

The following web sites are hot-linked at *The Psychology Major's Handbook* web site at *http://info.wadsworth.com/kuther*

Study Tips

http://www.utexas.edu/student/utlc/handouts/stutips.html

At this site, you'll find a collection of pages addressing common problems such as motivation, time management, reading, and other issues.

Interactive Study Tips

http://www.ohiou.edu/aac/tip/

Quizzes and interactive exercises on time management, memory, reading, notes, exam preparation, and other topics make this site an essential stop on your next trip online.

How to Study

http://www.howtostudy.org/resources.htm

This site organizes a collection of links for all aspects of study skills.

Learning Strategies: Maximizing Your Academic Experience

http://www.dartmouth.edu/~acskills/success/index.html

These pages provide a variety of suggestions and resources for maximizing your aca-demic experience. View an online video, read about helpful strategies, or download a handout. In-depth tips for time management, reading, studying, and other problems.

JOURNAL EXERCISES

I'm at My Best When . . .

When are you at your best? When do you find it easiest to concentrate on difficult tasks? Are you a morning person—someone who accomplishes the most in the early morning? Do you work better at night? Why do you think you have these working patterns? What are the implications for scheduling classes and studying? How can you use this knowledge to help yourself?

Analyzing My Time

List all the demands on your time. What are your responsibilities? What takes up your time (e.g., family, classes, research, meetings, social life, activities)? Are you doing too much? Identify places where you can cut back. What can you not do? Choose two places to cut back.

Ideal Day

Suppose that you managed your time well. What would an ideal day look like? Write about it—realistically. Dealing with life as it is now, not as a fantasy, what would you do? How would you handle yourself in all situations? What two things would you do to bring yourself closer to that ideal? Suppose you suddenly had an extra 2 hours each day. How would you spend the time? Why?

Evaluating Time Management Strategies

After you've had a chance to try the time management strategies described in this chapter, freewrite about your experience. Which strategies worked well? How might you modify them to fit your style and needs?

CHAPTER 5

Writing a Literature Review

Chapter Guide

It's the first day of class, and the professor has just handed out the course guidelines and syllabus. Oh, no! A 15- to 20-page paper is due on "the topic of your choice." You wonder, "Fifteen pages! How am I supposed to know what I want to write 15 pages about before taking the class? How can I write a paper on anything without knowing a little about it first?" Don't get stressed out. Feeling overwhelmed is common when you're confronted with an ambiguous assignment to write a paper. The best thing you can do is to start thinking about it early. Don't wait until the last minute. This chapter will walk you through the steps in writing a literature review, from selecting a topic to proofreading the final draft.

What Is a Literature Review?

A literature review, sometimes called a term paper, presents and critically evaluates the literature (i.e., existing scholarly journal articles) on a given topic. Your goal is to critically discuss what has been published on a topic, organizing your presentation according to a research objective, thesis, problem, or issue. This means that you must choose a method of organizing your paper (a thesis, problem statement, or other organizational device) and then identify, synthesize, and evaluate the published work relevant to your topic. In other words, what's the main point that you want to make in this paper? Your paper should present literature in a way that tells a story about your topic, supporting and leading readers to the main point. Discuss the history of your topic, what is known and not known about it, and what research has been conducted on it. Another way of thinking about a literature review is that it answers a question. What's the question you'd like to answer? Present your initial question and then answer it for your readers using your research to support the answer. The final paper will give readers a detailed summary of what exists in the literature on your topic, as well as your informed evaluation of the literature.

At this point most students wonder, "Is my instructor a sadist? Why assign such a difficult project?" The answer is that writing is an integral part of learning psychology. It's an opportunity to learn about a topic of interest and acquire a host of skills:

- Collecting information
- Reading psychological research
- Evaluating an author's claims
- Integrating ideas from multiple sources to support your ideas
- Developing writing skills and vocabulary, enabling more effective communication
- Exploring new topics and subjects within psychology
- Thinking and writing like a psychologist

You'll use information-seeking and critical thinking skills to complete your paper. Information-seeking skills enable you to find useful articles and other materials and to scan the literature efficiently. Critical thinking skills entail applying principles of analysis to identify valid studies; evaluating the literature; and organizing your review into sections that identify themes, major issues, or trends. Thus, in writing a literature review, your job is not to list as many articles as possible but rather to present a comprehensive discussion about what has been published on your topic. A literature review should accomplish the following objectives.

- Discuss the major findings relating to your topic.
- Summarize what is and is not known about the topic.
- Evaluate the existing research, identifying controversy when it appears in the literature.
- Discuss further questions for research (i.e., identify gaps in the knowledge base. What questions remain? What direction should further research take?).

SELECTING A TOPIC

Choosing a topic is one of the most important tasks in writing a paper because "the paper can be no better than the topic" (Sternberg, 1993, p. 17). How can you choose a topic that is well researched and will sustain your (and your reader's) interest? Plan ahead and pay attention to the tips discussed in the following sections.

Where to Look for Topics

Believe it or not, you're surrounded by ideas for papers. Paper topics might come from watching television, reading magazines and books, observing people, or observing yourself. Pay attention to the social world around you, observe people's behavior, and ask, "Why?" You'll never be at a loss for ideas. You may also find ideas by using the following resources, which are often overlooked.

Your Textbook Leaf through the text and carefully scan the table of contents, which lists all the topics covered in the text. Once you find a topic that sounds interesting, turn to that section of the text and skim through it. Textbook chapters usually provide short overviews of topics that condense broad areas of theory and research into a few pages. If you're still interested after reading more, you've found a potential paper topic. You may have to read several sections of the text to get to this point, so it's important to start early in the semester and try not to get discouraged. Once you've found a topic of interest, use the material in your text as a starting point to expand the topic into a paper. Read the appropriate sections of your text and take note of any references that look promising.

Encyclopedias and Dictionaries The reference section of most libraries contains behavioral science dictionaries and encyclopedias in which you can find overviews of specific areas. Table 5.1 lists commonly available psychology reference books. These resources can often help you in selecting and narrowing a topic, but remember that they are only a starting point. Also, realize that the more recently the book was published, the more useful it will be in guiding your research. In most cases you should not cite an encyclopedia in your paper but use it to develop an initial understanding of the breadth and depth of the topic at hand.

Psychology Journals For a paper in an introductory psychology course, look through general psychology journals that have articles spanning all the fields within psychology. This will help you to get a feel for the wide range of psychological topics available for you to choose from. For example, *Current*

TABLE 5.1 PSYCHOLOGY DICTIONARIES AND ENCYCLOPEDIAS

Dictionaries

Colman, A. M. (2003). *A dictionary of psychology.* Oxford, UK: Oxford University Press.

Corsini, R. J. (2001). *The dictionary of psychology.* Florence, KY: Taylor & Francis.

Reber, A. S., & Reber, E. S. (2002). *Penguin dictionary of psychology.* New York: Penguin.

Roeckelein, J. E. (1998). *Dictionary of theories, laws, and concepts in psychology.* Westport, CT: Greenwood Press/Greenwood Publishing Group.

Schmidt, R. O. (2000). *The student's dictionary of psychological terms.* Bristol, IN: Wyndham Hall Press.

Encyclopedias

Craighead, W. E, & Nemeroff, C. B. (2001). *The Corsini encyclopedia of psychology and behavioral science* (3rd ed., Vols. 1–4). New York: Wiley.

Friedman, H. S. (1998). *Encyclopedia of mental health,* Vols. 1–3. San Diego, CA: Academic Press.

Kazdin, A. E. (2000). *Encyclopedia of psychology.* Washington, DC: American Psychological Association.

Levinson, D., Ponzetti, J. J., & Jorgensen, P. F. (1999). *Encyclopedia of human emotions,* Vols. 1–2. New York: Macmillan.

Strickland, B. B. (2000). *The Gale encyclopedia of psychology.* New York: Gale Group.

Wilson, R. A., & Keil, F. C. (1999). *The MIT encyclopedia of the cognitive sciences.* Cambridge, MA: MIT Press.

Directions in Psychological Science publishes short review-type articles that may spark some ideas. Also, take a look at *American Psychologist* and *Psi Chi Journal of Undergraduate Research*. If you're writing a paper for a more specialized class, such as one in developmental psychology, look through more specialized psychology journals to find recent articles and get ideas. For example, if you're searching for a topic for an adolescent psychology paper, leaf through recent issues of journals specializing in adolescent development (e.g., *Journal of Research on Adolescence, Journal of Adolescence, Journal of Adolescent Research, Adolescence*). Once you find an article that's interesting, read it carefully and examine the reference section to find related articles.

Professors If your professor has provided a list of possible topics, give them serious consideration. Recognize that he or she can be an important source of information and ideas. However, professors are more likely to offer you help if you've done some work first. Approach your instructor for feedback but understand that you should come with several ideas and ask for advice. Don't expect your professor to provide you with a topic for your paper.

The Media Television, magazines, and newspapers can offer ideas for papers. For example, each Tuesday, the *New York Times* includes a science section that usually has at least one article about psychology. These articles are a fantastic source of information and ideas. As you read or watch television, stop and consider the topic of the article or the program. Ask why—Why does the problem occur? How can it be prevented? What do we know about it? Ideas are everywhere; finding them requires an inquiring mind.

The Internet The World Wide Web offers an overwhelming array of resources for learning about psychology and coming up with ideas for research papers. Where do you start? Try these specialized psychology search engines and lists of resources.

- PsychCrawler—http://www.psychcrawler.com/
- AmoebaWeb—
  http://www.vanguard.edu/faculty/ddegelman/amoebaweb/
- Encyclopedia of Psychology—http://www.psychology.org/
- American Psychological Association—http://www.apa.org
- American Psychological Society—http://www.psychologicalscience.org
- Psych Wurld MegaPsych—
  http://www.tulsa.oklahoma.net/~jnichols/bookmarks.html

Browse these resources; when you find something interesting, try searching for more material. Use synonyms for your topic to obtain the most information possible. Remember that you'll have to go beyond web searches when it comes time to find resources for your paper. Most instructors require the use of articles from psychology journals as references for student papers; Internet links can provide a start but cannot serve as the basis of your paper.

Begin Reading Now

The best thing you can do is to start thinking about your paper early. Don't underestimate the amount of time it will take you to decide on a topic. Choosing a topic obviously requires thinking, but students are sometimes surprised to discover that it also requires reading. How can you choose a topic when you don't know much about the literature? How can you decide what to write about without knowing a little about the course and the topic first? Take time to scan the literature before deciding on your topic. Is the area well researched? Is the topic narrow enough? Is the topic too narrow? You won't be able to determine the answers to these questions without searching and reading through some of the literature.

How can you locate additional readings to narrow your topic and get started? First, check your textbook to see if additional readings are provided. Frequently, the final page of each chapter lists additional resources that can serve as a useful starting point. The next step is to search for other sources of information. As you begin your search, remember that the Internet is a valuable tool for locating information but that it cannot replace a trip to the library. A literature review is a scholarly paper that integrates information from reputable sources such as academic journals and scholarly texts, which are often not available on the Internet.

Consult the Reference Librarian Your best source of information about library resources and holdings is the reference librarian. Discuss your paper with him or her and explain what you're looking for (which is why it's important to select a preliminary topic beforehand). Ask the librarian to suggest sources of information. He or she can help you devise specific search strategies to find what you need more quickly and efficiently.

Locate Sources of Psychological Research The American Psychological Association (APA) publishes an important resource for locating journal articles: PsycINFO, a web database of abstracts from journal articles, book chapters, books, and dissertations published in psychology and the behavioral sciences. Each article entry includes bibliographic information (helps you locate the article) and an abstract (provides summary information to help you decide if the article is useful for your paper). PsycINFO is updated frequently and indexes articles from 1887 to the present, permitting a thorough search of the literature. Most institutions maintain a subscription to PsycINFO, and some also have a subscription to PsycARTICLES, a new service that provides full text articles from journals published by the American Psychological Association from 1985 to the present.

PsycINFO and other databases of articles that your institution's library subscribes to make it easy to conduct a thorough literature search, saving you lots of time in your research *if* you know how to use them effectively. Skill, flexibility, and creativity are required to get the most from computer databases. Sometimes the search for a topic yields few results because the wrong search words have been used.

How do you determine the appropriate search terms? The *Thesaurus of Psychological Index Terms,* published by the American Psychological Association and linked to PsycINFO, can help you select search terms as it lists all descriptors or index terms (called key terms) used for PsycINFO. Use it before beginning your search to brainstorm the most appropriate descriptors, and you'll save time and hassles. Also, after locating an article that is useful for your paper, look for the key terms under which the article is listed. Use these key terms to find additional articles.

Additional features that make PsycINFO especially useful are the tools for refining searches; you can combine the results of several searches and limit the results of a search. Table 5.2 illustrates the steps in using an electronic

TABLE 5.2

Conducting a Literature Search With PsycINFO

Before beginning your search, remember that you won't find everything in one pass. Instead, you'll need to refine your searching strategies and, depending on your topic, may have to conduct several searches. For example, consider a paper on the influence of parents and peers on early adolescent drinking.

1. Doing the Initial Search

To gather articles about alcohol use, I typed in "alcohol or drinking" as keywords and found that more than 8,000 articles have "alcohol"or "drinking" in their title, in their abstract, or as a subject.

2. Narrowing the Search

Because the paper is for a course in adolescence, I decided that I would limit my findings to only those that examine adolescence. This required a two-step process. First, I typed "adolescent or adolescents or adolescence or teen" as search terms and found nearly 15,000 results. Next I combined this search with my initial search (see step 1) to narrow down the number of articles to a little more than 1,100. That was still too much for my paper!

3. Combining with "And"

Because my paper will examine parental and peer influences on adolescent alcohol use, I decided to limit my search to those articles that discuss parents or peers. I entered "parents" as a keyword and found 12,000 references. I then entered "peers" as a keyword and got over 2,800 results. The third step required combining the results of the two searches, which I did by using "and" to find all the references that examine both parents and peers and found nearly 600. Finally, I combined this search with my initial search on adolescent alcohol use (see step 1) and narrowed the results to 25, a manageable number.

4. Combining with "Or"

Alternatively, I might want to search for articles that examine parents *or* peers. If I combine the "parent" search with the "peer" search using "or," I get 14,000 articles. After combining this search with the initial search on adolescent alcohol use (see step 1), I find more than 250 references that examine adolescent alcohol use and either parents or peers. If I limit the results to journal articles published within the past 5 years, I get 182 results.

database, including how to combine the results of several searches and how to limit the results of a search.

Finally, note that if your institution does not subscribe to PsycINFO, you can access it online free through the American Psychological Association web site (http://www.apa.org). You'll have to obtain the articles through your school (or purchase them for a fee online), but this online resource permits you to do a great deal of research at home.

Read Journal Articles Journal articles are the most important sources of current findings in psychology. Students often wonder why journal articles are preferred over books. Journals are published more frequently and have a more rigorous review and acceptance process than do books. As a psychology major, you will need to become familiar with journal articles—if you aren't already.

How are journal articles different from magazine articles? Magazines pay writers, whereas journals do not pay their authors. Magazine articles might be checked for accuracy, but they do not undergo peer review and are not scrutinized to the same extent as journal articles. Journal articles document the sources of ideas and evidence more extensively; articles in magazines are rarely as extensively documented. Most important, journal articles on psychology are published after a process of peer review whereby several professionals review article submissions before an acceptance decision is made. When an author submits a manuscript to a journal, the journal editor sends copies of it out for review by the author's peers. This means that other psychologists are asked to read the article and determine whether it is suitable for publication. The peers who review the articles are called referees. Sometimes peer-reviewed journals are referred to as refereed journals.

How do referees evaluate manuscripts? Although each reviewer may use slightly different criteria, manuscripts are reviewed based on scholarship. A scholarly manuscript offers an important contribution to the field of psychology and includes a comprehensive review of the literature, concise writing, appropriate methodology and statistical analyses, and an understanding of the audience (Landrum, Davis, & Landrum, 2000). Once the editor receives the reviews, a decision is made whether to reject the paper, accept it, or suggest that the author make some changes and resubmit it. As you might imagine, this is a long, tedious process, but it ensures that the articles appearing in scholarly journals have scholarly merit.

Journal articles can lead you to other articles and sources for your research. When you find a current article that is especially useful, examine the references and you'll find other sources that are relevant to your paper. After you've examined the reference list for each article that you cite in your paper, you'll find that a great deal of your research is complete. However, it is important not to rely on this as your only strategy for locating articles because you may end up with a distorted view of the literature. Some authors may not cite other seminal works because of bias and differences of opinion. If you obtain all your sources from the reference lists for other articles, you might miss some important pieces of research, and you will certainly miss out on new research.

Find Recent Books About Your Topic When you consider books as sources for your paper, understand that the more recently a book was published, the more likely it is to contain current theory and methodology (Scott, Koch, Scott, & Garrison, 1999). Edited books, which contain chapters written by many different authors, are often good sources of information. Because each chapter is written by a different author, it usually presents a different view of your topic.

Before you spend a great deal of time searching for books, be familiar with your professor's recommended and required resources. Some instructors advise their students not to use books as sources because they're too long for student papers. In addition, many books are not scholarly or may not be academically acceptable. Many popular self-help books on the market are of questionable scientific value. Therefore, some professors discourage students from using books as sources because it can be difficult to evaluate their scholarly value.

If you decide to use books as source material for your paper, examine each one carefully. How do you determine the academic trustworthiness of a book?

- Examine the author's background. What are his or her academic credentials and experience?
- Examine the reference section because the number and type of references can indicate how well the book has been researched. How many of the references are the author's?
- How sound are the book's facts, methodologies, and findings?
- Does the book have an index? Scott et al. (1999) suggest that "in addition to making your search for relevant material easier, an index suggests a certain amount of professionalism on the part of the authors. Also, browsing through an index can give you a feel for the book's level of professionalism" (p. 109).
- Skim the introduction, preface, forward, or first chapter to find clues about the book's purpose, intended audience, and scholarly quality.

Choose an Interesting Topic

Another reason for starting early is that you'll have time to select a topic that will maintain your interest. Allow yourself an opportunity to consider several topics and choose the one that appeals to you most. In other words, don't procrastinate. Procrastinating is a mistake because you'll need time to think about the topic of your paper before you can begin to write. Too often, students wait until the last possible moment to select a topic. Then they choose hastily and end up with a subject they are only marginally interested in. Be nice to yourself and take the time to find an interesting topic. Few things are worse than working on an uninteresting paper.

Choose an Appropriate Match to Your Abilities

Try not to choose a topic that is too easy or too "safe" for you; also, try to avoid choosing a topic that's too difficult (Sternberg, 1993). The purpose of writing a paper is to learn something about a subject. Choose a topic that you're relatively unfamiliar with to maximize your learning opportunity. Choosing a safe topic (e.g., one you've already written papers on) deprives you of the opportunity and challenge of gaining competence in a new area.

As already mentioned, the opposite is also true; try not to choose a topic that is too difficult. Scan the abstracts of articles on your topic to be sure that you can understand the purposes and the underlying concepts and ideas presented. Avoid topics that you can't adequately discuss and evaluate from the information presented in these articles. In other words, be "certain that the topic you choose does not require an understanding of concepts that your background does not permit you to grasp" (Sternberg, 1993, p. 18).

Narrow Your Topic

Once you have an initial idea for a topic, you're still not yet ready to begin writing your paper. Before committing yourself to a topic, be sure that there is adequate literature on it. Can you find articles that address your topic or do you find too many? The most common mistake that students make in choosing a paper topic is to choose one that is too broad. A literature review, by its very nature, provides comprehensive coverage of a topic. In order to provide comprehensive coverage, you'll need to choose a narrow topic (otherwise you will be writing a book, not a class paper). Table 5.3 provides an example of how to narrow your topic.

Narrowing your topic means that you'll target your paper to a specific line of research or aspect of your topic. Unless you are already knowledgeable about the research area, you can't preselect a topic that is narrow enough. This is another reason why you shouldn't procrastinate, because choosing an appropriately narrow topic requires reading and getting a handle on the literature. Once you have tentatively chosen a topic, scan the literature (using the techniques described earlier in this chapter) to determine how well researched it is and then narrow it down if necessary. This is a good time to visit your professor or teaching assistant to get some feedback on your choice.

TABLE 5.3 NARROWING AND BROADENING A TOPIC

1. Initial Topic: Violence

A search using PsycINFO reveals more than 10,000 sources. This is much too broad a topic.

2. Narrowed: Child Abuse, Spouse Abuse, School Violence, Community Violence, Dating Violence, Bullying

Even these topics are too broad for an assignment calling for a 10-page paper. For example, consider Child Abuse; it yields nearly 10,000 sources on PsycINFO.

3. How to Narrow a Topic

Consider the problem more specifically. Ask who, what, when, where, how? For example, consider Child Abuse:

Who?	What population are you researching?
What?	Are you interested in causes of abuse? Prevention? Treatment programs?
When?	Historical? Recent trends?
Where?	The entire world? United States? Urban? Suburban?
How?	How does the abuse take place? What form of abuse? Physical? Sexual? Emotional? Neglect?

4. Sample Narrowed Topic: Child Abuse

Who?	Infants
What?	Causes
When?	Recent
Where?	United States
What?	Physical Abuse

After entering each of these terms into PsycINFO, I end up with 0 results.

5. How to Broaden a Topic

Broaden the topic by deleting some terms. When I delete Infants, Recent, and United States, my search yields 56 results.

Think you have a good understanding of how to use PsycINFO to locate articles as well as to broaden and narrow searches? Try Exercise 5.1 to test your competence.

EXERCISE 5.1

Using PsycINFO

Choose a research area in which you are interested (e.g., the effects of child abuse on development). Be specific in order to narrow the results of your PsycINFO search to yield a manageable number of articles. For example, instead of examining the effect of child abuse on development, use more narrow terms such as abuse in infancy; rather than development, use a more narrow term such as cognitive development or memory development.

1. What is your research question?
2. Write down the search terms that you will use.
3. Enter your search terms into PsycINFO. How many results do you get? Were your terms too narrow or too broad? Print out the first page of your results.
4. Try narrowing your topic. Write down the search terms used. How many results do you get? Print out the first page of your results.
5. Take a closer look at the results on the first page of your narrowed search. How do these results differ from those for your first search? Discuss any patterns that you notice in article titles.
6. Try broadening your topic. Write down the search terms used. How many results do you get? Print out the first page of your results.
7. Take a closer look at the results on the first page of your broadened search. How do these results differ from those in your narrowed search? Discuss any patterns that you notice in article titles.
8. Return to the results page for your narrowed topic search. Choose one article that is particularly interesting. Retrieve the first page of this article using your library's full-text and print resources. The reference librarian can assist you if you experience difficulty. Print the first page of the article.

READING

As your mass of journal articles and other research sources grows, it's easy to feel overwhelmed. Don't! Reading the articles and synthesizing the ideas into a cohesive paper may seem like a daunting task, but you can break it down into smaller pieces so that it will be more manageable. If you've taken your time choosing a topic and have narrowed it down appropriately, you've already begun reading some of the literature or at least scanned some of it.

Define Your Purpose

Once you begin reading, it's easy to forget the purpose of your paper. Instead, you may find yourself describing each detail of each article. Stay focused. Before you begin reading and taking notes, clarify the purpose of your paper. Remain focused as you read and consider articles, and your paper will seem more manageable.

Also, before you begin reading, consider your thesis, problem, or research question. What is your angle? Are you considering issues of theory, methodology, or policy? What is the scope of the review? How have you limited the literature? For example, a student might limit the scope of a paper about conduct disorder to examining evaluations of behavioral interventions. Defining the scope of the review involves restating a narrow topic and setting rules for including or excluding articles. Write down your ideas about the purpose, angle, and scope of your paper.

At first, concentrate on reading the abstracts for the articles that you've chosen. If you've defined your purpose well, you may find that after reading only the abstracts, you can eliminate some articles from consideration because they're not relevant to your paper. As you read, take occasional breaks to reread your stated purpose. Consider whether what you've read is within the scope you have delineated for your paper. Perhaps your reading has suggested that you should change your focus or narrow your paper. Realize that your ideas about your paper will change and become more refined with your reading. Be open to change and take notes on how you might refocus your paper.

Hints on Reading

The most important tip about reading, as with all aspects of preparing your paper, is to begin early. Lots of time and effort will be spent before you begin to write. You'll need plenty of time to think about your paper and collect articles and read them before any writing occurs. Reading for your paper is a process of information gathering and synthesis. As you read, you might encounter references that seem important. Return to the library to gather these new sources.

Understand the Layout of Research Articles Even those who are unfamiliar with journal articles quickly see that research articles have a specific format and layout. Understanding this layout will make articles more comprehensible. Chapter 6 discusses how to prepare research papers and provides information about the sections of a research article, but here is a brief overview.

An empirical article consists of several sections: abstract, introduction, method, results, discussion, and references. Each section has a specific purpose. The abstract (usually located below the article title and above the text of the article) briefly summarizes the study. The introduction is the first section of an article. It provides an overview of the research question, reviews the literature, and identifies the purpose of the study (the specific purpose and hypotheses are usually found at the very end of the introduction section). The method section explains how the research was conducted; it describes the participants, measures, instruments and equipment, and procedure. The results section presents statistical analyses that address the research questions. The study findings are presented here, with information displayed in graphs and tables. In the discussion section, the author examines the significance of the study's findings in light of prior research, discusses the limitations of the study, and offers suggestions for further research. For more information about empirical articles, see Chapter 6.

Scan the Article Thoroughly reading an article requires several passes. Your first pass should be an initial scan to determine whether the study is essential for your paper. Reading and taking notes is time-consuming; therefore, you want to be sure that the article suits your needs before you spend a great deal of time on it. During your initial scan of the article, determine the research question, specific hypotheses, findings, and interpretation. After you've scanned for this material, stop and consider whether the article fits with the purpose of your paper. Is it relevant? How does it apply to your paper? How will you use it?

Read for Depth If you've decided that an article is relevant to your paper, your next task is to read for depth. What is the problem or issue addressed? Discern the theories tested and the methods used. Who were the participants, and how were they tested? How were the findings interpreted? Consider the following:

- Is the author's hypothesis ambiguous or clearly articulated?
- What is the author's research orientation and theoretical framework? What are the author's underlying assumptions? From what theoretical framework does the author address the problem? (You can find clues in the author's choice of citations and how often particular references are cited.)
- Could the problem have been approached more effectively from another perspective?
- Has the author evaluated the literature relevant to the issue? Were any areas of literature excluded from the author's review?
- Does the author have a balanced perspective and include articles that take contrary positions?
- Is the sample large and representative of the population the author wishes to address? How were participants selected?
- What measures were used? Are the psychometric properties of the instruments presented? How valid are the instruments? Do they measure the intended constructs?
- Were the data analyzed properly? What are the findings? Are the findings meaningful? Sometimes researchers find differences between variables that are statistically significant but small; these differences may not be meaningful when applied.
- How are the findings interpreted? Do you agree with the interpretation?
- What are the strengths and weaknesses of the study? (Every study has strengths and weaknesses.)
- Do the findings have applied or policy implications?

Take Time It takes time to digest the volumes of information that you'll need to absorb. Give yourself enough time to read and evaluate the research. When should you stop reading and taking notes? You'll know that you have done a thorough review when you notice that article authors cite studies that you have already reviewed. But this doesn't mean that you're ready to write your paper. Understand your sources, take notes, and think carefully about their implications before beginning to write. Consider how the articles fit together and how you might organize your review.

Recording Your Research: Take Notes

As you read, summarize the main findings and methods of each study that you think are important enough to include in your paper. If you consistently take the time to write a brief summary of each article that you plan to include, your literature review will be largely done by the time you sit down to formally write. Summarize each article in a page or less but don't write down everything. Avoid copying from a source word for word; doing so makes it too easy to commit plagiarism without realizing it. (We'll talk more about plagiarism later.) Note taking is a skill; it requires critical thinking and evaluation to record only the most essential features of a study (purpose, method, findings, and interpretation).

How to Take Notes

The method that you use to take notes is a personal choice. I've found that I can save a great deal of time by taking notes using a word processing program. If you take notes on a computer, clearly mark each reference and print out a hard copy. You'll find that most of the notes that later become the prose of your first draft have already been typed. You can then edit them, adding transitions, analysis, and interpretation (after making a "safe" copy). You can also cut and paste the material to organize it, making writing a lot easier.

Others (e.g., Landrum et al., 2000; Sternberg, 1993) suggest using a note card system. Use 5-by-7-inch cards organized by topic. Use a separate card for each article. Write the APA-style reference on the back of the card and your notes on the front. (If you're not sure what an APA-style reference is, see Chapter 6 for a discussion of APA style). Note cards allow you to physically rearrange information and sort it into topical categories that will help you to organize the outline of your paper. Note cards travel well and offer a handy way of arranging and rearranging information.

Whatever method you choose, remember that good notes concisely and accurately summarize the main points of a source. Be precise in indicating paraphrases and direct quotes (see the next section). It's also essential that you take time to write references using correct APA style. Nothing is more frustrating than hunting for a reference that you haven't recorded. It can sometimes take hours to locate a source once you've begun writing; it takes only a few minutes to record the information properly while you're taking notes.

Avoid Plagiarism

Plagiarism means using another person's work (i.e., ideas, research, writing, web sites, charts, data, or other original work) without giving credit and without clearly acknowledging its source. The rules of plagiarism apply to all sources, both published (books, magazines, newspapers, web sites, and textbooks) and unpublished (class lectures, notes, handouts, speeches, and student papers). To avoid plagiarizing, writers must give credit whenever they use information from a source. Citations giving the source of information must accompany discussions of another person's ideas, arguments, or theory; facts that are not common knowledge; quotations of a person's spoken or written words; and paraphrases of another person's spoken or written words.

How can you avoid plagiarism? By using your own words to express the ideas of others and then giving credit to the originators of those ideas. Try to convey the author's main idea without using his or her words or sentence structure. Always cite information and ideas that are learned through your research, no matter where you find them (even if it is on the Internet or in an encyclopedia). Common knowledge is not cited, but be careful what you consider common knowledge. Examples of common knowledge are well-known dates and familiar sayings. Generally, information that can be found in a number of general sources (e.g., popular magazines) may not have to be cited. Whenever in doubt, cite. It is better to be safe and overcite your sources than to accidentally plagiarize someone else's work.

Appropriate Use of Quotations When you repeat an author's exact words, you must indicate that the material is a direct quote and give its source. APA style requires that you enclose the material in quotation marks and cite the author's last name, the year of publication, and the page number for the quote (American Psychological Association, 2001). Here is an example of a short quotation given within the text:

> Bornstein and Arterberry (1999) argued that "perception begins our experience and interpretation of the world, and is crucial to the growth of thought" (p. 231). This is . . .

If the quotation contains 40 or more words, it should be displayed as a free-standing block, with the quotation marks omitted:

> Bornstein and Arterberry (1999) argued that
>
> > Perception begins our experience and interpretation of the world, and is crucial to the growth of thought, to the regulation of emotions, to interaction in

> social relationships, and to progress in most aspects of our development. The input, translation, and encoding of sensory information in perception is requisite to reflection and action (p. 231).

In summary, it is permissible to include a direct quote in your paper as long as it is appropriately documented. Enclose the material in quotation marks and cite the authors, year of publication, and page numbers. Quoting a source without providing documentation is plagiarism.

Now that you've reviewed the appropriate use of quotes, be aware that it's best not to use too many of them in your paper. A paper represents the synthesis and analysis of what you've read. When you use direct quotes too often, the resulting paper is just a string of other people's words and ideas rather than your own analysis, interpretation, and expression of their ideas. Be careful not to quote because of laziness; it is much easier to use direct quotes than it is to paraphrase. Quote directly from a source only when you cannot capture the original ideas in your own words. Use quotes only when the author's language is distinctive and enhances your argument. In other words, record quotations only when "(1) the language of the original was especially important or vivid and therefore worth preserving, and (2) when you wanted to invoke the authority of your source" (Meyer, 1985, p. 78). I ask that students use quotes no more than every other page—at most—and integrate them within sentences.

Appropriate Paraphrasing Paraphrasing refers to restating an author's ideas or information in your own words. Even though you are using your own words, you must cite the source of your information. In APA style, appropriate citation of paraphrases includes the author's last name and the year of publication but not the page number. Note that you should provide the page number only when quoting directly from a source. For example, a paraphrase of the text quoted earlier might read as follows:

> Perception is essential to cognitive, emotional, and social development because it determines how we interpret and react to the sensory world around us (Bornstein & Arterberry, 1999).

As you can see, the paraphrase concisely restates the main idea of the passage using different words and sentence structure.

How do you paraphrase? First, be sure that you understand the information you wish to paraphrase. Your goal is to restate the idea and convey the same meaning, so it is essential that you understand the original passage before trying to paraphrase it. Realize that you may have to edit your paraphrase several times. Write your paraphrase; then reread the original passage to check for accuracy and to be sure that you haven't borrowed language or structure. Revise your paraphrase as needed. Remember to use your own grammatical structure, restate the material in your own words, and cite the source. Practice is essential because appropriate paraphrasing is difficult. Paraphrasing allows you to summarize an author's main points concisely and in your own writing style, contributing to the "flow" of your paper.

Test your ability to quote and paraphrase, as well as learn about how your institution views plagiarism and its consequences, by completing Exercise 5.2.

EXERCISE 5.2

Understanding and Avoiding Plagiarism

1. Identify an interesting passage from your textbook. Write a short paragraph about the topic, including the quotation, using appropriate APA style to indicate that it is a quotation and not your own words.
2. Now write a short paragraph that paraphrases instead of quotes the passage. Note that paraphrasing entails more than using a thesaurus to replace a few words. Appropriate paraphrasing requires conveying the ideas in a new set of words and sentence structure entirely different from the original.
3. Reflect on the process of paraphrasing. Was it challenging? Why? How might you gain experience and become more comfortable with this new skill?
4. Identify reasons why students might plagiarize.
5. Look up your institution's definitions and policies about plagiarism. What are the consequences of plagiarism at your institution?

More on Academic Honesty Frequently, students commit plagiarism without realizing it by incorrectly quoting and paraphrasing material. Remember that ignorance of the rules is no excuse for plagiarizing. Many professors don't provide a "get-out-of-jail-free card." In other words, if you inadvertently plagiarize, you might find yourself with an F or a zero on an assignment and no way to make it up.

Writing papers is difficult. Take your time and do it right. Some students take the easy way out by

- recycling an old paper used in a prior class;
- buying a paper online;
- downloading a paper online;
- cutting and pasting from Internet pages;
- using a service that writes papers for students;
- asking someone else to write a paper for them.

Recognize that these are not appropriate ways of completing an assignment to write a paper. You'll cheat yourself of the learning and skills that are developed by researching and writing papers. Professors also have ways of discovering the use of these techniques, so success with these devious methods is unlikely. For more information and resources to help you understand the scope of plagiarism, as well as quizzes to determine if you really understand acceptable use of information and how to appropriately cite material, see the web sites listed at the end of this chapter.

WRITING YOUR PAPER

Now that you've read your articles, taken notes, and spent time thinking about the articles, it is time to organize and write your paper. Where do you begin?

Organize Your Ideas

Consider the theme, issue, or research question that you plan to explore in your paper. Organize the paper to highlight your major theme, issue, or research question. The introduction section establishes the research question and explains why it is worth examining. The last paragraph of the introduction section should outline the organization of the paper.

Within the body of the paper, present evidence from research studies to support your points. Describe and evaluate each study and make comparisons among the studies. Compare studies based on assumptions, theories tested, hypotheses, research designs, methods, findings, and interpretations. How do these studies support the theme of your paper?

In the final section of the paper, draw conclusions, discuss implications, and suggest avenues of further research. Based on the studies reviewed and the comparisons and evaluations made, what conclusions can you draw? What research is left to be done? Recommend future studies.

Prepare an Outline

Before you begin writing, prepare an outline. It's much easier to prepare an outline once you've completed your reading and taken notes, so save this step until you have a set of notes from your reading and have had time to think about what you've read. Outlining gives you a better understanding of your paper because it forces you to list your ideas and to arrange them logically. Perhaps most important, an outline is a plan for your writing. It will not only help you stay on track (i.e., keep you from introducing irrelevant topics) but will also keep you from leaving important material out of your paper. You'll find that you can write your paper more quickly because you'll know exactly what to put in each section. An outline doesn't have to be fancy. Just jot down the points you want to make and then order them so that they make sense. It's easier to do this with a computer, using a word processing program to cut and paste your ideas as you wish.

Some students and professors dislike using outlines and think they are a waste of time. Typically, if you are experiencing difficulty structuring your outline, it means that your ideas are too vague and fuzzy. Read and think about your project, and organizational themes will emerge. Outlining is a valuable skill, but if you really can't use an outline, then just begin writing. Some authors prefer to write rough drafts of their papers, allowing thoughts and creativity to flow freely. Once you're written a rough draft, read through it and outline what you've written. The resulting outline will help you to see the structure of your argument. You can then reorder the outline as needed to make sense and present your argument skillfully.

All good literature reviews can be outlined easily. The first sentence of each paragraph should provide an overview of the paragraph, and thus by examining the first sentence of each paragraph, one can compile an outline of the structure of the paper. Once you have done so, examine the structure. First, ask yourself whether each paragraph has a purpose. Then examine the ordering of the paragraphs. What idea is expressed in each paragraph? Are the ideas ordered in a logical fashion? Reorder them as needed.

Write

Students often worry about how to start writing and then don't begin. An outline (simply a list of points to address) helps to prevent writer's block. Once you have an outline, your paper is organized, and you can work on filling in the outline. Don't worry about starting at the beginning. Don't get stuck on a first sentence or paragraph. Just start anywhere. Write with a word processing program on a computer, which will allow you to cut and paste your writing into endless patterns. Take advantage of this technological capability and begin writing whatever part of your paper flows most naturally. You can arrange and rearrange your writing later.

Remember that this is your first draft. Not every word will stay, and not every word has to be perfect. Don't worry about errors. Just get the ideas out; you'll catch the errors later as you edit. Write anything that appears relevant and think about where to put it and how to reorganize it later. Save your work regularly on the computer's internal hard drive as well as on other media in case a virus or other malfunction occurs. Print a hard copy at the end of each writing session and preferably more often (e.g., after completing two or three pages or an hour's worth of work).

Begin working early to give yourself time to write and rewrite. Time is essential in writing a comprehensive review of the literature; take time to read, let your ideas simmer, write, gain a perspective on what you've written, and revise. As you work, you may find that some elements of your research are incomplete. Go back to the library and gather additional resources to fill in any gaps in your research or argument.

Revise

The most important part of writing is rewriting, so be prepared for lots of edits and rewrites. Once you have a draft, spend at least 24 hours away from it. Let it sit for a day or two, and you'll be able to approach it with fresh eyes. You'll be surprised at the number of changes that seem obvious. With time, you'll find it easier to separate yourself from your work and become more objective.

Before you begin the editing and revising process, make a safe copy of your paper in case you decide to undo some of your revisions. Read through your draft and note what needs to be done. Is the organization consistent with your outline? Are you happy with the outline or should it be modified based on your paper? As you read, you might want to list gaps in the paper's organization that need to be filled, missing details to be provided, and other tasks to be completed, such as checking spelling and grammar or tracking down an errant reference. Recognize that you will revise the paper several times; don't feel the need to complete the final draft right away.

Read your paper aloud. Reorganize sections, edit them, or even delete them if you deem them unnecessary. Examine the order of sentences and paragraphs. Sometimes moving a sentence to a different place within a paragraph (or even deleting it) makes a world of difference. As you revise your paper, consider whether you've left anything out. Can anything be deleted; are there extraneous details or sections? Are the paragraphs and sections coherent and logical? Have you used transitions between paragraphs and sections so that the paper flows? Have you used a consistent style throughout? Have you used the proper guidelines as stipulated by your instructor or APA style? (See Chapter 6 for more on APA style.)

Think you're finished? Print out your final draft and proofread it aloud. Check for the placement of commas and your use of grammar. You might be surprised by the errors that you find. Take your final draft to the writing center at your college or university. You'll get an extra pair of eyes to read your work and some helpful feedback on how to improve your paper. Then make your corrections and print out your final draft.

Remember that good writing is the result of practice. The process gets easier with experience, but we all begin writing papers with at least a little trepidation. Start early and take time to read and mull over your articles. Revise your paper several times, waiting a day or two between each draft to gain distance. Use the questions in Checklist 5.1 as a guide in writing your literature review. Finally, don't procrastinate or let fear stop you from writing.

CHECKLIST 5.1

Literature Review Checklist

- ❑ Is the topic appropriate (i.e., is it a topic within the field of psychology)?
- ❑ Does the title of your paper describe the topic of your review?
- ❑ Does your review include an introduction section that defines the purpose of the review and its significance?
- ❑ Does the introduction section explain the organization of the literature review?
- ❑ Does your review include journal articles as sources?
- ❑ Does your review include the most current (and appropriate) articles as sources?
- ❑ Does your review discuss the major findings relating to your topic?
- ❑ Does your review evaluate existing research?
- ❑ Have you explained why particular studies and sets of findings are strong?
- ❑ Have you explained why particular studies and sets of findings are weak?
- ❑ Have you included enough detail about each study to help the reader determine the significance of each article?
- ❑ Have you described relationships among studies?
- ❑ Have you noted and explained gaps in the literature?
- ❑ Have you described any controversies in the field?
- ❑ Have you chosen a method of organizing the literature reviewed in your paper?
- ❑ Have you outlined your paper after writing it to examine its organization?
- ❑ Does your literature review answer an identifiable question?
- ❑ Does each study you reviewed correspond with a specific part of your topic outline?
- ❑ Have you deleted studies that do not relate to your purpose or argument?
- ❑ Does each part of your review flow logically from the preceding part?
- ❑ Do you use transitions between paragraphs to indicate the flow of major points in your outline?
- ❑ Does your review include a conclusion section?
- ❑ Does your review discuss further questions for research?
- ❑ Does your conclusion address the purpose identified in the introduction?
- ❑ Did you revise your manuscript several times?
- ❑ Did you spell check the manuscript?
- ❑ Are quotations used only when needed?
- ❑ Are quotations cited appropriately? Can any quotations be paraphrased?
- ❑ Are all paraphrases cited appropriately?
- ❑ Have you avoided the use of slang, abbreviations, and contractions?
- ❑ Have you used the past tense to refer to research studies?

SUGGESTED READINGS

Rosnow, R. L., & Rosnow, M. (2003). *Writing papers in psychology*. Belmont, CA: Wadsworth.

Scott, J. M., Koch, R. E., Scott, G. M., & Garrison, S. M. (1999). *The psychology student writer's manual*. Upper Saddle River, NJ: Prentice Hall.

WEB RESOURCES

The following web sites are hot-linked at *The Psychology Major's Handbook* web site at *http://info.wadsworth.com/kuther*

Writing in Psychology

http://webpub.alleg.edu/dept/psych/Writing.html

This web site contains an excellent guide to all forms of writing in psychology. Essential reading!

Writing a Review Article for Psychological Bulletin

http://comp9.psych.cornell.edu/dbem/psych_bull.html

At this site, you'll find a classic article, by Daryl Bem, on how to write a scholarly literature review.

Writing a Psychology Literature Review

http://depts.washington.edu/psywc/handouts/pdf/litrev.pdf

An excellent handout describing the steps in writing a literature review paper and providing helpful advice for student writers.

PsycINFO Guide

http://www.library.auckland.ac.nz/docs/helpsheets/psycinfoguide.pdf

Everything you need to know about using PsychINFO is in this handy guide. A must read that will make finding relevant articles much easier.

Plagiarism Tutorial

http://www.lib.usm.edu/research/plag/plagiarismtutorial.php

An excellent site with several lessons and two quizzes to assess your understanding of plagiarism.

What Is Plagiarism?

http://education.indiana.edu/~frick/plagiarism/item1.html
An educational quiz that will help you to learn the scope of acceptable use.

Journal Exercises

How I Feel About Writing

How do you feel about writing? Imagine receiving a paper assignment in class. What are your initial thoughts and emotions? Would you like to change any of these reactions? Which ones? How would you prefer to react? What small steps can you take to make it easier to react in a more satisfactory way?

What I Like to Write

Which writing experiences do you find fun? Do you prefer freewriting or do you like writing papers, essays, or creative pieces? How are these different for you, and what do you prefer about each? What topics do you most like writing about? Why?

My Habits

What are your habits and typical ways of completing a writing assignment? Do you find that you procrastinate? How? Is there any way that you can prevent this? How can using some of the techniques described in this chapter make the writing task quicker and easier?

CHAPTER

WRITING AN EMPIRICAL PAPER

6

CHAPTER GUIDE

In Chapter 5, we discussed how to write literature review papers; however, most psychology students must also learn how to prepare lab reports and other empirical papers. Psychology is a science, and part of your education as a psychology major entails learning how to read, understand, and contribute to the scientific literature. All colleges and universities require psychology majors to complete at least one course in research methodology. These courses usually require students to prepare lab reports and empirical papers describing research they have conducted. Therefore, understanding how to write an empirical paper is essential for all psychology students, not just honors students who are interested in research. Also, as discussed in Chapter 7, employers often look for psychology graduates with skills in research, statistics, and report writing, so learning how to conduct effective research is vital to your future career.

After you complete data collection and analysis for your lab project or other empirical assignment, it's time to write your paper. Easier said than done, I know. Where do you start? Never fear; in this chapter you'll learn how to write an empirical paper. After briefly discussing the *Publication Manual of the American Psychological Association*, we will examine each section of an empirical paper. The chapter closes with a sample template for your empirical paper.

APA STYLE: THE *PUBLICATION MANUAL OF THE AMERICAN PSYCHOLOGICAL ASSOCIATION*

While reading journal articles, you've probably noticed the distinct style of scientific communication. Why is this style so structured? Consider the purpose of written reports—communication. The goal is to tell readers about your research, explaining what you did and what you found. Scientific communication entails providing enough information to enable readers to critically evaluate the procedure, judge the quality of the research, and replicate (or reproduce) the results. Scientific writing presents facts that are appropriately paraphrased and documented. Because publication space in scholarly journals is limited, authors attempt to provide complete information in as few words as possible; each word is carefully chosen for its precision. A scientific style of writing promotes clear communication, but it is very different from other types of writing and often requires more practice to master.

In psychology, reports and articles are expected to follow the format specified by the fifth edition of the *Publication Manual of the American Psychological Association* (2001). A standard style of scientific communication makes research findings easier for researchers to report and for readers to comprehend. This chapter provides a brief overview of APA style and the structure of research reports. Remember that this presentation is brief and cannot replace the *Publication Manual*, which exceeds 400 pages. If you have questions about specific issues, consult the *Publication Manual* or your instructor.

Structure of an Empirical Paper

As we've discussed, an empirical paper or research article is a highly structured, concise, professional way of communicating the results of a research study. It consists of several sections, each with a specific purpose. The abstract provides a brief summary of the study. The introduction is the first section of an article. It gives an overview of the research question, reviews the literature, and identifies the purpose of the study. The method section explains how the research was conducted; it includes a description of the participants, measures, instruments and equipment, and procedure. The results section presents statistical analyses that address the research questions, with information displayed in graphs and tables. The discussion section explores the significance of the study's findings in light of prior research, the limitations of the study, and suggestions for further research. Last but not least is the references section, which provides accurate references for all the material cited in the paper. Now let's examine each section of an empirical paper.

Title

Don't underestimate the importance of a title. The title gives readers a mini introduction to your paper and helps them to decide if they want to read your abstract and your paper. The title should offer a concise summary of the paper—the topic, variables, and theoretical issue under study—all in 10 to 12 words. According to the *Publication Manual,* "a title should be fully explanatory when standing alone" (American Psychological Association, 2001, p. 11). A good title is hard to write; plan to spend some time on it. It's often easier to write the title once the paper has been completed.

- The title appears in upper- and lowercase letters centered on the first page of the paper.
- The author's name appears in upper- and lowercase letters centered on the line below the title.
- The institutional affiliation appears in upper- and lowercase letters centered on the line following the name(s) of the author(s).
- The manuscript page header consists of the first two or three words of the title of the paper (even if the two or three words alone do not make

sense). The manuscript page header appears flush at the top right-hand side of the page followed by five spaces and the page number.

- The running head is typed flush left (all uppercase) following the words "Running head:" on the line below the manuscript page header. The running head consists of a maximum of 50 characters and is a short version of the title that summarizes the title and makes sense.
- The title page is double-spaced, is in the same font as the rest of the paper, and is not in bold type, italicized, or underlined.
- For a sample title page, see the sample paper at the end of this chapter.

Abstract

Like the title, the abstract gives readers a quick overview of your study, permitting them to decide if they want to read the article itself. Write the abstract after you've completed your paper (i.e., it should be the last part that you write) and have a firm perspective on the findings and their importance. Describe the problem under investigation, presenting the major hypotheses, participants, materials, and procedure. Summarize the results and conclusions, indicating the implications or applications. A good abstract interests readers and convinces them that the study is worth reading. The abstract should be self-explanatory, self-contained, and not exceed 120 words. It is a challenge to keep to the word limit. Most writers begin by composing a longer summary and slowly pare it down by deleting unneeded words.

Introduction

Consider the introduction as three separate sections. The first section, a paragraph or two in length, introduces the problem. What is the topic under study, and how will it be approached? Why is it important? The second section of the introduction provides a literature review of what is known about the topic (review Chapter 5 for suggestions on how to conduct a literature review). What has prior research shown? What were the limitations of prior research? How is your study an extension of prior research? The third section of the introduction states the purpose and rationale of your study and provides a brief overview. Now, let's consider each part of the introduction in greater depth.

Introductory Paragraphs The introductory paragraphs lure readers into your paper. These paragraphs are often the most difficult to write, so consider saving them for later, after you've written the rest of the paper. Use the funnel approach to structure the introduction. Begin with a general statement and get more specific with each sentence until the final sentence introduces the purpose of your study. An additional introductory paragraph should explain why the research question addressed by your study is important. Your goal is to make readers see the point of your study and to convince them that your project tackles an important question or issue.

Literature Review The next component of the introduction, the literature review, is typically several pages long, expanding and supporting the rationale for your study. The literature searching and summarizing strategies discussed in Chapter 5 illustrate how to search the literature, take notes, and organize a literature review. Your goal is to inform readers about the published literature on your problem, demonstrate the importance of the question, and justify the rationale for your methods (Scott, Koch, Scott, & Garrison, 1999). As you review the literature, it is important to remain focused on your research topic. Discuss only research that is pertinent to your project. The review should "emphasize pertinent findings, relevant methodological issues, and major conclusions" (American Psychological Association, 2001, p. 16). Refer readers to published reviews that examine more general issues so that they can obtain additional information if desired.

The literature review should orient readers to the literature and answer several questions (Austin & Calderon, 1996; Landrum, Davis, & Landrum, 2000; Sternberg, 1993):

- What is the purpose of the study?
- What do we know about this area of research?
- How does the study relate to prior research? How does it draw on and extend prior work? What is the nature of your contribution?
- Why is the study important or interesting?
- What rationale links the research questions and the research design? How did you choose the research design, and how does the design address the question?

It is vital that you demonstrate the logical continuity between prior research, your research question, and your research design. Unquestionably, this is the most difficult part of writing the introduction. As you write, keep your purpose in mind: Your goal is to interest readers, explain why your study is relevant, and motivate them to continue reading (Sternberg, 1993). Finally, be very careful to appropriately cite the sources of information in your literature review. If you are unsure of the overall use of citations or how to appropriately quote or paraphrase sources, see the section on plagiarism in Chapter 5 and in the *Publication Manual*.

Purpose and Rationale The final component of the introduction section explains the purpose and rationale for your study. Explain your hypotheses (your specific predictions about the research results) and provide a brief overview of your study. How does your research design relate to the theoretical issue that you wish to address?

Method

Your paper's introduction answers the questions *what* and *why*. The method section explains *how*. The purpose of the method section is to clearly describe how you conducted your study. The method section should provide enough pertinent details so that readers can replicate your research. Typically the method section contains several sections—participants, apparatus materials or measures, and procedure.

Participants The participants section answers the questions, "Who participated in the study?" and "How were they selected?" In this section, describe the demographic characteristics of the participants. Include any demographic details that might affect your study, including age, sex, ethnicity, geographic location, and number of participants assigned to each treatment group. Explain how participants were selected and how they were assigned to groups. What were the circumstances under which they participated, and were any inducements offered (e.g., extra credit)?

Apparatus, Materials, or Measures Depending on your study, this section might be entitled "Apparatus," "Materials," or "Measures." Here, you describe the equipment or instruments used to conduct the study. If you used specialized equipment in your research, describe it and explain how it was used. If the equipment was a manufactured item, include information on the manufacturer and the model number. If you developed an apparatus or any materials for your study, describe them in enough detail so that readers can reproduce them. If standardized tests or measures were used, describe them, include their psychometric properties (e.g., reliability and validity), and explain how they were coded or scored. As you write this section, remember that your goal is to describe how you measured your variables and what methods you used to collect data.

Procedure The procedure section describes the steps you took in conducting your research. Tell readers what was done, how it was done, and in what order. Clearly explain what happened to participants from the time they walked into the lab until the time they left—from the beginning to the end of the study. If you administered surveys to participants, describe the survey conditions and instructions provided. If your research was experimental, explain how participants were exposed to the independent variable; include a description of any instructions that participants received. Describe your methodology and any control features of the design, such as counterbalancing or the use of control groups. Again, your goal is to provide sufficient detail so that the reader can replicate your study.

Results

The results section provides answers to your research questions. What analyses did you conduct, and what did you find? This section should include descriptive and inferential statistics. Descriptive statistics summarize the data. Inferential statistics examine your hypotheses and test the likelihood that the results are not due to chance. As you report tests of statistical significance, include the name of the test, degrees of freedom, and significance level. If you use tables to display your data (e.g., means and standard deviations), they must be self-explanatory (e.g., have titles and be fully labeled) and should not repeat information presented in the text. The *Publication Manual* provides detailed explanations of how to construct tables to present data. When tables are used, discuss the data and explain what they mean without repeating the results in the table.

Before you write the results section, ask yourself, "What did I find? How can I say what I found in a careful, detailed way? Is what I am planning to say precise and to the point? Have I left out anything of importance?" (Rosnow & Rosnow, 2001, p. 58). Sternberg (1993) suggests that you report the most interesting results first or those that are most relevant to the hypotheses tested. Save results that are less interesting and less relevant for later in the results section. "You may wish to report first a general conclusion or interpretation, followed by some descriptive statistics that support your assertion, followed only at the end by the inferential statistics that buttress the conclusion" (Sternberg, 1993, p. 51). In other words, think about the importance of your findings and present them accordingly. Don't just give your readers a laundry list of findings. Instead, carefully consider how to present the results, including the order and style of presentation.

Discussion

The discussion section describes the significance of your findings, places them in context, and discusses their implications. As you structure the discussion section, ask yourself, "What was the purpose of my study? How do my results relate to that purpose? Were there any serendipitous findings of interest? How valid and generalizable are my findings? Is there an alternative way to interpret my results?" (Rosnow & Rosnow, 2001, p. 60).

Begin the discussion section by reminding readers of the purpose of your study. Next, consider your data. Was there support for your hypotheses? If the data do not fit your hypotheses, can you provide another interpretation? If so, clearly state that your interpretation is speculative and that further research is needed to confirm it. Then, discuss your findings within the context of prior research. How do your findings compare with those of other researchers? Does your work extend earlier findings? What are the implications of your findings? What are the theoretical or practical implications of your findings?

As you write this section, remember that your goal is to connect your findings with prior research but not to present the results of statistical analyses not reported in the results section. In other words, don't present data in the discussion section; instead, explain the value and implications of your work.

Discuss the limitations or shortcomings of your study (every study has weaknesses). What factors might limit the extent to which you can generalize your results? Try to think of objections someone might make to the conclusions that you draw (whether the objections are correct or not) and either answer them or qualify your conclusions to take them into account. If you think that possible objections are weak, explain why. Help readers to understand exactly what can and cannot be concluded from your study. Finally, consider avenues for future research. Please try not to end your discussion section with the sentence, "More research is needed." Instead, inform readers about the unanswered research questions. What research is left to do? Provide questions and ideas for further research.

References

The reference section lists all the articles and books that you cited in your paper, including enough information so that an interested reader can locate them. If a work is listed in the reference section, it must be cited within the paper. List only the works that you used. The most common sources of reference material in student papers are journal articles, books, and perhaps material from reputable sources on the Internet. The *Publication Manual* lists slightly different formats for journal articles, books, and Internet sources, as well as slight differences depending on the number of authors. Table 6.1 illustrates how to cite journal articles, books, and Internet sources. Let's examine each type of citation.

List journal articles in the following way:

- The author's last name and first initial appear first.
- The year of publication follows, in parentheses, with a period.
- The article title comes next. Don't capitalize each word of the title; only the first word of the article title is capitalized. If the article title contains a colon, the first word after the colon is capitalized as well. Follow the article title with a period.
- The title of the journal and volume number come next and are italicized. Note that only the number is used to indicate volume; don't use "V," "Volume," or "Vol."
- Last are the page numbers, followed by a period. Again, note that only the numbers themselves are used to indicate pages; don't use "page," "p," or "pg."
- The first journal article example in Table 6.1 illustrates an article by one author, the second example illustrates one by two authors, and the third illustrates one by three authors.

TABLE 6.1 **APA-Style References**

Journal Articles

Kuther, T. L. (2000). Moral reasoning, perceived competence, and adolescent engagement in risky activity. *Journal of Adolescence, 23,* 599–604.

Kuther, T. L., & Higgins-D'Alessandro, A. (2000). Bridging the gap between moral reasoning and adolescent engagement in risky behavior. *Journal of Adolescence, 23,* 409–422.

Dawson, G., Hessl, D., & Frey, K. (1994). Social influences of early developing biological and behavioral systems related to risk for affective disorder. *Development and Psychopathology, 6,* 759–779.

Books

Pollack, W. (1998). *Real boys: Rescuing our sons from the myths of boyhood.* New York: Henry Holt.

Kronenfeld, J. J., & Whicker, M. L. (1997). *Getting an academic job.* Thousand Oaks, CA: Sage.

Furstenberg, F. F., Brooks-Gunn, J., & Morgan, S. P. (1987). *Adolescent mothers in later life.* New York: Cambridge University Press.

Chapters in Edited Books

Berzonsky, M. D. (2000). Theories of adolescence. In G. Adams (Ed.), *Adolescent development: The essential readings* (pp. 11–27). Malden, MA: Blackwell.

Berndt, T. J., & Savin-Williams, R. C. (1993). Variations in friendships and peer-group relationships in adolescence. In P. Tolan & B. Cohler (Eds.), *Handbook of clinical research and practice with adolescents* (pp. 203–219). New York: Wiley.

Cook, T. D., Anson, A. R., & Walchli, S. B. (1993). From causal description to causal explanation: Improving three already good evaluations of adolescent health programs. In S. G. Millstein, A. C. Petersen, & E. O. Nightingale (Eds.), *Promoting the health of adolescents* (pp. 339–374). New York: Oxford University Press.

Internet

Kuther, T. L. (2001). *Piaget's theory of cognitive development.* Retrieved June 15, 2001, from http://www.suite101.com/article.cfm/7054/58943

American Psychological Association (2001). *Psychology: Scientific problem solvers. Careers for the 21st century.* Retrieved June 15, 2001, from http://www.apa.org/students/brochure/homepage.html

List books as follows.

- The author's last name and first initial appear first.
- The year of publication follows, in parentheses, with a period.
- Next comes the book title, italicized. As in the journal article format, only the first word of the book title is capitalized. If the book title contains a colon, the first word after the colon is capitalized as well.
- Finally, list the place of publication, a colon, and the publisher.
- The first book example in Table 6.1 illustrates a book by one author, the second example illustrates one by two authors, and the third illustrates one by three authors.

What if you're citing a book chapter in an edited book? List it as follows.

- The chapter author's last name and first initial appear first.
- The year of publication follows, in parentheses, with a period. The title of the chapter follows, with only the first word capitalized, ending with a period.
- Next indicate the editors by first initial and last name, followed by "Ed." in parentheses, with a comma.
- List the title of the book, capitalizing only the first word.
- Provide the page numbers in parentheses, signified by "pp." Note that this is the only time that "pp." is used in APA style.
- Finally, provide the place of publication, followed by a colon, and the publisher.
- The first example of chapters in edited books in Table 6.1 lists a single-authored chapter in a book edited by one person. The second example illustrates a book with two authors and two editors, and the third example illustrates one with three authors and three editors.

List Internet sources as follows.

- Cite Internet sources by the author's last name (if no author appears, then cite the organization).
- Also, indicate the year of publication (if listed) in parentheses. If the year of publication is not listed, then use "n.d." to indicate no date, in parentheses.
- The title of the page appears next, in italics (with only the first word capitalized).
- Next, list the date that you retrieved the information and the Internet address (and don't use a period after the Internet address).
- As shown in Table 6.1, the first Internet example lists an author, and the second lists an organization.

Conclusion

As you can see, an empirical paper entails writing in a highly structured, scientific style. Use Exercise 6.1 to help you determine whether your paper meets the major guidelines set by APA style. While it is challenging to learn, a scientific style of writing enables the clear communication of research questions, findings, and conclusions.

Exercise 6.1
Understanding Journal Articles

Using PsycINFO, locate an empirical journal article in an area of interest. Retrieve the article using your library's full text and in print resources. The reference librarian can offer assistance if you experience difficulty. Read the article and answer the following questions:

1. Write the article's citation in APA style.
2. Examine the abstract of the article. Based on the abstract, what do you expect to learn from this article?
3. What was the purpose of the study? Where did you find this information?
4. How was the study conducted? Describe the methodology. Where did you locate this information?
5. What were the findings of the study? Where did you look to learn about the findings?
6. What were the author's conclusions? How did the results of this study compare with prior research? Where did you look to learn about the findings?
7. Reflect back on the abstract. How well did it reflect the content of the article? Did you learn what you thought you would?

SUGGESTED READINGS

American Psychological Association. (2001). *Publication manual of the American Psychological Association.* Washington, DC: Author.

Rosnow, R. L., & Rosnow, M. (2003). *Writing papers in psychology*. Belmont, CA: Wadsworth.

Scott, J. M., Koch, R. E., Scott, G. M., & Garrison, S. M. (1999).*The psychology student writer's manual*. Upper Saddle River, NJ: Prentice Hall.

Szuchman, L. T. (2002). *Writing with style: APA style made easy*. Belmont, CA: Wadsworth.

WEB RESOURCES

The following web sites are hot-linked at *The Psychology Major's Handbook* web site at *http://info.wadsworth.com/kuther*

APA Style Online

http://www.apastyle.org/previoustips.html

This site from the American Psychological Association presents an overview of APA style, along with answers to frequently asked questions.

Writing the Empirical Journal Article

http://comp9.psych.cornell.edu/dbem/writing_article.html

Daryl Bem provides excellent advice on how to write up your research.

The Elements of Style

http://www.bartleby.com/141/index.html

This web site gives you access to Strunk and White's classic volume on how to write clearly and concisely.

How to Write a Research Report in Psychology

http://www.psych.upenn.edu/~baron/labrep.html

At this site you'll find an overview of the sections in an empirical paper, as well as additional advice on grammar.

APA Style Guide Resources

http://www.psywww.com/resource/apacrib.htm

Links to a variety of guides on APA style (5th edition).

JOURNAL EXERCISES

My Rationale

Freewrite about your research project. Don't use your notes or readings but write as much as you can about your project. What is your research question? How did it evolve? Where did you get the idea? How is your study an improvement over prior studies? Why is your study important?

My Findings

Tell a story about your research project. What did you set out to do, and what did you find? Try to explain what your statistical analyses tested. Pretend that you're explaining your project to a friend or a high school student. How would you explain your results in a way that a student could understand?

Implications

Without looking at your notes or readings, freewrite about the possible implications of your study. Be grandiose and try to think about far-reaching implications for laws, social policy, regulations, education, and so on.

If I Could Do It All Over

Pretend that you are going to revise your study. What would you do differently? Why?

Chapter 6 Appendix: Sample Paper

My Paper 1

Running head: TEMPLATE PAPER

My Paper: A Template From Which to Work

Jane J. Smith

Your State University

My Paper 2

Abstract

The abstract should be self-explanatory, self-contained, and should not exceed 120 words. Describe the problem under investigation, the major hypotheses, participants, materials, and procedure. Summarize the results and conclusions, indicating the implications or applications. A good abstract interests readers and convinces them that the study is worth reading.

My Paper 3

My Paper: A Template From Which to Work

Begin the introduction with a general statement about your topic area. Consider your readers and attempt to pique their interest. Use the funnel effect in the first paragraph of your introduction so that you begin with general statements, each one becoming more narrowly focused until you end with a statement of the problem under study.

A second paragraph of the introduction might explain the importance of the research question. What is its theoretical or applied relevance?

After introducing the problem, the second component of the introduction section provides a literature review of what is known about the topic. What has prior research shown? What are the limitations of prior research? How is your study an extension of prior research? As you write the literature review, cite only those studies that are most pertinent to your research question (and use appropriate documentation, as described in Chapter 5). The literature review is typically several pages long.

End the introductory section with a clear statement of the purpose and rationale of your study. Discuss hypotheses and set the stage for the method section.

Method

The method section explains how the study was conducted. Provide enough detail so that a reader could replicate your research. Typically the method section contains several sections: participants, apparatus, materials or measures, and procedure.

Notice that three levels of headings are used. First-level headings are written in upper- and lowercase letters, centered. Second-level headings

My Paper 4

are written in upper- and lowercase letters, flush left, and are italicized. Third-level headings are indented and italicized, with only the first letter of the first word capitalized, and are followed by a period. Headings can be used to organize your introduction section. Review the *Publication Manual* to learn more about the use of headings.

Participants

The participants section describes the characteristics of the participants and explains how they were selected. Explain any demographic details that might affect your study, including age, sex, ethnicity, geographic location, and number of participants assigned to each treatment group. Report any inducements to participate (e.g., money, extra credit).

Apparatus/Measures

Depending on your study, this section might be entitled apparatus, materials, or measures. Briefly describe the equipment or instruments used in the study. If the equipment is a manufactured item, include information on the manufacturer and the model number. If you developed an apparatus or materials for your study, describe them in enough detail so that the reader could reproduce them. If standardized tests or measures were used, describe them, their psychometric properties (e.g., reliability and validity), and how they were coded or scored.

Procedure

Describe each step in conducting the study. Clearly explain what happened to participants from the time they walked into the lab until the time they left, from the beginning to the end of the study. Describe your methodology and any control features of the design, such as counterbalancing or the

My Paper 5

use of control groups. What instructions were provided to participants? How were participants debriefed at the end of the study?

Results

Begin your results section by explaining the main findings. Follow up by explaining the analyses in detail. Report all relevant results, even those counter to your hypothesis. As you report tests of statistical significance, include the name of the test, degrees of freedom, and significance level. Provide enough detail to justify the conclusions that you will make in the discussion section. Include tables to display complex sets of data (e.g., means and standard deviations, the results of complex analyses). For information on how to construct tables, see the *Publication Manual*.

Discussion

Begin the discussion section by reiterating the purpose of the study. Provide a statement in support of your original hypotheses. Next, examine your findings. Explain what the results mean, consider them in the context of the literature, and discuss their implications. Identify the possible limitations of your study. Close with a discussion of venues for future research.

My Paper 6

References

Note that the reference section includes only articles that were cited in your study. List these references in alphabetical order. See Table 6.1 for sample article, book, and Internet references. Further examples of references appear in the *Publication Manual*.

What Can I Do With a Bachelor's Degree in Psychology?

CHAPTER 7

Chapter Guide

If you're considering majoring in psychology, you're not alone. In 2002, more than 76,000 students earned bachelor's degrees in psychology (National Center for Education Statistics, 2003b). Each year, psychology is consistently among the top five most popular bachelor's degrees awarded (Chronicle of Higher Education, 1999; National Center for Education Statistics, 2003b). Why are so many students attracted to psychology? Perhaps it's because psychology is applicable to everyday life; we all seek to understand human behavior and the environment around us. Psychology courses cover a range of fascinating topics, such as how we think, learn, use our memory, feel emotions, cope with adversity, change throughout our lives, and others. Much of what we study in psychology is directly relevant to our environments and our lives.

Many undergraduate students choose psychology because of their desire to become psychologists or to work with people. However, careful study of this book and discussions with your professors will reveal that a bachelor's degree in psychology will not qualify you to be a psychologist. Becoming a psychologist requires earning at least a master's degree, and more commonly a doctoral degree, which entails several years of education, training, and supervision beyond the bachelor's degree.

So why major in psychology? Although a baccalaureate in psychology won't qualify you to formally practice psychology, you'll learn skills that are applicable in a variety of jobs, including some that allow you to work with people. This chapter describes the educational goals of most undergraduate psychology programs, the skills that employers seek, the many careers that you can pursue with a bachelor's degree in psychology, and how you can cultivate useful skills and enhance your employability.

Goals of an Undergraduate Education in Psychology

A psychology major is a general liberal arts degree that prepares graduates for "lifelong learning, thinking, and action" (McGovern, Furumoto, Halpern, Kimble, & McKeachie, 1991, p. 600). A liberal arts education provides students with training in critical thinking and analytic skills. From a liberal arts education, you'll learn how to think independently, understand how you learn, be able to demonstrate mature and reasoned decision making, and exercise self-control (Bare, 1988). Because psychology is a liberal arts major, students gain knowledge and skills that are generalizable to the world outside the classroom. Undergraduate programs in psychology seek to promote the following range of skills and abilities in students (Allen, Noel, Deegan, Halpern, & Crawford, 2000; Hayes, 1996; McGovern et al., 1991):

- **Knowledge of Psychology.** Psychology is a very broad field encompassing subfields of biology, development, perception, emotion, and others. An undergraduate education in psychology provides an understanding of the major facts, theories, and issues in the discipline. This conceptual framework can serve as a base for lifelong learning about human behavior.
- **Research Methods and Statistical Skills.** Psychology students pose questions about human behavior and experience, and they become familiar with the research methods used to answer these questions. Students develop a basic understanding of statistics and learn how to interpret data summaries.
- **Thinking and Problem-Solving Skills.** Exposure to the diverse perspectives within psychology trains students to think flexibly and to accept some ambiguity. Introductory psychology students often ask for the "right" answer; they soon learn that answers often aren't black or white but many shades of gray. Psychology students acquire skills in problem solving, critical thinking, and evaluation, which are all important tools for making reasoned decisions.
- **Information Acquisition and Synthesis Skills.** Because our knowledge base is constantly changing, the ability to gather and synthesize information is essential. Psychology students learn how to use a range of sources including the library, computerized databases, and the Internet to gather information. More important, psychology students learn how to synthesize information into coherent, persuasive arguments.
- **Computer Literacy.** Psychology students develop familiarity with computers and understand how to use common statistical, word processing, and spreadsheet programs. They also understand how to learn to use new software and computer programs, and they have the basic skills needed to use and access e-mail as well as to browse the Internet.
- **Reading and Writing Skills.** Psychology students develop reading, writing, and presentation skills required for effective oral and written communication. They learn how to comprehend and present arguments from a psychological standpoint.
- **Communication and Intrapersonal Skills.** Effective communicators are aware of, and sensitive to, others. They are sensitive to issues of culture, race, class, and ethnicity. Psychology students develop the ability to communicate, lead, and work in groups—teamwork skills. Students of psychology also develop intrapersonal awareness or self-knowledge. They are able to monitor and manage their own behavior.
- **Adaptability.** Psychology students quickly learn that a perfect experiment is an unattainable goal toward which all researchers strive. Students learn how to design the best research studies possible given limited resources.

These skills (certainly not an exhaustive list) emphasized by most psychology departments will help you to develop into a well-rounded, well-educated person. The blend of education in statistical, thinking, research, writing, and interpersonal skills supports the goals of a liberal education and will provide you with valuable tools applicable to a broad range of careers (Kierniesky, 1992).

At this point, those of you with a healthy dose of skepticism may wonder, "Yeah, but what about all those people who ask, 'You're a psychology major? What can you do with a degree in psychology?' If a psychology degree is so great, then why do people react that way?" You may encounter many people who argue that because you cannot be a psychologist with a bachelor's degree, a psychology major is useless (Carroll, Shmidt, & Sorensen, 1992). This is far from true.

A psychology major is the first step toward becoming a psychologist, and it is also the first step toward a range of other careers, as we'll discuss later in this chapter. Consider other professional areas such as law and medicine. Is a student who has completed the premedical or prelaw curriculum ready to practice medicine or law when they graduate from college? We all recognize that physicians and lawyers require additional, specialized education that builds on the foundation of knowledge and skills developed in college. The same is true for students who seek to enter the field of professional psychology (University of Texas at Austin, 2000).

These myths about the psychology major cause many psychology students to feel anxious and uncertain about their abilities and their job potential. Many graduates with psychology degrees believe that they are no more perceptive or knowledgeable about human behavior than are other people. Yet they are often wrong. Psychology students often fail to recognize their skills or cannot articulate their abilities because they have deeply internalized their knowledge about human behavior. Once we internalize psychological knowledge, it becomes automatized and difficult for us to recognize when we are applying it (Hayes, 1996). Therefore, psychology students apply a sophisticated understanding of human behavior without realizing it. Students' scientific training teaches them to not accept knowledge at face value; thus, psychology students question their abilities.

At the same time, "a psychology graduate venturing into the outside world is often surprised at how other people appear to overlook the obvious. The style of thinking which one acquires while studying for a psychology degree may feel intuitively obvious, but it actually involved a long and arduous process of discarding prior assumptions" (Hayes, 1996, p. 134). The automatized skills typical of psychology students contribute to their communication, interpersonal, and problem-solving abilities.

As you can see, the combination of a liberal arts education and training in human behavior makes the psychology degree very special. It satisfies the objectives of a liberal arts education, which include critical and analytical thinking, independent thinking, leadership skills, communication skills, understanding how to learn, being able to see all sides of an issue, and understanding human diversity (Winter, McClelland, & Stewart, 1981). Training in research design and statistical analysis, as well as in human behavior, makes the psychology major unique among liberal arts degrees.

SKILLS AND ABILITIES SOUGHT BY EMPLOYERS

As you've already seen, a psychology major offers students opportunities to develop expertise in many areas. A bachelor's degree in psychology lays the foundation for a variety of career paths in the mental health professions, science, and business. When considering possible careers, evaluate and think carefully about the skills and knowledge that you've acquired over your college years. It may help for you to reconsider your answers to the exercises in Chapter 2. A thorough understanding of your talents and proficiencies is particularly important because it is unlikely that you will see classified ads stating "Psychology Majors Wanted." While it is rare to see classified ads explicitly recruiting psychology majors, don't be fooled. Your major has helped you to develop a host of skills that employers want.

What do employers look for in a new hire? Table 7.1 lists the most desirable qualities in prospective employees according to surveys of a broad sample

TABLE 7.1 TEN MOST DESIRABLE QUALITIES IN PROSPECTIVE EMPLOYEES

Personal Qualities	Description
1. Communication skills	Writing, public speaking, and social skills
2. Motivation/influence	Commitment to lifelong learning, ability to meet challenges
3. Teamwork skills	Ability to work with others
4. Leadership abilities	Ability to lead groups, communicate, and work effectively with others
5. Grade point average/academic skills	Broad education, good grades
6. Interpersonal skills	Interacts well with others, has social skills
7. Flexibility/adaptability	Can cope with change and tolerate stress
8. Technical skills	Computer skills, Internet skills
9. Honesty/integrity	Ethics, personal responsibility
10. Analytic skills/problem-solving skills	Reasoning and thinking abilities

Source: National Association of Colleges and Employers, 2000.

of employers. Carefully examine the list, and you'll quickly notice that interpersonal skills—including the abilities to communicate, influence others, and work in groups—are highly valued. These results indicate that "people skills" typical of psychology majors, honed through course work, practica, and extracurricular activities, provide an advantage in the job market.

Many other surveys have yielded similar results. Following is a compilation of the conclusions of these studies, providing a detailed description of the skills employers seek in prospective employees (Appleby, 2000; Edwards & Smith, 1988; Grocer & Kohout, 1997; Landrum, Davis, & Landrum, 2000; Lloyd & Kennedy, 1997; Sheetz, 1995).

- **Communication and Interpersonal Skills.** Prospective employees must have good listening skills and the ability to communicate orally in a clear, concise, accurate, logical fashion. Graduates who can interact effectively with others and are sensitive to social signals are in demand. Group or teamwork skills, including discussion, team building, and conflict management, are also important. Employees who can share responsibility with others and who have a tolerance for and an understanding of individual differences are desired.
- **Thinking and Problem-Solving Skills.** Successful employees have good judgment and decision-making skills. They can apply information to solve and analyze problems on the basis of personal experience and psychological principles. Analytic and decision-making skills are important because many of today's jobs require higher levels of complex, critical thinking than ever before.
- **Information Acquisition and Synthesis Skills.** Successful employees understand how they absorb and retain information. They know how to learn, where to find information, and how to evaluate and use it. A commitment to learning is essential in today's marketplace.
- **Reading and Writing Skills.** Prospective employees can extract important ideas through reading and have the writing skills to document their ideas. Strong writing skills, including the ability to write reports, proposals, and summaries, are useful.
- **Career-Related Work Experience.** Successful job applicants have obtained hands-on practical experience through cooperative education, internships, practica, part-time jobs, or summer work experiences. They have a real-world work orientation and can apply their school-based knowledge in practical settings.
- **Psychological Knowledge.** Employers often desire specific knowledge from psychology graduates, such as how attitudes are formed and changed or how people think, solve problems, and process information. Also useful is an understanding of group dynamics and knowing how people perceive and sense their environments.
- **Data Analysis Skills.** Employers seek prospective employees with

computational skills, the ability to reason numerically, and the ability to identify problems in data. Graduates who can collect, record, and report statistical information will find success.

- **Computer Literacy.** A knowledge of computer applications—including word processing, spreadsheet, and database software—and familiarity with the Internet and e-mail are essential.
- **Self-Management.** Employers desire personal qualities and traits such as self-esteem, confidence, and social skills. Tolerance for stress and ambiguity are helpful qualities. Self-management skills such as the ability to set and pursue goals, control one's emotions, and engage in appropriate behavior are sought.
- **Adaptability.** Employers seek employees who are adaptable, flexible, and capable of handling multiple tasks. A broad knowledge base outside the field of psychology provides a background for enhancing your adaptability. The ability to utilize resources in order to effectively complete tasks (e.g., creating a schedule, writing a budget, assigning space, and managing others) is essential.

Now that you have a general understanding of what employers seek, consider the goals of a psychology education. The goals of an undergraduate education in psychology match employers' expectations well. Over the course of your undergraduate years you will not be able to achieve all these skills or abilities, but you will gain proficiency in many of them.

Where should you focus the most attention? What skills should you seek to develop? Consider what employers expect specifically from psychology graduates. Table 7.2 lists employers' views of the top five most useful skills and knowledge areas attained specifically by psychology students as ranked by 118

TABLE 7.2 FIVE MOST USEFUL SKILLS AND KNOWLEDGE AREAS AS RATED BY EMPLOYERS

Skills	Knowledge Areas
1. Writing proposals and reports	1. Attitude and opinion formation and change
2. Ability to identify problems and suggest solutions based on research findings and knowledge of psychology	2. Principles and techniques of personnel selection
3. Conducting interviews	3. How people think, solve problems, and process information
4. Doing statistical analyses	4. Group dynamics and structure
5. Knowledge of how to design and carry out research projects	5. How the physical environment influences our feelings and actions

Source: Edwards & Smith, 1988.

organizations that hire psychology graduates. Perhaps what's most important to take away from these results is the fact that employers will expect you to know something about your major (Landrum et al., 2000). While cramming may get you through an exam, you probably won't retain the material well enough to satisfy an employer who needs your expertise. (See Chapter 4 for study tips to help you learn and retain material more effectively.)

So where should you focus your energy? First, consider your own strengths and weaknesses (reviewing the assessments you completed in Chapter 2 may help). Seek improvement in the areas you identify as weaknesses. Second, focus on the two components of the psychology major desired most by employers—people skills and research skills. People skills include knowledge and an understanding of psychological principles and group dynamics, as well as interpersonal skills—self-management skills. Employers also value research skills such as report writing, the ability to carry out a research project, and the ability to conduct statistical analyses. The blend of liberal arts and science is what makes the psychology major unique, and it's what makes you very employable.

JOBS FOR PSYCHOLOGY MAJORS

Contrary to popular belief, most students who graduate with a bachelor's degree in psychology do not go to graduate school (Borden & Rajecki, 2000). It has been estimated that about one-quarter of recipients of undergraduate psychology degrees attend graduate school immediately after graduation (Tsapogas, 2004). Instead, psychology baccalaureates head into the job market and find success. According to the National Science Foundation (2001), only 6% of 1999 and 2000 psychology degree recipients were unemployed in 2001. So what kinds of jobs do psychology majors obtain? Jobs that require people skills (the ability to communicate effectively with others), analytic skills, writing skills, and research skills. These skills are found in many settings, and so your potential job options are varied. As you consider job options and look for a position, remember that many people do not understand psychology. It is your responsibility to educate them about how your degree has prepared you for a position with their organization or company.

Most recipients of bachelor's degrees in psychology work in jobs that are not directly related to psychology (although an understanding of human behavior obviously is helpful in most positions) (Borden & Rajecki, 2000; Finney, Snell, & Sebby, 1989; Keyes & Hogberg, 1990; Littlepage, Perry, & Hodge, 1990). About two-thirds of psychology graduates work in business settings (American Psychological Association, n.d.); other graduates work in social service settings (McGovern & Carr, 1989; Quereshi and Kuchan, 1988). Table 7.3 lists common jobs that psychology majors have obtained after graduation. It is not a complete list; many other opportunities are out there waiting for you.

TABLE 7.3 **POSITIONS OBTAINED BY PSYCHOLOGY MAJORS**

Business Field	Education/Academic Fields	Social Fields
Administrative assistant	Administration	Activities coordinator
Affirmative action officer	Child care provider	Behavioral specialist
Advertising trainee	Child care worker/supervisor	Career counselor
Benefits manager	Data management	Case worker
Claims specialist	Laboratory assistant	Child protection worker
Community relations officer	Parent/family education	Clinical coordinator
Customer relations	Preschool teacher	Community outreach worker
Data management	Public opinion surveyor	Corrections officer
Employee recruitment	Research assistant	Counselor assistant
Employee counselor	Teaching assistant	Crisis intervention counselor
Human resources coordinator/manager/specialist		Employment counselor
Labor relations manager/specialist		Group home attendant
Loan officer		Occupational therapist
Management trainee		Probation officer
Marketing		Program manager
Personnel manager/officer		Rehabilitation counselor
Product and services research		Residence counselor
Programs/events coordination		Mental health assistant
Public relations		Social service assistant
Retail sales management		Social worker assistant
Sales representative		Social worker
Special features writing/reporting		Substance abuse counselor
Staff training and development		Youth counselor
Trainer/training officer		

Source: DeGalan & Lambert, 1995; Fretz, 1976; Lloyd, 1997; University of Texas at Austin, 2000.

Positions in Business Settings

Business employers tend to view liberal arts majors, especially psychology majors, favorably (McGovern & Carr, 1989). The psychology major's skills in quantitative analysis and computer applications offer an advantage over many other majors. Graduates who obtain positions in business often work in human resources, public relations, retail, and advertising.

Human Resources Careers in human resources focus on helping employers work with their employees. Human resource positions encompass many titles (personnel administrator, employment specialist, human resources coordinator/specialist/manager, affirmative action coordinator, employee relations manager) and serve various functions (employment and placement, wage and salary administration, training and development, benefits administration, research, and information management). For example, human resources personnel work to attract the most qualified employees, match them to the jobs for which they are best suited, and help them to succeed in their jobs. Activities include recruiting and interviewing potential employees, training and development of workers to help them develop and improve their morale and performance, organization development (helping companies and businesses deal with change), and career development (helping employees manage their careers) (DeGalan & Lambert, 1995). Human resources personnel often collect applications and résumés for jobs, assemble applicant files, perform background checks, orient new employees, educate employees about salary and benefits, and assess departmental needs for staffing. Human resources positions involve not only working with people but also a great deal of paperwork and information management; accurate record keeping relating to employment salary and benefits is essential to the work of human resources personnel.

Public Relations Public relations specialists work in businesses, government, universities, hospitals, schools, and other organizations to build and maintain positive relationships with the public. Public relations specialists work to improve their organization's communication with the community; with consumer, employee, and public interest groups; and with the media. Part of the job entails informing the community and the media about an organization's policies, activities, and accomplishments, but public relations specialists must also keep an organization's management and administrative personnel aware of the attitudes and concerns of the public and of special interest groups. Typical activities might include setting up speaking engagements for management or helping to prepare speeches. Titles include public relations specialist, information officer, press secretary, communications specialist, public affairs specialist, and others.

Retail About one-fifth of workers in the United States are employed in the retail sector (U.S. Bureau of Labor Statistics, 2004b). Retail sales workers sell goods, provide customer service, and help buyers make informed purchases. Many large retail stores have management training programs in which a worker learns about all aspects of the business and then is placed as an assistant manager or store manager. An understanding of consumer behavior is important in order to learn the appropriate sales techniques to achieve success. As one advances in retail to manager status, one becomes responsible for managing the activity of part or all of a store, including managing staff, tracking inventory, marketing products, devising techniques to attract customers, and promoting sales and good customer relations. Although the working hours are often unusual, positions in retail sales are busy, people-oriented jobs with many opportunities for advancement.

Advertising There are many different kinds of entry-level positions in advertising. Administrative assistants perform much of the paperwork and organizational tasks that keep a firm running. Assistant account managers, also called account coordinators, work in the account management department, which identifies and solicits new clients and ensures that clients' advertising needs are met. Assistant media planners work in the media department, which places ads; they study what people read and watch in order to determine where to place advertising, and then attempt to place the right ad at the right time to reach the intended audience. Assistant media buyers help media buyers secure ad time and space and ensure that advertisements appear as planned and according to the intended budget.

Positions in Social Service Settings

What if you're interested in obtaining a position has something to do with psychology in the more traditional sense? What are your options? Table 7.4 presents employment data from the *Occupational Outlook Handbook* (U.S. Bureau of Labor Statistics, 2004b) on general categories of psychology-related positions, listing common titles, salary information, and long-term outlook. Following are several general categories of psychology-related jobs.

Counselor There are many different kinds of counselors with different educational and training standards. Although school counselors and mental health counselors are typically required to have master's degrees, psychology graduates often work as counselor aides, and there are many other types of counselors. Rehabilitation counselors assist people in coping with the personal, social, and vocational effects of disabilities. National certification for rehabilitation counselors is voluntary through the Commission on Rehabilitation Counselor Certification, although some employers require certification. Employment and career counselors help people make career decisions and conduct job searches. Other counselor positions include youth counselor, residential care counselor, gerontology counselor, and multicultural counselor. In nearly all states counselors must be certified (U.S. Bureau of Labor Statistics, 2004b). If you're interested in counseling, seek information from your school's career development office because requirements for certification or licensure often vary by state. Although entry-level positions may be available to baccalaureate graduates, turnover is often high in these positions because the jobs are challenging and the pay is often low. Advancement and additional opportunities come with a master's degree.

TABLE 7.4 PSYCHOLOGY-RELATED POSITIONS: TITLES, SALARIES, AND OUTLOOK

Area	Titles	Median Salary in 2002 ($)	Outlook for Increase[a]
Preschool teacher/child care worker	Preschool teacher	19,270	Faster than average
Correctional officer	Child care worker	32,670	Much faster than average
Counselor[b]	Rehabilitation counselor	25,840–30,180	Faster than average
	Employment or career counselor		
	Mental health counselor		
	Gerontology counselor		
Human resources worker	Human resources specialist/manager/officer	39,410–64,710	Faster than average
	Labor relations specialist/manager		
	Benefits manager/analyst		
	Personnel officer		
	Trainer/training specialist		
Human services worker and assistant	Social services worker	23,370–31,280	Much faster than average
	Case management worker		
	Social work assistant		
	Community support worker		
	Alcohol or drug abuse counselor		
	Gerontology aide		
	Mental health worker		

(Continued)

TABLE 7.4

Psychology-Related Positions: Titles, Salaries, and Outlook (*Continued*)

Area	Titles	Median Salary in 2002 ($)	Outlook for Increase[a]
	Community outreach worker		
	Life skills counselor		
Occupational therapy assistant[b]	—	22,040–36,660	Much faster than average
Occupational therapist[b]	—	51,990	Faster than average
Social worker[b]	Child welfare social worker	33,150–37,380	Faster than average
	Family services social worker		
	Child or adult protective services social worker		
	Health care social worker		
	Occupational social worker		
	Gerontology social worker		

Source: U.S. Bureau of Labor Statistics, 2004b.

[a] Expectations for increases, as compared with the average occupational increases, through 2012.

[b] Certification, licensure, or credentialing necessary, depending on state regulations.

Social Worker As in the case of counselors, there are many different types of social workers, with differing standards of education and training. Clinical social workers offer psychotherapy and counseling and usually have master's degrees. A bachelor's degree is the most common minimum requirement for most other social work positions, although a master's degree has become the standard for most (U.S. Bureau of Labor Statistics, 2004b). Child welfare social workers and family services social workers assist children (and their families) who are experiencing social and emotional difficulties. Child or adult protective services social workers investigate claims of abuse and domestic violence. Health care social workers assist patients who are coping with illnesses such as cancer, AIDS, Alzheimer's disease, and others. Occupational social workers help employees with job-related problems, stress, and personal problems. Gerontological social workers offer support and assistance to older adults and their families.

While it is possible to obtain many social work positions with a bachelor's degree, continuing education in the form of a part-time master's program will increase your job security, opportunities for advancement, and ability to start a private practice (U.S. Bureau of Labor Statistics, 2004b). All states have licensing or certification requirements for private practice and use of the title "Social Worker." Standards for licensing vary by state, so it's a good idea to check with your school's career development office.

Human Services Worker This category of positions includes various job titles such as social services worker, case management worker, social work assistant, community support worker, alcohol and substance abuse counselor, mental health worker, community outreach worker, life skills counselor, child care worker, and gerontology aide (U.S. Bureau of Labor Statistics, 2004b). Each of these positions is a paraprofessional position or "a support role that overlaps with job duties and responsibilities of a psychologist; however, the paraprofessional does not have the education, responsibility, nor salary of the psychologist" (Landrum et al., 2000, p. 17). Human services workers provide direct and indirect services to clients. Typical duties include assessing clients' needs and eligibility for services, helping clients obtain services (such as food stamps, Medicaid, and other human services programs) and providing emotional support (U.S. Bureau of Labor Statistics, 2004b). In communities, group homes, and government-supported housing programs, human services workers assist clients in need of counseling, assist adults with daily living skills, and organize group activities.

Salary Information

What can you expect to earn with your bachelor's degree? Salaries vary by occupation, region, and experience. In 2001, the median salary of 1999 and 2000 bachelor's degree recipients was $28,000 (U.S. Bureau of Labor

Statistics, 2004b). The average starting salaries for psychology majors of the class of 2001 was $30,338 (National Association of Colleges and Employers, 2000). Work experience has a favorable effect on salary; with experience, your salary will increase. According to the U.S. Bureau of Labor Statistics (2004c), the 2003 median earnings for all employed persons with bachelor's degrees (regardless of major or job experience) was $46,800.

Alumni Satisfaction

Alumni surveys have shown that the graduates most satisfied with their decision to major in psychology are those who enter graduate study (Lunneborg, 1985; McGovern & Carr, 1989;) or perceive that their jobs are related to psychology (Kressel, 1990; McGovern & Carr, 1989). In addition, during bleak economic times such as recessions, college graduates with degrees in psychology tend to be successful in finding employment (McGovern & Carr, 1989, p. 54).

Graduates tend to perceive that their psychological skills and knowledge are best used in social services positions such as therapy and teaching but tend to be more disappointed with the salaries in these positions (Lunneborg, 1985). Positions in counseling, residential care, and human services can be rewarding, but they also can be draining because of the many challenges and the generally low pay. Alternatively, psychology graduates employed in business settings often are more satisfied with their salaries but tend to be less satisfied with their positions and duties (Lunneborg, 1985). If you're planning to enter the business world, take some courses in related areas, seek a practicum in a business setting to hone your skills, and prepare yourself psychologically to give yourself an edge.

Acquire Useful Skills and Enhance Your Employability

As you've seen, a psychology major is quite useful, with its blend of liberal arts and science. New graduates agree, noting that their experiences with writing, computers, and research were particularly important in preparing them for their first jobs (American Psychological Association, 1997).

So, what can you do to enhance your marketability and help your psychology education work for you? First, plan your career goals. This is a difficult task, but try to think about where you'd like to be in a few years. The counseling center or career development center at your school can help you select your goals through personality, ability, and vocational interest assessments and counseling. The career development center may also offer alumni contacts who can tell you about their experiences and offer advice.

After you've considered what types of careers interest you, take a few elective courses outside psychology that are specific to your goals. For example, if you plan to enter the business world, a course in management or accounting certainly wouldn't hurt. If you would like a job in human services, take courses in social work, communication, criminal justice, sociology, or anthropology. Regardless of your career plans, classes and experiences that enhance your communication skills (e.g., courses in writing, speech, and communications; writing for the campus newspaper) are a good investment because employers view communication skills favorably (Edwards & Smith, 1988; Grocer & Kohout, 1997; Landrum et al., 2000; Lloyd & Kennedy, 1997; National Association of Colleges and Employers, 2000).

Seek research experience by assisting professors with their research or by developing an independent research project. Research experience demonstrates your ability to work independently and sharpens your analytic and critical thinking skills. It also provides employers with evidence of your motivation, initiative, and willingness to go beyond the basic requirements. Chapter 3 discusses research experience in greater detail.

Secure an internship or practicum to obtain hands-on experience. Internships provide wonderful opportunities for learning and training that you can use later. Another advantage of an internship is that it lets you sample a potential career. Do you really want to work with people? Your internship experiences may surprise you. The career center at your school can place you with an internship that provides valuable hands-on experience. In addition, internships can lead to contacts in the field, a possible offer for paid employment after graduation, and someone who can provide a reference or recommendation based on your ability to apply your knowledge of psychology in a real-world setting.

Work experience is invaluable. There are many part-time and summer jobs that allow you to sharpen your interpersonal skills and try out potential careers. Try a job as a camp counselor, residence hall advisor, child-care worker, or human services worker. According to the Collegiate Employment Research Institute, 82% of employers rate career-related employment as extremely important for prospective hires (Gardner, 2000).

Extracurricular activities can help you develop useful skills and enhance your marketability. Similar to internships and work experience, such activities can provide opportunities to test career paths, develop contacts, and work on your communication skills. In addition, employers value volunteer work for campus and community organizations because it shows that you're a good citizen. Extracurricular participation gives employers evidence of your leadership skills, your ability to work effectively in a group, and your initiative and motivation. Finally, be open to new possibilities. Flexibility is an important life skill; it is critical in coping and for optimal development throughout adulthood. Employers also rate adaptability as highly desired in new employees (National

Association of Colleges and Employers, 2000). Keep an open mind and explore multiple possibilities to find a job that you'll love. Exercises 7.1 and 7.2 will help you to research employment options and plan a career that's right for you.

EXERCISE 7.1
Career Research Exercise

Consider the jobs discussed in this chapter as a starting point. There are many other types of jobs out there for psychology graduates. Conduct some research to learn about a job that sounds interesting to you.

1. What is this job? What are typical titles?
2. Describe the nature of the work.
    a. List at least three job duties or work tasks performed in this occupation.
    b. What kind of work would someone be doing if he or she were hired as a college graduate with no prior experience in this field?
    c. What other occupations are related to this job?
    d. What is the history of this occupation and what does it do for society?
3. Training/licensing/certification and other qualifications
    a. What is the lowest level of education needed for entry into this occupation?
    b. What is the most desirable education level?
    c. Is special licensing or certification required? If so, please explain.
    d. Which major(s) or courses of study or training are most desirable?
    e. What kinds of skills are needed? Please be as specific as possible.
    f. Does this occupation have specific physical requirements and/or desirable personal traits (friendliness, patience, etc.)? If so, please describe them.
4. Advancement and job outlook
    a. What are the opportunities for advancement in this job?
    b. What is the turnover rate for employees in this occupation?
    c. List at least three kinds of organizations that employ people in this occupation.
    d. What is the projected employment outlook for this occupation?
5. Salary and benefits
    a. What is the potential salary range for this occupation?
    b. What other benefits are generally associated with this job?

Source: Nauta, 2002.

EXERCISE 7.2
Planning for Your Future

1. Identify one (or two) specific occupations for which you are preparing.
   a. What is the work environment of a person employed in this area (e.g., workload, hours, deadlines, travel)?
   b. Why is this occupation a good fit for you in terms of your characteristics, skills, interests, abilities, and values (refer to Chapter 2)?
   c. How much and what kind of education will you need for this career?
2. Examine your course catalog and the materials that the psychology department provides to its majors at your school. What skills can you develop if you take full advantage of these opportunities during your undergraduate years?
3. What electives should you choose to prepare yourself for your chosen career? Electives help you develop the knowledge and skills you will need to succeed in your chosen career. Choose your electives wisely to demonstrate that you are a person who knows what you want to do and who has made wise choices in preparation for that goal. For example, if you are considering a career working with juvenile offenders, appropriate electives might include classes in the departments of criminal justice, sociology, social work, public policy, communications, human development, anthropology (e.g., ethnic identity, social and cultural behavior, urban anthropology), and English (e.g., literature for adolescents).
4. Identify opportunities for outside-of-class experience through research, internships, or work experience. The psychology department course catalog and web site, your advisor, and the career services office at your school can provide assistance with this task.
   a. Describe the activity.
   b. When should you make contact and whom should you contact?
   c. How will this experience enhance your education? What will you learn? What skills will you gain? What will be the outcomes of this experience?

SUGGESTED READINGS

Kuther, T. L., & Morgan, R. D. (2004). *Careers in psychology: Opportunities in a changing world.* Belmont, CA: Wadsworth.

Morgan, B. L., & Korschgen, A. J. (2001). *Majoring in psych? Career options for psychology undergraduates*. Needham Heights, MA: Allyn & Bacon.

Web Resources

The following web sites are hot-linked at *The psychology major's handbook* web site at *http://info.wadsworth.com/kuther*

Occupational Outlook Handbook

http://www.bls.gov/oco/home.htm

"A nationally recognized source of career information, designed to provide valuable assistance to individuals making decisions about their future work lives. Revised every two years, the *Handbook* describes what workers do on the job, working conditions, the training and education needed, earnings, and expected job prospects in a wide range of occupations."

Occupational Information Network Resource Center

http://www.onetcenter.org/

Administered and sponsored by the Employment and Training Administration of the U.S. Department of Labor, this site provides career exploration tools, testing and assessment guides, occupational listings, and other information.

Psychology Careers for the 21st Century

http://www.apa.org/students/brochure/index.html

This American Psychological Association (APA) brochure describes the field of psychology, including employment settings, the job outlook, and career preparation.

Careers in Psychology

http://www.psywww.com/careers/index.htm

Margaret Lloyd's web site discusses entry-level and graduate-level careers in psychology, as well as how to prepare for them.

Pursuing Psychology Career Page

http://www.uni.edu/walsh/linda1.html

Linda Weber provides a list of links to excellent materials on career development and resources for psychology majors.

Psi Chi: The National Honor Society in Psychology

http://www.psichi.org

The Psi Chi web site offers a variety of resources for psychology students, including full-text access to all the articles published in *Eye on Psi Chi,* the organization's quarterly newsletter. Articles cover areas in psychology, career preparation, personal growth, and other subjects.

Journal Exercises

My Dream Job

Describe your dream job. What does it entail? What skills are required? How can you work toward your dream?

My Strengths and Weaknesses

Consider the skills that a liberal arts degree builds as well as the skills employers seek. Identify your strengths. What do you do well? What do you enjoy? What are your weaknesses? How do you feel about your weaknesses? How might you strengthen these areas?

Finding a Job With Your Bachelor's Degree

CHAPTER 8

Chapter Guide

As the saying goes, "Time flies when you're having fun." Before you know it, graduation will be here. If you've decided to seek employment with your bachelor's degree, start planning early and hone your job-seeking skills. This chapter is your key to job-seeking success. You'll learn about how to find a job with your bachelor's degree, including where to look, how to prepare a résumé, the importance of cover letters, interviewing, and other important information.

Finding Job Openings

The first stop in your job search should be the career services office at your college, where you'll find skilled professionals who can help you with all aspects of the job search. Most career services offices have a variety of resources for locating available positions, including books, databases, and lists of employers who have contacted them seeking college students and recent graduates.

Newspaper advertisements are another common way to locate job openings; check your local paper. The Internet is a valuable resource for locating positions. A variety of sites on the Internet provide lists of job openings and advertisements (see the Web Resources at the end of this chapter). Don't forget to call the human resources department of major businesses and corporations in your town to inquire about applying for a position.

Remember the most important job-hunting resource of all: You! Applicants commonly overlook their own personal networks when scouting for available positions. Think about it. Through school, friends (and their parents), part-time jobs, and internships, you've already made many connections. Tap into these professional connections. If you've completed an internship or practicum, you may already have a foot in the door and a potential employer has already had a peek at your work habits. Even if the organization where you did your internship is not hiring additional staff, your supervisor probably has outside contacts. Tapping into your personal connections, as well as making new ones, is essential. It has been estimated that only about 15% of jobs are formally advertised, meaning that the majority of available jobs don't appear in newspapers or other ads (DeGalan & Lambert, 1995, p. 62). You can learn about these unadvertised positions only by word of mouth. Networking, or establishing connections, will help you to become more knowledgeable about the so-called hidden job market.

Completing Job Applications

Many employers require applicants to complete a job application form or even a large packet of forms. Carefully complete all job applications because they reveal a great deal about you. Your job application tells potential employers about your work habits, your ability to follow instructions, your personality and character, your personal achievements and job performance, and your potential to succeed (Landrum, Davis, & Landrum, 2000). Neatness, spelling, and grammar count regardless of the position for which you're applying. Be honest and accurate and remember to notify the people you plan to use as references (you should approach these individuals before submitting a job application). Some applications include personality inventories and other kinds of psychological assessments, so be truthful. Finally, understand that the job application form is never a substitute for a résumé; always supplement your application with a copy of your résumé.

Preparing Your Résumé

A résumé is a summary of your educational history, work experience, and career objectives. Employers always expect to see a résumé (even if it isn't stated in the advertisement). As you prepare your résumé, remember that it is often the only impression an employer has of you. It is a chance to present your strengths, to communicate that you have valuable skills, and to emphasize the aspects of your educational and employment background that make you unique. Writing a résumé may seem to be an overwhelming task, but you'll soon see that it is simply a matter of showcasing your skills.

Before you write, take time to assess your skills and abilities. Look back to the self-assessments you completed in Chapter 2. Outline your skills and abilities as well as your work experience and extracurricular activities to make it easier to prepare a thorough résumé. As you assess your skills, keep in mind the qualities that employers seek, as shown in Checklist 8.1.

Checklist 8.1
Skills and Qualities That Employers Seek

- ❑ Public speaking ability
- ❑ Writing ability (e.g., report and proposal writing)
- ❑ Problem identification and solving
- ❑ Small-group and teamwork skills
- ❑ Interpersonal and communication skills (including listening)
- ❑ Leadership skills
- ❑ Motivation
- ❑ Flexibility
- ❑ Tolerance for ambiguity
- ❑ Organizational skills
- ❑ Desire and willingness to learn
- ❑ Survey construction and methodology
- ❑ Statistics and mathematical reasoning

- ❑ Understanding of human cognition and behavior
- ❑ Understanding of how attitudes form and change

Source: Edwards & Smith, 1988; Landrum, Harrold, & Davis, 2003.

How many of these items match your abilities? Be sure that your résumé highlights your strengths. Remember that a résumé is your ticket through the door; its purpose is to convince an employer to interview you. Most employers glance at a résumé for 20 to 30 seconds (Krannich, 1991); therefore, if the first few lines don't catch his or her attention, the opportunity is lost. How do you make it past the 20-second test? Consider the main question that employers ask themselves as they read résumés: Why should I read this or contact this person for an interview? Keep this question in mind as you prepare your résumé, making sure that you answer it, and you'll have a unique résumé. All this hard work is essential; a good résumé gets you to the next stage, whereas a poor résumé stops you from going anywhere. There are many types of résumés, but chronological and functional résumés are the two most common.

Chronological Résumé

A chronological résumé is most commonly used by applicants (DeGalan & Lambert, 1995). It is easy for employers to understand and read because it discusses the chronological progression of your education and career. A brief description of the content of each section of a chronological résumé follows; a sample chronological résumé appears in Box 8.1.

Heading All your contact information should go at the top of your résumé. Include your name, permanent address (this is particularly important if you live on campus and will be moving home after graduation), phone (with area code), fax (if available), and e-mail address. In the 21st century, e-mail is essential, but be sure that your e-mail address is professional. Fun e-mail addresses such as "butterflygirl," "temptress," and "crazycat" are not professional. If possible, use your last name in your e-mail address. Include a web site address only if it reflects your professional ambitions.

Objective An objective informs potential employers about the sort of work you hope to do; it focuses your résumé. The objective statement is difficult to write because it must be concise yet provide a frame of reference for employers; it tells employers about your goals and your career focus (DeGalan & Lambert, 1995). Be specific about the job you want. For example: "To obtain an entry-level position within a financial institution requiring strong analytic and organizational skills" or "To obtain an entry-level position within a social service agency requiring strong interpersonal skills."

Education New graduates without a lot of employment experience should list the education section first. Include the name of the degree that you have

BOX 8.1

Sample Chronological Résumé

CHRISTINE JONES

Student Dorms #321
Your University
Purchase, NY 11234
(914) 555-1414
Jones@yourstateu.edu

7 Pleasant Street
Pleasantville, NY 11245
(914) 555 -6677
Fax (914) 555-9999

OBJECTIVE: Entry-level position in human resources utilizing interpersonal and organizational skills.

EDUCATION: Your University, Purchase, NY
Bachelor of Arts in Psychology, May 2001
Minor: Communications

EXPERIENCE: Resident Assistant, Your University, Purchase, NY, May 1999–Present

Assisted the director of a 360-resident living unit on campus. Assisted in creating and implementing policies and procedures for managing the residence. Developed and presented programs on a variety of subjects including alcohol awareness, career development, leadership, and safety.

Intern, *Purchase Daily News,* Purchase, NY August 1998–May 1999

Researched and wrote weekly articles on breaking news. Interviewed and researched local residents for weekly "Local Profile" articles.

Cashier, Purchase Delicatessen, Purchase, NY, June 1997–August 1999

Assisted customers in locating products, operated computerized cash register, handled large sums of cash, stocked shelves, and monitored store inventory.

ACTIVITIES: Theater Society, active member, two years, chorus member in three plays

Psychology Club, active member, three years, organized fund-raisers, participated in tutoring groups, and invited local speakers to club meetings.

REFERENCES: Available on request

received or will receive (AS, BS, BA, etc.), institution name and address, month and year of graduation, major, minor/concentration, grade point average (only if it is higher than 3.0), and academic honors, if applicable.

Experience Discuss your work experience, listing your most recent job first and working your way backward. For each job, indicate the position title, company or organization name, address, and dates of employment. Include all relevant employment experiences: part-time jobs, internships, cooperative education, and self-employment. Recruiters are interested in the skills that you've developed, not in whether or how much you were paid. For each position, briefly describe your duties and responsibilities as they relate to the position you are seeking, and emphasize specific skills and achievements. Use active words to describe your duties and the results that you produced. Table 8.1 provides a list of action verbs to help you construct this section of your résumé.

TABLE 8.1 **ACTION VERBS TO SPICE UP YOUR RÉSUMÉ**

Achieved	Coached	Decreased
Acquired	Collaborated	Defined
Acted	Collected	Demonstrated
Adapted	Communicated	Designed
Administered	Compared	Determined
Advised	Compiled	Developed
Allocated	Completed	Devised
Analyzed	Composed	Diagnosed
Applied	Computed	Directed
Arranged	Conceptualized	Discovered
Assembled	Condensed	Documented
Assessed	Conducted	Drafted
Assisted	Consolidated	Earned
Attained	Consulted	Edited
Averted	Constructed	Eliminated
Balanced	Contributed	Empowered
Briefed	Controlled	Encouraged
Budgeted	Converted	Enforced
Built	Coordinated	Ensured
Calculated	Counseled	Established
Clarified	Created	Estimated
Classified	Decided	Evaluated

(Continued)

TABLE 8.1

Action Verbs to Spice Up Your Résumé (Continued)

Examined	Managed	Reinforced
Expanded	Mapped	Repaired
Expedited	Marketed	Represented
Facilitated	Measured	Researched
Financed	Met	Resolved
Formulated	Modified	Reviewed
Gathered	Monitored	Revised
Generated	Motivated	Scheduled
Guided	Negotiated	Served
Handled	Observed	Showed
Headed	Obtained	Simplified
Helped	Operated	Sketched
Identified	Organized	Sold
Illustrated	Oversaw	Solved
Implemented	Participated	Staffed
Improved	Performed	Streamlined
Improvised	Persuaded	Studied
Increased	Planned	Submitted
Informed	Predicted	Summarized
Initiated	Prepared	Supervised
Innovated	Presented	Supported
Installed	Processed	Synthesized
Instituted	Produced	Systematized
Instructed	Projected	Tabulated
Integrated	Proposed	Taught
Interpreted	Qualified	Tested
Introduced	Quantified	Trained
Invented	Questioned	Translated
Investigated	Realized	Undertook
Learned	Received	Updated
Lectured	Recommended	Utilized
Led	Recorded	Verified
Maintained	Reduced	Wrote

Source: Appleby, 1997; DeGalan & Lambert, 1995; Lock, 1992

Activities and Affiliations List any professional affiliations (e.g., a student affiliate of APA) that are relevant to the objective stated on your résumé. Include activities and awards only if they are significant experiences and are in some way related to the objective stated on your résumé. If you can draw a valid connection between your objective and the activity, keep it in. If not, take it out.

Functional Résumé

A functional résumé organizes information by specific accomplishments. It enables you to make sense of your work history by highlighting skills and accomplishments that might not be obvious in a chronological résumé. Like a chronological résumé, a functional résumé begins with a heading and an objective statement. Box 8.2 on page 153 illustrates a functional résumé.

After the objective statement, a functional résumé includes a statement about specific accomplishments. This is the section that makes a functional résumé radically different from a chronological résumé. Rearrange your employment, volunteer, and internship history into sections that highlight areas of skills and accomplishments. Each skill or accomplishment section must contain statements relating to your experience in that category (as well as employers and dates of employment). Organize accomplishments in their order of importance with regard to the position that you seek. The experience and education sections follow and are identical to those in a chronological résumé, but because they appear toward the bottom of the page, they are less important visually.

FORMATTING AND STYLE

Make your résumé as professional looking as possible. Be concise; a new graduate's résumé should be no more than one page in length. Carefully proofread your résumé because typographical, spelling, and grammatical errors are unacceptable and will cost you an interview. Print your résumé on white or off-white paper using a laser printer. See Checklist 8.2 for more résumé tips.

CHECKLIST 8.2
Résumé Checklist

- ❑ Clearly communicate your purpose and value.
- ❑ Communicate your strongest points first.
- ❑ Don't make statements that you can't document.
- ❑ Be direct, succinct, and expressive with language.
- ❑ Don't use lengthy sentences and descriptions. This is the only time that sentence fragments are acceptable; just use them judiciously.

- ❑ Don't use the passive voice.
- ❑ Don't change the tense of verbs throughout the résumé.
- ❑ Confine your information to one page.
- ❑ Use space to organize your résumé; it should not appear cramped.
- ❑ Aim for overall visual balance on the page.
- ❑ Use a font size of 10 to 14 points.
- ❑ Choose a simple typeface and stick to it (i.e., don't change fonts).
- ❑ Use ample spacing and boldface for emphasis (but don't overdo it).
- ❑ Don't fold or staple your résumé.
- ❑ Check spelling, grammar, and punctuation.
- ❑ Proofread.
- ❑ Ask someone else to proofread.
- ❑ Get outside help. Get feedback from two or three people, including someone who regularly evaluates résumés and hires employees.
- ❑ Do not include your reference information on your résumé (see sample).
- ❑ Before giving their names to a potential employer, ask your references if they are willing to serve as references.

Source: Appleby, 1997; DeGalan & Lambert, 1995; Krannich, 1991.

Writing a Cover Letter

The cover letter is an introduction to your résumé that enables you to tailor your application to a prospective employer. Your cover letter must be concise, tell who you are, and explain what you can offer an employer. Three paragraphs will suffice. In the first paragraph, state your reason for writing (e.g., "to apply to the research assistant position advertised in the *Daily News*"). The second paragraph should explain what you can offer the employer. Highlight the most important aspects of your background that are relevant to the position and/or organization. The final paragraph provides contact information, thanks the reader, and reiterates your interest in the position.

Remember that the cover letter is an introduction that should motivate the reader to examine your résumé. An effective cover letter is written with the needs of the audience (i.e., the prospective employer) in mind. Before writing a cover letter, ask yourself, "What is the purpose of this letter? What are the needs of the reader? What benefits will an employer gain from me? How can I maintain the reader's interest? How can I end the letter persuasively so that the reader will want to examine my résumé and contact me?" Be explicit and communicate what you can do for the employer, not what the job can do for you. Box 8.3 illustrates a sample cover letter. Checklist 8.3 provides tips for writing a cover letter.

BOX 8.2 **SAMPLE FUNCTIONAL RESUME**

CHRISTINE JONES

Student Dorms #321 Your University Purchase, NY 11234 (914) 555-1414 Jones@yourstateu.edu	77 Pleasant Street Pleasantville, NY 11245 (914) 555-6677 Fax (914) 555-9999

OBJECTIVE:	Entry-level position in human resources utilizing interpersonal and organizational skills.
INTERPERSONAL EXPERIENCE:	Resident Assistant, Your University, Purchase, NY, May 1999–Present Assisted the director of a 360-resident living unit on campus. Assisted in creating and implementing policies and procedures for managing the residence. Developed and presented programs on a variety of subjects including alcohol awareness, career development, leadership, and safety. Cashier, Purchase Delicatessen, Purchase, NY, June 1997–August 1999 Assisted customers in locating products, operated computerized cash register, handled large sums of cash, stocked shelves, and monitored store inventory.
LEADERSHIP AND ORGANIZATIONAL EXPERIENCE:	Psychology Club, active member, three years, organized fund-raisers, participated in tutoring groups, and invited local speakers to club meetings.
WRITING EXPERIENCE:	Intern, *Purchase Daily News*, Purchase, NY August 1998–May 1999 Researched and wrote weekly articles on breaking news. Interviewed and researched local residents for weekly "Local Profile"articles.
PUBLIC SPEAKING:	Theater Society, active member, two years, chorus member in three plays
EDUCATION:	Your University, Purchase, NY Bachelor of Arts in Psychology; Minor: Communications, May 2001

BOX 8.3 **SAMPLE COVER LETTER**

April 17, 2000

Mr. John Jones
Director of Personnel
Children's Aid Center
123 Centre Street
New York, NY 11234

Dear Mr. Jones:

I am writing to apply to the residential counselor position that was advertised in the April 11 issue of the *Purchase News*. As indicated by my resume, I will receive a bachelor of arts degree in psychology from Your University in May 2000.

The advertisement indicated that you were looking for someone with good interpersonal skills who is capable of working with a clinical team, and who holds a degree in psychology. I believe that you will find my educational and work history, as outlined on my résumé, interesting and relevant. Over the past 6 years, I have gained experience in several counseling contexts including camp counseling, volunteer work at a homeless shelter for youth, and an internship at a residential center for emotionally disturbed adolescents. I have taken a variety of courses in psychology and communications to supplement these professional experiences.

I would like to meet with you, at your convenience, to discuss how my education and experience would be consistent with your needs. I will contact your office within the next week to discuss the possibility of an interview. If you have any questions or require additional information, please contact me at (914) 555-1414. Thank you for your attention and consideration.

Sincerely,

Timothy Smith

CHECKLIST 8.3
Cover Letter Checklist

- ❑ Address the letter to an individual using the person's name and title. If answering a blind newspaper advertisement, use the following: "To Whom It May Concern."

- ❑ Indicate the position for which you are applying and explain why you are qualified to fill it.
- ❑ Include a phone number where you can be reached.
- ❑ Ask someone to proofread your letter for spelling, grammar, and punctuation errors.
- ❑ Indicate how your education and work skills are transferable and relevant to the position for which you are applying.
- ❑ Keep a copy of each cover letter for your records; on your copy of the cover letter write notes from any phone conversations that might take place.
- ❑ Make a connection with the company through a person you know, some information you've researched, or a specific interest.

Adapted from Appleby, 1997; DeGalan & Lambert, 1995; Krannich, 1991.

INTERVIEWING

Congratulations! You've been asked to come in for an interview. An interview is the most important criterion for hiring; it beats out grades, related work experience, and recommendations (Krannich, 1991). It helps companies identify which applicants they'd like to take a closer look at. Often, second, and sometimes even third, interviews occur. This is your chance to impress the prospective employer. How do you do it? Display good communication skills, clearly defined professional goals, and an honest, outgoing personality (Appleby, 1999). Interviews are stressful, but you can increase your confidence by being thoroughly prepared.

Prepare

Understand the purpose of a job interview and keep the interviewer's objectives in mind. From your perspective, the purpose of the interview is to get a second interview or a job offer; but for employers, the purpose of the interview is to whittle down the list of applicants to one or two finalists. The interviewer is interested in answering several questions:

- Why does this person want to work for us?
- What position is this person suited for?
- What are his or her qualifications?
- Why should I hire him or her?
- Does this person meet my employment needs?
- Is he or she trustworthy?

The interviewer looks for reasons why you should not be hired; interviewers are interested in identifying your weaknesses. Your job is to communicate your strengths. This means that you must understand yourself, but you must also understand the company or the organization to which you are applying.

Research the company. What is the relative size and growth of the industry? What product lines or services are offered? Where is the headquarters? Identify the competition. Be familiar with any recent items in the news. Try to predict what will be asked during the interview and prepare answers. Table 8.2 presents questions commonly asked during interviews.

You will also be judged on the questions that you ask. Ask thoughtful, intelligent questions about the company and the position. Table 8.3 provides sample questions that an applicant might ask during an interview.

TABLE 8.2 **COMMON INTERVIEW QUESTIONS**

What do you hope to be doing 5 or 10 years from now?

Why did you apply for this job?

Tell me about yourself.

What are your strengths and weaknesses?

What can you offer to us and what can we offer you?

What are the two or three accomplishments in your life that have given you the greatest satisfaction?

Do you work well under pressure?

Have you ever held any supervisory or leadership roles?

What do you like to do in your spare time?

What other jobs are you applying for?

Is there anything else we should know about you?

Why do you feel that you will be successful in this position?

What courses did you like best? Least? Why?

What did you learn or gain from your part-time and summer job experiences?

What are your plans for graduate study?

Why did you choose your major?

What can a psychology major do for this organization?

How did you finance your education?

If you could do it all again, what would you change about your education?

Did you do the best you could in school? Why or why not?

Why did you leave your last employer?

What job did you like the most? The least? Why?

Have you ever been fired?

Why do you want to join our organization?

Why should we hire you?

When will you be ready to work?

TABLE 8.2 COMMON INTERVIEW QUESTIONS (CONTINUED)

What do you want to do with your life?

Do you have any actual work experience?

How would you describe your ideal job?

Are you a team player? Explain.

What motivates you?

Tell me about some of your recent goals and what you did to achieve them.

Have you ever had a conflict with a boss or professor? How did you resolve it?

If I were to ask one of your professors to describe you, what would he or she say?

Why did you choose to attend your college?

What qualities do you feel a successful manager should have?

What do you know about our company?

What kind of salary are you looking for?

Adapted from Appleby 1997; DeGalan & Lambert, 1995; Krannich, 1991; Landrum et al., 2000.

TABLE 8.3 POSSIBLE QUESTIONS TO ASK DURING AN INTERVIEW

What are the duties and responsibilities of this job?

How long has this position been in the company?

What type of person would be ideal for this position?

What kinds of skills or personality characteristics are ideal for this position?

Whom would I be working with?

What am I expected to accomplish during the first year?

How will I be evaluated?

Are promotions and raises tied to performance criteria?

What is unique about working for this company?

What does the future look like for this company?

Adapted from Appleby, 1997; DeGalan & Lambert, 1995; Krannich, 1991.

What to Wear

It may not be politically correct, but physical appearance counts. Dress appropriately for your interview because your appearance communicates messages about your level of seriousness and professionalism. During the first 5 minutes of an interview, interviewers make initial judgments or create expectations about your professionalism and "fit" for a position based on your appearance and demeanor. Use this to your advantage by dressing appropriately. Even if you are applying to a company with a casual dress code, dress up for the interview to communicate your enthusiasm for the position.

Whether you're a man or a woman, you can't go wrong with a classic navy or gray suit. Men should wear a white or blue oxford shirt with an understated tie. Women should wear a modest blouse, with understated hair and makeup. Keep jewelry to a minimum: a watch, simple earrings (for women only), and a ring. Remember that these are merely general rules. You might want to see how others in your field dress for appropriate cues.

During the Interview

Be enthusiastic. Remember that your interviewer is committed to his or her position and to the company and wants to hire someone who is similarly committed. Demonstrate your enthusiasm by discussing what you've learned from your research and preparation. Ask questions to fill in any gaps in your understanding. Convey a sense of long-term interest by asking about opportunities for further professional education and advancement.

Throughout the interview, be aware of your body language and keep fidgeting to a minimum. Lean very slightly toward the interviewer to communicate your interest in what he or she is saying (Krannich, 1991). Maintain eye contact to convey interest and trustworthiness. Smile to convey a positive attitude. Don't forget that your tone of voice can indicate how interested you are in the interview and in the organization. Here are some other helpful tips for acing interviews.

- Bring a copy of your résumé. It comes in handy if you have to fill in applications and provides initial information for your interviewer.
- Allow the interviewer to direct the conversation.
- Answer questions in a clear and positive manner.
- Never speak negatively about former employers or colleagues, no matter what.
- Let the interviewer lead the conversation toward salary and benefits. Try not to focus your interest on these issues (at least not during the initial interview).
- When discussing salary, be flexible.
- If the employer doesn't say when you'll hear about their decision, ask when you can call to follow up.
- Thank the employer for the interview.

Thank-You Note

Immediately after your interview, send a thank-you note. Few applicants do, so you'll stand out (Appleby, 1997; Krannich, 1991). Express your appreciation for the opportunity to be interviewed and for the interviewer's time and consideration. Restate your interest and highlight any noteworthy points made in your conversation. State when you'll contact the employer to follow up and inquire about your status (and remember to call as you said you would).

THINKING ABOUT A JOB OFFER

Job offers are usually made over the phone or in person (e.g., toward the end of an interview). No matter how the offer is delivered, you're likely to be surprised. The most appropriate response to an offer in person or by phone is to ask any questions that come to mind and then request time (a day or two) to think about the offer.

Before accepting an offer, be sure that you understand the conditions and elements of the job. In many cases, salaries for entry-level positions leave little room for negotiation. Take your lead from the employer as to whether the salary is negotiable. If it isn't, you must decide whether you're still willing to accept the position and what, if anything, would make it more attractive. As you think about whether to accept the job offer, consider the scope of the position, how it fits your career goals, opportunities for professional growth, and pragmatics (geographical location, benefits, salary, work hours, etc.). If you decide to accept the offer, be sure to inform any employers still actively considering you. Also, contact your references to inform them of your new job as well as to thank them for their assistance.

If you decide not to accept the job, notify the employer as soon as possible by phone. Timeliness is important because other applicants are also waiting for a response. Be polite, thank the employer for the offer, and wish him or her success. Follow up with a polite letter as well.

SUGGESTED READINGS

Bolles, R. N. (2005). *What color is your parachute? A practical manual for job-hunters and career-changers.* Berkeley, CA: Ten Speed Press.

DeGalan, J., & Lambert, S. (1995). *Great jobs for psychology majors*. Chicago: VGM Career Horizons.

Farr, M. J. (1995). *The quick interview and salary negotiation book*. Indianapolis, IN: Jist Works.

Fry, R. (2001).*Your first resume: For students and anyone preparing to enter today's tough job market.* Belmont, CA: Thomson.

Greene, B. (2004). *Get the interview every time: Fortune 500 hiring professionals' tips for writing winning résumés and cover letters*. Princeton, NJ: Kaplan.

Web Resources

The following web sites are hot-linked at *The Psychology Major's Handbook* web site at *http://info.wadsworth.com/kuther*

Job Hunter's Bible

http://www.jobhuntersbible.com/

Richard Bolles, author of *What Color Is Your Parachute? A Practical Manual for Job-Hunters and Career-Changers,* maintains this site of job hunting and career development resources.

Quintessential Careers

http://www.quintcareers.com

This web site offers an extensive online guide to job hunting and career exploration, complete with resources on résumés, cover letters, interviewing, and other topics.

College Grad Job Hunter

http://www.collegegrad.com/

This is a job site designed for college students and others who are just getting started in the world of work.

JobWeb

http://www.jobweb.com

Here you'll find links to job search guides, articles, and other valuable resources on the web.

MonsterTrak.com

http://monstertrak.com/

This site features job search tools, articles, a salary search center, and other information.

Journal Exercises

Who Am I?

Who are you? What are your interests, skills, abilities, and aspirations? Freewrite about yourself and your goals. After you've completed this exercise, look back over the exercises in Chapter 2. Do you notice anything different, or can you add anything to your responses?

Thinking Ahead

Try to imagine your ideal life 5 years from now. What are you doing? Where do you live? How do you spend your days?

Interview Preparation

In preparation for an interview, take notes on the prospective employer. What kinds of questions might the interviewer ask? How might you respond? Which of your characteristics match the job description well? Which might need some work?

What Can I Do With a Graduate Degree in Psychology?

CHAPTER 9

Chapter Guide

The well-rounded liberal arts grounding of psychology makes it a consistently popular major. Each year more than 76,000 students graduate with baccalaureate degrees in psychology (National Center for Education Statistics, 2003a). Most go out into the world and secure jobs after graduation; about one-quarter to one-third enroll in graduate school (National Science Foundation, 2001). Why do students pursue graduate degrees?

REASONS FOR PURSUING A GRADUATE DEGREE: SKILLS OBTAINED THROUGH GRADUATE STUDY

Why go to graduate school? First and foremost, students enter graduate study in psychology and related fields because of a deep interest in understanding human behavior. Successful graduate students have a love of learning; they thirst for knowledge and thrive on discovery. Graduate study provides a unique opportunity to contribute to the discipline and enhance our knowledge base of the causes and correlates of human behavior. Many students pursue graduate study in order to contribute to society, help others in need, and improve the quality of life for people (Seton Hall University, 2000). It is unquestionable that graduate degrees offer prestige and opportunities for career and economic advancement (American Psychological Association, 1996).

Many students pursue graduate degrees because education pays. Not only does it provide personal enrichment and knowledge, but it also allows graduates to increase their salaries substantially. In the United States, the median salary of all bachelor's degree holders, regardless of field and experience, is $46,800; for master's degree holders it is $55,328; and for doctoral degree holders it is $70,148 (U.S Bureau of Labor Statistics, 2004c). Of course, salaries vary by field and experience; as you accumulate experience after graduation, your salary will increase. In 2002, the median annual earnings wage of clinical, counseling, and school psychologists (at both the master's and doctoral levels) were $51,170, with the middle 50% earning between $38,560 and $66,970 (U.S. Bureau of Labor Statistics, 2004c). Later in the chapter we'll examine salaries in more detail. There are also many intangible and nonfinancial benefits of a graduate education.

As you are aware, undergraduate training in psychology provides students with opportunities to learn many valuable skills. Graduate education further hones these skills and provides other opportunities for personal and professional development. Although the particular set of skills developed varies depending on the student, program, advisor, and experiences, generally speaking, graduate training in psychology gives students an opportunity to develop and master the following abilities and competencies (American Psychological Association, 1998; Landrum, Davis, & Landrum, 2000).

Specialized Knowledge of Psychology and Appreciation of Multiple Perspectives

A graduate education provides a depth of knowledge in a particular area of psychology. Students are exposed to diverse perspectives within a specialized area of psychology, enhancing their awareness that professionals trained in different disciplines may see a given problem differently and permitting them to gain an appreciation for different perspectives and an understanding of the advantages of different viewpoints.

Thinking and Problem-Finding, Problem Definition, and Problem-Solving Skills

Training in research design and methodology offers graduate students valuable experience in identifying, defining, and solving problems, further honing their critical thinking and problem-solving skills. Given limited or ambiguous information, graduate degree holders learn to identify central issues and extrapolate the most important problems to be addressed. Research, clinical, and applied experiences teach graduate students that there is often more than one acceptable way to solve a problem.

Information Acquisition, Management, and Synthesis

Some of the most highly valued skills obtained in graduate school include the ability to gather, summarize, synthesize, and draw conclusions from information. Students gain experience with a variety of methods for gathering information—literature searches, interviewing techniques, survey construction, content analysis, experimental design, and observational skills. Through direct instruction and experience, they learn the importance of avoiding bias and preconceptions in conducting information searches. A graduate education gives students the cognitive tools needed to deal with inconsistent and uncertain information, extract key ideas from information rapidly, impose structure on ambiguous or messy data, and translate information into meaningful conclusions and recommendations.

Methodological and Quantitative Skills

Graduate students in psychology develop inferential skills, statistical reasoning ability, and analysis skills. With experience, they become able to draw appropriate inferences from numerical data and learn how to present data to a nontechnical audience. The scientific and methodological skills developed through graduate education motivate students to understand phenomena by examining the data rather than avoiding it. An understanding of experimental and quasi-experimental design, survey and sampling techniques, and qualitative analysis enables graduates not only to conceptualize phenomena based on cause and effect but also to understand the limitations of conclusions given particular methodological approaches.

Planning and Leadership Skills

Conducting therapy and engaging in long-term research projects encourage graduate students to develop planning skills. They learn how to identify the steps needed to complete a given project, from beginning to end, and gain expertise in identifying and anticipating problems. Conducting research in a faculty member's lab often gives students experience in teamwork and collegiality.

Interpersonal and Intrapersonal Awareness and Agility

Working closely with others in research contexts provides valuable opportunities for learning how to be a team player. Experience as teaching assistants or instructors—opportunities that are commonly available to graduate students—enable them to learn leadership, organizational, motivational, and negotiation skills. Training in psychology offers an understanding and appreciation of the capabilities and limitations of people from cognitive, perceptual, physical, motivational, and developmental as well as other perspectives. Graduate students often learn how to extend interpersonal skills to an intrapersonal context; they learn how to become more self-aware and self-observant. The challenges of a graduate education lead to an enhanced awareness of one's abilities and limitations, as well as an understanding of how to motivate oneself.

Reading, Writing, and Communication Skills

Graduate students learn how to structure and evaluate written and oral arguments, as well as how to write concisely in a professional style. Research presentations and teaching assistantships give students opportunities to learn how to communicate research and theoretical concepts to professional and lay audiences.

Application

The ability to apply psychological, research, and methodological knowledge in real-world settings is highly valued in applied research, clinical, and business settings. Graduate education provides opportunities to learn how to apply research-based knowledge to solve real-life problems and to use psychological principles and methods to change behaviors and mental processes in clinical and organizational settings. These are important skills that place holders of advanced degrees at an advantage in a variety of career settings.

Adaptability

Graduate education trains students to think flexibly and accept some ambiguity. They learn to become action-oriented and develop the ability to work on and consider several problems at once. Successful graduate students learn the value of initiative, motivation, and responsibility and successfully embody these qualities.

Graduate-Level Careers in Psychology

Graduate education opens the door to many possibilities and opportunities. Generally speaking, graduate degrees can be placed into two categories: master's- and doctoral-level degrees. There are many different kinds of master's and doctoral degrees, as we'll discuss. If you're wondering exactly what careers are possible with a graduate degree, read on. Here's an overview of what you can do with a graduate degree; however, you should note that no one program will prepare you for all these careers. Before you decide on a graduate degree and program, it's important to consider all the types of careers that you might enjoy and choose a degree and program that will not limit your options. Also carefully research the many specializations in psychology because they offer varying career opportunities, as completing Exercise 9.1 will illustrate.

EXERCISE 9.1
Exploring Psychology Specializations

1. Identify two areas of specialization in psychology that interest you. Why do these areas interest you? What are typical topics of study within these areas?
2. What kinds of jobs do individuals with master's degrees in these areas hold? Include information about typical settings, salary, and other aspects.
3. What kinds of jobs do individuals with doctoral degrees in these areas hold? Include information about typical settings, salary, and other aspects.
4. How has what you have learned about this specialization influenced your views about graduate study in this area? Is a graduate degree a good career option? Which degree offers more opportunities? Conduct a cost analysis of the pros and cons of seeking a master's degree verses a doctoral degree in this specialization.

Teaching Careers

Many students seek graduate degrees in order to teach at a high school or at a 2- or 4-year college. Holders of master's degrees can teach psychology in a high school (although additional certification may be necessary, depending on the state) or community college setting. In recent years, faculty positions at 2-year and community colleges have become more competitive; many are held by holders of doctoral degrees. Similarly, although holders of master's degrees may be hired to teach at 4-year colleges on a part-time basis, they are unlikely to be hired for full-time positions (Peters, 1992).

If your goal is to teach at the college level, it's in your best interest to pursue a doctoral degree, which will provide you with the most opportunities for employment, mobility, and advancement as a faculty member (Actkinson, 2000; Lloyd, 2000). Graduates with doctoral degrees can teach undergraduate, master's, and doctoral students in a variety of educational settings, including universities, professional schools, and medical schools. When you consider a career as a professor, recognize that there is more to a professorate than lecturing in front of a classroom each day. Spending time in the classroom is only the most obvious job a professor has.. His or her career involves many roles, usually including research and service to the campus and community (advising, committee work, administrative work). During a typical week, a professor may give lectures, spend time writing an article or book, conduct statistical analyses and continue with his or her research, conduct literature searches, sit in on faculty meetings, advise students, write letters of recommendation, spend time grading papers, give a talk at a professional meeting, engage in consulting work, serve as an advisor for community agencies, and perform many other activities.

Research Careers

A graduate degree in psychology is excellent preparation for a career in research. Research psychologists conduct basic and applied studies on human behavior and may participate in research programs sponsored by universities, government, and private organizations (Kuther & Morgan, 2004). For example, a psychologist working at a university- or hospital-based clinic might study smoking cessation; another working at a traumatic brain injury center might study the effects of particular kinds of brain injuries on behavior, as well as resilience to brain injury and rehabilitation strategies. Some psychologists work in military research programs, examining the effects of exposure to trauma, for example, whereas others act as research and development officers for pharmaceutical companies and businesses (Lloyd, 2000). Medical schools are emerging as an important employment setting for research psychologists who conduct research and teach medical students. Fields such as anatomy, biochemistry, physiology, pharmacology, and microbiology are merging; as a result, interdisciplinary study is playing an increasingly important role in university life and is leading to more research (and teaching) opportunities for psychologists outside psychology departments (Balster, 1995). Many research positions are available to holders of a master's degree, especially in business and private organizations. Particularly in academic settings, a doctoral degree offers more flexibility, opportunities for advancement, and opportunities to serve as the primary investigator in research studies funded by federal grants (Lloyd, 2000).

Applied Careers

Graduate degrees open the door to a wide variety of careers outside teaching and research. However, a discussion of the opportunities that the various graduate degrees afford for applying psychological knowledge to the real world is incomplete without emphasizing the importance of licensure and credentialing.

Licensure and Credentialing A license is a form of quality control, a credential issued by a state that ensures a minimum level of competence for professionals (Kuther, 1996; Kuther & Morgan, 2004). It is a way of protecting the public from individuals who are not competent to practice. Licensure has personal, professional, and economic implications because it provides statutory recognition and thus has a legitimizing and enhancing effect. A license gives mental health professionals the legal authority to work independently (Kuther, 1996); in order to have any type of private practice in which psychological services are offered, you must be licensed.

The various graduate degrees differ in the opportunities they afford for certification and licensure. The term *psychologist* is regulated by state licensing boards; in order to use the title "Psychologist," you must be licensed (Lloyd, 2000). All states and the District of Columbia have such requirements. Laws vary by state but generally require a doctorate in psychology, completion of an approved internship, and 1 to 2 years of professional experience in order to be licensed as a psychologist (Kuther & Morgan, 2004). Most states also require that applicants pass a standardized test and, in some instances, additional oral or essay examinations.

With a master's degree in psychology, you cannot be licensed as a psychologist. Instead, you must be supervised by licensed psychologists. As we will discuss, there are other alternatives to becoming a psychologist that allow autonomy and the possibility of establishing an independent practice. For example, clinical social workers can be licensed in all states. In most states, those holding master's-level clinical and counseling degrees can be licensed as marriage and family therapists and licensed professional counselors. In addition, those with master's degrees are often eligible for certificates—quality control credentials awarded by professional organizations.

Practice Recipients of graduate degrees have a variety of opportunities to engage in service delivery. Mental health professionals with graduate degrees, including clinical and counseling psychologists, engage in a variety of practice activities including, but often not limited to (a) conducting psychotherapy with persons with psychological disorders, crises, or problems of living; (b) administering and interpreting psychological tests of personality, intellect, and vocational aptitude; (c) facilitating psychoeducational and psychotherapy groups; (d) giving talks or workshops on specialty areas; (e) directing and administrating mental health programs; (f) supervising the clinical work of other therapists; and (g) responding to crises or emergency situations (Himelein, 1999; U.S. Bureau of Labor Statistics, 2004b).

There are many myths and misconceptions about the competencies and abilities of master's- and doctoral-level clinicians. Generally speaking, a doctoral degree in clinical or counseling psychology allows for the most autonomy in providing direct service, with some exceptions. In all states, a person with a master's degree in psychology can be certified as a psychological assistant. Psychological assistants perform many direct service activities including administering psychological tests, implementing behavioral interventions, and conducting limited amounts of therapy. The major caveat to be aware of in becoming a master's-level psychological assistant is that you must be supervised by a doctoral-level psychologist; however, there is a "loophole" that permits more autonomy.

Most states allow several forms of licensure for master's-trained individuals, usually as counselors, which provides a great deal of autonomy (Actkinson, 2000). Master's-level counselors and social workers (with degrees in psychology, counseling, or social work) perform many of the same services as those with doctoral degrees: They provide assessment and intervention services for community-based programs, public and private institutions, and programs dealing with special problems such as substance abuse, spouse abuse, crisis intervention, and vocational rehabilitation (Himelein, 1999). In institutional settings, holders of master's degrees can work as behavior change specialists, who design and implement programs to serve special populations. Finally, if you're considering a graduate degree for the purpose of setting up a private practice, be aware that many licensed mental health workers, including social workers and psychologists, are leaving private practice because they cannot compete with health maintenance organizations (HMOs) (Himelein, 1999; Humphreys, 1996).

Administration Holders of graduate degrees in psychology and related fields work as managers and administrators in hospitals, mental health clinics, government agencies, schools, universities, businesses, and nonprofit organizations, where they may oversee research and applied activities (Bat-Chava, 2000). The ability to effectively administer in each of these settings is enhanced by the research skills obtained in graduate school. Such skills are essential for evaluating programs and making decisions based on evaluations. Many administrative positions can be obtained with a master's degree and some experience, especially in smaller institutions and organizations. As in other applied careers, additional opportunities are available to doctoral-level administrators.

Consulting Holders of graduate degrees in psychology are often hired by organizations to provide consultative services on problems in their area of expertise. These services can include designing a marketing survey, organizing outpatient mental health services, conducting individual assessments, providing expert testimony in court, and designing web pages, as well as many other activities.

Health psychologists, for example, may be hired as consultants to design and implement programs to help people become healthier, stop smoking, lose weight, or manage stress. Some consultants work in policy: They conduct, interpret, and disseminate research to help national planners and policy makers reach decisions (Flattau, 1998). Trial consultants work in several areas: They may help with jury selection, work with witnesses, or develop effective trial strategies in order to shape juror perceptions (Stapp, 1996). Those trained in forensic or clinical psychology may conduct clinical work in corrections settings, serve as consultants for trial lawyers or as expert witnesses in jury trials, and conduct assessments used in trials. As in the other areas that we've discussed, some opportunities are available to recipients of master's degrees, and additional opportunities for advancement are open to holders of doctoral degrees.

Business/Human Resources Many holders of graduate degrees find jobs in business, where they select and train employees, engage in human resources development, and produce employee assistance programs. Typical activities include designing and validating assessment instruments; determining the fairness of assessment and vocational tests, particularly for minority applicants; and creating work environments that maximize employee satisfaction in public and private settings (U.S. Bureau of Labor Statistics, 2004b).

The research skills honed in graduate school are applicable and are valued in a corporate setting; for example, in market research (Garfein, 1997). Like other research psychologists, market researchers design studies, construct questionnaires and other research instruments, analyze data, draw conclusions, and write reports. However, instead of conducting and publishing research to advance theory, a market researcher conducts applied research in an effort to help clients become more productive, competitive, and profitable (Krauss, 1996). Business offers a variety of opportunities for holders of master's degrees because, unlike the situation in many other applied psychology careers, doctoral degrees do not necessarily offer much of an advantage over master's degrees. For recipients of both master's and doctoral degrees, advancement becomes possible with additional work experience.

Publishing Journalism and publishing offer new opportunities for holders of advanced degrees in psychology. Some psychologists pursue careers as acquisitions editors. An acquisitions editor works for a publishing company and engages in a variety of tasks, including reading book proposals, interpreting reviews of proposals, deciding whether to offer book contracts to authors, approaching potential authors with book ideas, discussing works in progress with authors, negotiating journal-publishing agreements with professional societies, and working on practical issues in publishing such as the design of book covers (Amsel, 1997). Positions in publishing offer important opportunities for master's degree holders with an interest in writing and the ability to think critically and solve problems effectively. More advanced positions in publishing are held by doctoral degree holders and master's degree recipients with experience in the field.

The Master's Degree

Myths abound about the master's degree because students and advisors often know little about master's degrees in psychology and related fields (Actkinson, 2000). The value and professionalism of the master's degree has been questioned repeatedly (Quereshi & Kuchan, 1988; Trent, 1993), even by the

American Psychological Association (APA) (Actkinson, 2000; Woods, 1971). The field of psychology cannot seem to agree on the appropriate service delivery roles of master's degree holders (Actkinson, 2000; Dale, 1988; Hays-Thomas, 2000).

Despite possible biases against, and lack of discussion about, the master's degree in psychology, it is a very popular degree (Actkinson, 2000). Nearly 15,000 master's degrees in psychology were conferred in 2002 (National Center for Education Statistics, 2003b). Between 1973 and 1993 the number of master's programs quadrupled (from 178 to 931; Norcross, Hanych, & Terranova, 1996); clearly, the master's is a popular degree. A far greater number of students pursue master's degrees than doctoral degrees. Can master's-trained individuals provide effective therapy? Studies have shown that there are no convincing differences in therapeutic outcomes as a function of the practitioner's level of training (Christensen & Jacobson, 1994; Seligman, 1995). Therefore, some psychologists argue that a form of licensure should be extended to master's-level psychologists (Hays-Thomas, 2000).

Perhaps some of the confusion and miscommunication about the master's degree derive from its origin. Peters (1992) points out that "U.S. master's degrees began in the seventeenth century as fund-raising devices that catered to people who liked titles after their names. Any student who successfully completed the bachelor's and refrained from ungentlemanly activities for three years while paying college fees was automatically awarded a master's degree" (p. 109). In the mid-1800s to late 1800s, the "rules" changed so that master's degrees became "earned" degrees. Even today, the status of master's degrees is befuddling and lacks standardization. There are many different types of master's degrees, the most common being the standard master of arts (MA) or master of science (MS). Master's degrees require from 1 to 3 years of study, depending on the program. The diversity in type and quality of programs leads to considerable confusion.

In most cases, 2 years of full-time graduate study are needed to earn a master's degree in psychology or counseling. Requirements for service-oriented fields such as clinical, counseling, and school psychology usually include practical experience in an applied setting. As illustrated by Exercise 9.2, states vary in their requirements for masters-level practitioners. Research-oriented areas such as experimental and developmental psychology usually require a master's thesis based on a research project.

Because of the diversity in master's programs, Peters (1992) advises that good programs offer at least two kinds of experiences that go beyond mere course work. "First are integrative experiences that help the student pull together knowledge learned in courses and translate it into practice. . . . Second are summative experiences which test the students' knowledge and ability to do this integration on a higher than undergraduate level" (p. 112). Examples of integrative experiences include internships, practica, and other research and/or field work. Examples of summative experiences include comprehensive examinations, theses, and research projects. Exercise 9.2 will help you learn more about practice opportunities with a master's degree in your state.

EXERCISE 9.2
Practicing With a Master's Degree

1. Opportunities to practice therapy with a master's degree vary by state. Research the requirements of your state. Under what conditions can an individual with a master's in psychology practice? What types of credentialing or licensure are necessary?
2. What other types of master's degrees offer practice opportunities in your state?
3. If you were to pursue a master's degree with the intent of practicing, which degree would you choose, and why?
4. Based on your research, with how much independence can an individual with a master's degree practice in your state?

Why Seek a Master's Degree?

What can you do with a master's degree? Depending on the program and curriculum, a master's degree enables graduates to: (a) teach psychology in high school (other certification may be needed); (b) become more competitive for jobs in government and industry; (c) practice clinical counseling or school psychology under supervision; (d) obtain certification or licensure for school psychology (depending on the state) and practice industrial/organizational psychology; and (e) pursue alternative careers in counseling such as marriage and family therapy, alcohol and substance abuse counseling, and social work.

Why do students choose to pursue a master's degree? A big consideration for some is that a master's degree takes much less time than a doctoral degree. Typically it takes 1 to 2 years to achieve a master's degree, as compared with 6 to 8 for a doctorate (Actkinson, 2000). A related factor is money; although a master's degree is expensive, both in tuition and in salary lost while attending school, it's cheaper than a doctoral degree (because it requires less time). However, note that while you're enrolled in graduate school, you will lose several income-producing years and will accrue debt in terms of loans for tuition and for living expenses. Other reasons why students pursue master's degrees include program availability. A doctoral program may not be available in a given geographical location, and students may not be able or willing to relocate to attend graduate school (Actkinson, 2000). Students with families must also consider how graduate education will affect the family unit. Doctoral programs place students under great stress for an extended period of time. Students with families may not be able or willing to place such stress on their families.

Other reasons for choosing a master's program are pragmatic. Master's degree programs often have lower admissions requirements. According to the American Psychological Association (1993), doctoral programs generally require a grade point average (GPA) of 3.2 and a Graduate Record Examination (GRE) minimum of 1200; master's degree programs often have lower admissions criteria. Master's programs are more likely than doctoral programs to offer part-time study, which allows time for employment and family responsibilities. In addition, most doctoral programs allow enrollment only in the fall semester, whereas master's programs often allow spring admissions (Actkinson, 2000). Many students pursue master's degrees because "a master's degree provides sufficient training and credentials for a large number of employment arenas: there are many career opportunities for master's degree holders" (American Psychological Association, 1993, p. 53). With changes in health care reimbursement and a movement toward managed care, there is a growing preference for hiring master's-level clinicians instead of pricier doctoral-level clinicians (Actkinson, 2000; Humphreys, 1996). Finally, some students are motivated to seek a master's degree simply because they want more education for its own sake (Peters, 1992).

Master's Degrees in Psychology

Clinical and Counseling Psychology Master's-level clinical and counseling degree recipients are trained to conduct practice-related activities, including conducting assessments of and therapy for people who are experiencing psychological problems. They work in community mental health centers, psychiatric hospitals, nonprofit organizations, and group practices, usually under the direction of a doctoral-level psychologist. The controversy surrounding the master's degree in clinical and counseling psychology is that degree holders are not able to practice independently; they must be supervised by a doctoral-level psychologist (Actkinson, 2000; Lloyd, 1997b). In contrast, master's-level social workers and counselors can be licensed or certified (varying by state) to practice independently. If you're considering a master's in clinical or counseling psychology with the intention of setting up an independent practice, carefully research your options beforehand because some clinical and counseling master's programs meet the requirements for licensure as counselors or marriage and family therapists (Levant, Moldawsky, & Stigall, 2000). Be sure to do your homework so that you will not be disappointed later.

School Psychology School psychologists provide direct service to children and adolescents within elementary and secondary school settings. Typically, school psychologists assess students' learning aptitudes, diagnose learning disabilities, identify and address special needs, and assess and promote personality, emotional, cognitive, and social development (Himelein, 1999). School psychologists consult with school personnel regarding students' academic and behavioral problems and recommend appropriate interventions or classroom placements. Although some school psychologists practice with a master's degree, national certification as a school psychologist (from the National Association of School Psychologists) requires a more advanced degree called a specialist's degree (Rittle, 2000). A specialist's degree falls between the master's and doctoral degrees and typically takes from an extra semester to a year of study to complete. Because 75% of nondoctoral school psychologists hold a specialist degree, and because it's required for certification, you should plan on taking the time to earn this degree if you're interested in school psychology (Himelein, 1999).

Industrial and Organizational Psychology There has been relatively little discussion about master's-level training in industrial and organizational psychology (Lowe, 1993). Holders of advanced degrees in these fields apply psychological principles and research methods in the workplace. They are employed in business, government, and private organizations as human resources specialists, directors, and managers. Typical activities include interviewing and assessing potential employees, engaging in employee development, initiating and leading strategic planning and quality management activities, and devising methods to help businesses cope with organizational change (American Psychological Association, 1996).

Research-Oriented Areas of Psychology Recipients of master's degrees in research-oriented fields such as quantitative psychology, developmental psychology, general psychology, and experimental psychology have developed useful methodological and quantitative skills. They are often employed in research positions in university research centers as well as in government, business, and private organizations. Others seek entry into doctoral programs.

Master's Degrees in Related Fields

Master's-level clinicians with degrees in clinical and counseling psychology generally experience little professional autonomy; however, their academic and clinical experience often meets the requirements for certification or licensure as professional counselors (varying by state). If you're considering a master's degree in clinical or counseling psychology because you want to work with people, be aware of the other educational paths that will enable you to work closely with people in a therapeutic relationship. Many psychology students instead pursue graduate education in fields that are related to psychology.

Social Work As a profession, social work is dedicated to promoting optimal functioning in everyday contexts and helping people to adapt and function as best they can in their environments (U.S. Bureau of Labor Statistics, 2004b). Social workers provide direct services or therapy, serving individuals, families, and communities. They work in hospitals, clinics, schools, correctional facilities, specialized programs, and private practice. Social workers assist clients in identifying problems, issues, and concerns, help them to consider and implement effective solutions, and guide them in locating reliable resources (U.S. Bureau of Labor Statistics, 2004b). The master of social work (MSW) degree enables holders to practice therapy independently because they are eligible for licensure in all the states (U.S. Bureau of Labor Statistics, 2004b). An MSW requires 2 to 3 years of study, depending on the program and when the supervised internship (900 hours for licensure) is scheduled. The MSW is a respected degree whose recipients provide major job competition for those holding a master's degree in psychology (Actkinson, 2000).

Counseling There are many different types of counselors, but all help people who are experiencing personal, family, or mental health problems. Counselors also help people make educational and career decisions. A school or guidance counselor, for example, helps students understand and deal with problems, as well as evaluates their abilities, interests, and talents so that they can develop educational and career goals that are realistic and achievable (U.S. Bureau of Labor Statistics, 2004b). Counselors work in schools, colleges, health care facilities, job training, career development centers, social agencies, correctional institutions, residential care centers, drug and alcohol rehabilitation programs, state and government agencies, group practice, and private practice.

Typically, a master's degree in counseling requires 2 years of course work including 600 hours of supervised clinical experience. Holders of master's degrees in counseling can conduct therapy independently and can seek licensure or certification. In 2003, forty-seven states had some form of counselor credentialing, licensure, or certification (U.S. Bureau of Labor Statistics, 2004b). If you're considering a master's in counseling, do your homework to learn about the form of licensure or credentialing available in your state. In addition, if you're considering programs in school counseling, be aware that all states require school counselors to hold state certification (U.S. Bureau of Labor Statistics, 2004b); some also require teaching certificates.

How is counseling different from social work? The two are related disciplines and share a helping orientation. According to the American Counseling Association (2000), social work education takes a more global perspective because it emphasizes understanding the "impact of social and economic forces on individuals and social systems," including understanding the patterns, dynamics, and consequences of discrimination, economic deprivation, and oppression. Although counseling also examines how the environment influences human behavior, it doesn't focus as heavily on social and economic forces at the societal level. Theoretically, it appears that counseling concentrates more on the individual, whereas social work emphasizes a more global perspective. In practice, this difference is probably not that important. What is important is that counseling education includes training in the selection, use, and interpretation of assessment techniques, methods, and instruments; in contrast, social work education is more limited in assessment (American Counseling Association, 2000).

Occupational Therapy Occupational therapists work with clients who are experiencing disabilities (emotional, mental, physical, and developmental) that influence their occupational performance or well-being (Himelein, 1999; U.S. Bureau of Labor Statistics, 2004b). Occupational therapists assess physical, mental, and emotional deficiencies and counsel patients to help them improve their abilities to function in their daily environments. For example, an occupational therapist might help a client to improve basic motor functions or reasoning abilities, as well as helping him or her to compensate for permanent losses of function.

Occupational therapists obtain positions in hospitals, offices, and clinics of occupational therapists and other health practitioners; school systems; home health agencies; nursing homes; community mental health centers; adult day care programs; job training services; and residential care facilities. Many occupational therapists work in private practice. The minimum requirement for entry into the field is a bachelor's degree in occupational therapy (U.S. Bureau of Labor Statistics, 2004b). For holders of baccalaureate degrees in fields other than occupational therapy, there are certification programs as well as master's programs in occupational therapy. All 50 states regulate occupational therapy, meaning that graduates must obtain licensure. Beginning in 2007, the minimum educational requirement for entry into this field will be a master's degree in occupational therapy (U.S. Bureau of Labor Statistics, 2004b).

Speech Pathology Speech pathologists assess, diagnose, and treat communication disabilities such as stuttering and impaired language. They work with clients who have difficulty understanding and producing language, including those with cognitive communication impairments such as attention and memory disorders. Speech pathologists help clients to develop and regain language (e.g., assist with making speech sounds). Their work also involves counseling clients and families to help them better understand the disorder and the treatment.

Speech pathologists provide direct clinical services in schools, nursing homes, mental health centers, private practices, and medical settings, often as part of a team of allied health professionals. A master's degree in speech pathology (requiring approximately 2 years of course work) is required for entry into the profession. Nearly all states require speech pathologists to be licensed, with 300 to 375 hours of supervised clinical experience needed for licensure (varying by state; U.S. Bureau of Labor Statistics, 2004b).

Job Outlook for Holders of Master's Degrees in Psychology and Related Fields

The future looks bright for recipients of master's degrees in psychology and related fields (Humphreys, 1996). According to the *Occupational Outlook Handbook* (U.S. Bureau of Labor Statistics, 2004b), master's degree clinician—including social workers, counselors, and master's-trained psychologists, as well as speech pathologists and occupational therapists—are expected to be working in some of the fastest growing occupations through the year 2012.

A 2003 survey of 2002 master's degree recipients in psychology revealed that 88% were either employed (67%) or attending graduate school (21%) (Singleton, Tate, & Kohout, 2003a). If your goal is to provide services to individuals, a master's degree may be the ideal choice. Given the movement toward managed health care, the greater recognition and expanded roles afforded master's-level professionals, and the great demand for master's-level clinicians, doctoral psychologists have been encouraged to search for new and innovative roles outside direct service settings (Humphreys, 1996; Robiner & Crew, 2000).

Where Are Holders of Master's Degrees Employed?

By 2003, of the 2002 recipients of master's degrees in psychology who were employed full-time, 25% were employed in school or educational settings including elementary and secondary schools, school system district offices, special education, and vocational or adult education (Singleton, Tate, & Kohout, 2003b). Twenty percent were employed in human services settings including counseling and guidance centers, student counseling centers, nursing homes, substance abuse facilities, mental retardation facilities, developmental disability facilities, head injury facilities, and other community social services agencies. Twenty percent worked in business or government, holding positions in consulting firms, private research organizations, government research, corporations, small businesses, the criminal justice system, the military, government agencies, and nonprofit organizations. Nineteen percent were employed in hospitals or clinics including outpatient mental health clinics, community mental health centers, and HMOs and other managed care settings. Thirteen percent worked in academics, including universities, colleges, medical schools, and community colleges. Only 3% worked in independent private practice. As you can see, master's degree recipients can find employment in a wide range of settings.

Are Master's Degree Recipients Satisfied With Their Positions?

About one-half of MA and MS (54% and 51%, respectively) of 2002 master's degree recipients surveyed by the American Psychological Association

(Singleton, Tate, & Kohout, 2003b) reported that their current positions were their first choices. Two-thirds reported being satisfied with opportunities for recognition in their current position. About three-quarters reported being satisfied with their supervisor and working conditions, and more than four-fifths reported being satisfied with their coworkers.

How Useful Was Graduate Training?

Most of the 2002 master's degree recipients surveyed by APA (Singleton et al., 2003b) reported that their graduate degrees had been essential (52%) or helpful (35%) in obtaining their present positions. Most also believed that their degrees in psychology had been essential (54%) or at least helpful (28%) in obtaining their current positions. The vast majority (90%) felt that their graduate training provided adequate preparation for their current positions.

What aspects of graduate study were particularly relevant to the positions currently held by graduates? Ninety percent of the 2002 recipients of master's degrees in psychology perceived graduate training in general to be related to their current work; more than four-fifths perceived the courses in their major subfields as relevant; three-quarters reported practicum or internship experiences as relevant; and two-thirds reported courses outside their major subfields as relevant to their current positions.

What Can You Expect to Earn With a Master's Degree?

Table 9.1 illustrates starting salaries for full-time positions held by 2002 recipients of master's degrees in psychology. The median starting salary ranges from $30,000 to $48,000, varying by specialty and setting. Table 9.2 lists the 2001 median salaries for all holders of master's degrees in psychology (regardless of when the degree was conferred). The median salary ranges from $42,000 to $67,000, depending on specialization and work setting (Singleton et al., 2003b). As you can see, salaries rise considerably with experience.What about salaries in related fields? Table 9.3 shows the median annual salaries for holders of master's degrees in fields related to psychology. Within social work settings, the median salaries range from about $29,000 to $44,000. Vocational and educational counseling shows more variability—median salaries range from about $27,000 to $49,000. Median salaries for speech pathology and occupational therapy range from about $44,000 to $53,000. If you're considering a graduate degree to increase your employment options and earning potential, a master's degree is a good bet. According to the *Occupational Outlook Handbook* (U.S. Bureau of Labor Statistics, 2004b), each of the fields that we've discussed shows promise for growth. Before committing yourself to any particular program, do your homework. Understand your state requirements for certification and/or

TABLE 9.1 **STARTING SALARIES FOR FULL-TIME EMPLOYMENT POSITIONS FOR 2001 AND 2002 RECIPIENTS OF MASTER'S DEGREES IN PSYCHOLOGY**

Setting	Median ($)	Mean ($)	SD ($)*
Direct human services			
Clinical psychology	30,000	31,623	7,230
Counseling psychology	33,000	33,854	8,162
School psychology	41,250	40,980	9,765
Administration of human services delivery	32,000	32,335	3,943
Applied psychology settings	48,000	50,121	21,703
Research	36,500	36,065	10,348
Administrative positions	34,911	36,704	15,502
Other	40,800	43,633	14,022

Adapted from Singleton et al., 2003a.

*Standard Deviation

licensure and determine whether the program provides the background for appropriate credentialing.

THE DOCTORAL DEGREE

A master's degree may allow you to work directly with people, but if you're planning to conduct research or teach at the college level, a doctoral degree is essential. A doctoral degree provides a greater range of flexibility and autonomy, but it usually requires 5 to 7 years of graduate work to complete. In clinical and counseling psychology, the requirement for a doctoral degree generally includes a year or more of internship or supervised experience. A doctoral degree requires a great commitment of time.

Why do students seek doctoral degrees? Generally they pursue these degrees for any of the following reasons: (a) to teach at a college; (b) to conduct research in a university or in a private organization in industry or business; (c) to practice clinical psychology without supervision; or (d) to engage in a variety of consulting positions that allow autonomy. Most psychologists engage in more than one of these roles. For example, a college professor doesn't spend all his or her time at the podium. Other activities include advising students, conducting research, and writing scholarly papers and books. With a doctoral degree, a psychologist can also serve as a consultant to private agencies and businesses or can have an independent private psychotherapy practice.

TABLE 9.2 MEDIAN SALARIES FOR ALL MASTER'S-LEVEL PSYCHOLOGISTS IN 2001

Position	Median Salary ($)
Faculty positions [a]	42,000
Educational administration [b]	66,000
Research positions [c]	47,000
Direct human service	
Clinical psychology [d]	46,000
Counseling psychology [e]	42,000
School psychology [f]	61,000
Other [g]	48,500
Administration of human services [h]	55,000
Other administration [i]	67,000
Applied psychology	
Industrial/organizational psychology [j]	63,000
Other areas of psychology [k]	63,000

Adapted from Singleton et al., 2003b.

[a] Includes 2- and 4-year colleges and is based on a 9- to 10-month salary.

[b] Based on an 11- to 12-month salary.

[c] Includes government organizations, university settings, hospitals, business/industry, and human service and nonprofit settings.

[d] Includes individual and group practices, hospitals and clinics, mental health centers, criminal justice systems, school settings, and human service settings.

[e] Includes individual and group practices, hospital settings, other human service settings, criminal justice systems, school settings, and business settings.

[f] Includes school settings, school system district offices, individual private practices, and clinics.

[g] Includes individual and group practices, other human service provider settings, school settings, hospitals, government settings, and clinics.

[h] Includes clinics, other human service provider settings, hospital settings, school settings, and criminal justice settings.

[i] Includes consulting firms, nonprofit organizations, government organizations, and community mental health centers.

[j] Includes primarily business/industry settings, consulting firms, government settings, and independent consulting.

[k] Includes consulting firms, business/industry settings, government settings, self-employment, and independent practice settings including individual private practice, group psychological practice, and independent consulting.

Doctoral Degrees: PhD, PsyD, and EdD

As you consider obtaining a doctoral degree—the highest academic degree attainable—one of the first decisions to make is whether to pursue a doctor of philosophy (PhD), a doctor of psychology (PsyD), or a doctor of education

TABLE 9.3 **MEDIAN ANNUAL EARNINGS IN FIELDS RELATED TO PSYCHOLOGY BY MASTER'S-LEVEL DISCIPLINE AND INDUSTRY IN 2002**

Social Work

Setting	**Median Salary ($)**
Child, family, and school social workers	
Elementary and secondary schools	44,100
Local government	38,140
State government	34,000
Individual and family services	29,150
Other residential care facilities	28,470
Medical and public health social workers	
General medical and surgical hospitals	42,730
Local government	37,620
State government	35,250
Nursing care facilities	33,330
Individual and family services	31,000
Mental health and substance abuse social workers	
State government	38,430
Local government	35,700
Psychiatric and substance abuse hospitals	34,610
Outpatient care centers	31,370
Individual and family services	31,300

Educational, Vocational, and School Counselors

Setting	**Median Salary ($)**
Elementary and secondary schools	49,530
State government	45,480
Colleges and universities	36,990
Individual and family services	26,910

Speech Pathology

Setting	**Median Salary ($)**
Hospitals	53,090
Offices of other health care practitioners	44,500
Elementary and secondary schools	46,060

(Continued)

TABLE 9.3 **MEDIAN ANNUAL EARNINGS IN FIELDS RELATED TO PSYCHOLOGY BY MASTER'S-LEVEL DISCIPLINE AND INDUSTRY IN 2002 (CONTINUED)**

Occupational Therapy

Setting	Median Salary ($)
Nursing and personal care facilities	53,930
Offices of other health care practitioners	53,660
Hospitals	53,210
Elementary and secondary schools	45,740

Adapted from U.S. Bureau of Labor Statistics, 2004b.

(EdD). What's with all the letters? These are the three different kinds of doctoral degrees that a psychology student can pursue. PhD refers to doctor of philosophy. Like the master's degree, the PhD degree is awarded in many fields. It is a research degree that culminates in a dissertation based on original research. If you're considering pursuing a PhD in psychology, note that courses in quantitative research methods and statistics, including the use of computers, are an integral part of graduate study and are needed to complete the dissertation independently (Lloyd, 1997b). A PhD in clinical or counseling psychology is a flexible degree—it trains people for research, teaching, writing, and clinical practice.

PsyD refers to doctor of psychology. It is offered only in clinical and counseling psychology and is considered a professional degree, much like a doctor of jurisprudence (JD, a lawyer's degree). How is a PsyD different from a PhD? The main difference is that a PhD has greater emphasis on research, requiring more courses in methodology and statistics. A PhD prepares graduates for research as well as practice, whereas a PsyD prepares graduates to be consumers of research (Lloyd, 1997b). A PsyD is usually based on practical and applied work, as well as on examinations. The dissertation, if required, is usually a theoretical paper. A PsyD is for those who aim to engage in clinical practice rather than conduct research.

An EdD, a third doctoral option for psychology students, is not as popular as the PhD or the PsyD. An EdD is offered by education departments rather than by psychology departments. According to Lloyd (1997b), the research requirements for many EdD programs are not as rigorous as those for PhD programs. Psychologists sometimes view an EdD degree as inferior because it is rarely offered by a psychology department and frequently offers less training in the principles of psychology. Nevertheless, many administrative positions in college and university settings do not discriminate between applicants with EdD degrees and those with PhD degrees (Himelein, 1999).

EMPLOYMENT OUTLOOK FOR DOCTORAL-LEVEL PSYCHOLOGISTS

Holders of doctoral degrees experience little difficulty securing employment. A survey of 1999 doctoral degree recipients conducted by the American Psychological Association revealed that two-thirds were employed full-time, 17% were completing postdoctoral studies, 10% were employed part-time, and less than 3% were unemployed and seeking employment (Kohout & Wicherski, 2004).

Where Are New Psychologists Employed?

Forty-four percent of 1999 doctoral degree recipients surveyed were employed in direct service settings including hospitals, community mental health clinics, managed care settings, independent and group practices, college counseling centers, clinics, and human services agencies (Kohout & Wicherski, 1999). Twenty-eight percent worked in academic settings at universities, 4-year colleges, and medical schools, within departments of education, psychology, business, administration, and research centers. Nineteen percent found employment in business and government, including consulting agencies, private research, government research, criminal justice, military, and nonprofit organizations. Nine percent worked in elementary and secondary schools or school district offices.

Are Doctoral Degree Recipients Satisfied With Their Positions?

Approximately 91% of 1999 doctoral degree recipients agreed or strongly agreed that their current positions are related to their fields of study (Kohout & Wicherski, 2004); 78% agreed or strongly agreed that their positions were commensurate with their levels of training. About 81% agreed or strongly agreed that their positions were professionally challenging. Surprisingly, only 55% agreed or strongly agreed that their present positions were similar to what they had expected, suggesting that we need to examine students' expectations about careers in psychology.

When considering more specific aspects of employment, such as salary and benefits, we see a greater range of responses. Table 9.4 lists the percentages of employed doctoral recipients who were satisfied or very satisfied with several aspects of their employment. About two-thirds of respondents were satisfied or very satisfied with their income or salary, and about one-half reported being satisfied or very satisfied with their opportunities for promotion. About three-quarters of respondents were satisfied or very satisfied with their opportunities for recognition, supervisors, and working conditions. About two-thirds were satisfied or very satisfied with opportunities for personal development. Although

TABLE 9.4 **Percentages of Employed 2001 Doctoral Recipients Who Are Satisfied or Very Satisfied With Several Aspects of Their Current Positions**

	Satisfied (%)	Very Satisfied (%)
Income/salary	46	17
Benefits	42	32
Opportunities for promotion	40	15
Opportunities for personal development	39	35
Opportunities for recognition	48	25
Supervisor	32	40
Coworkers	41	46
Working conditions	45	32

Adapted from Kohout & Wicherski, 2004.

there is a range of responses, it appears that most new psychologists were generally satisfied with their positions.

How Useful Is Graduate Training?

Most of the 2001 doctoral degree recipients surveyed by the American Psychological Association reported that their doctoral degrees had been essential (53%) or helpful (30%) in obtaining their present positions (Kohout & Wicherski, 2004). Most also agreed that their doctorates in psychology had been essential (53%) or helpful (34%) in obtaining their current positions.

What aspects of graduate study were particularly relevant to graduates' current positions? Seventy-two percent of the 2001 recipients of doctoral degrees in psychology perceived their graduate training in general to be closely related to their current work; 70% perceived the courses in their major subfield to be closely relevant to their current positions (Kohout & Wicherski, 2004). Recipients perceived predoctoral internships in clinical, counseling, and school settings (53%) and other practicum and internships experiences (36%) also to be closely relevant to their current work.

What Can You Expect to Earn With a Doctoral Degree?

Table 9.5 presents data on the starting salaries of employed 2001 recipients of doctoral degrees in psychology. As you can see, starting salaries vary considerably depending on the field and the setting. Median starting salaries ranged from $36,000 for those employed in adjunct or visiting faculty positions to $73,000 for psychologists in applied settings such as consulting firms, business, and industry. Doctoral-level psychologists have considerable opportunities to

TABLE 9.5 STARTING SALARIES FOR FULL-TIME POSITIONS FOR 2001 DOCTORAL DEGREE RECIPIENTS IN PSYCHOLOGY

Setting	Median ($)	Mean ($)	SD ($)
Assistant professor [a]	44,000	44,614	8,204
Adjunct/visiting faculty	36,409	36,167	10,156
Educational administration	58,000	59,549	15,953
Research positions [b]	53,500	54,511	15,261
Research administration	53,778	54,511	15,261
Direct human services			
Clinical psychology [c]	48,000	48,386	12,950
Counseling psychology [d]	45,000	46,486	8,579
School psychology [e]	57,444	61,460	18,695
Administration of human services [f]	51,500	55,889	19,813
Applied psychology [g]	73,500	75,162	26,420
Other administrative position	67,000	68,870	13,118
Other [h]	58,000	62,310	27,369

Adapted from Kohout & Wicherski, 2004.

[a] This is a 9- to 10-month salary and includes the following: university psychology, education, and other academic departments, 4-year college psychology departments, and medical school settings.

[b] Includes university research centers and institutes, private research organizations, medical school settings, businesses, government, and other research settings.

[c] Includes university and college counseling centers, hospitals, group practices, outpatient clinics, community mental health centers, rehabilitation facilities, the criminal justice system, other nonprofit organizations, schools, business settings, government, and other settings.

[d] Includes university and college counseling centers, community mental health agencies, hospitals, independent practice, and other human service settings.

[e] Includes elementary and secondary schools, and school district offices.

[f] Includes community mental health centers, hospitals, managed care settings, and other human service settings.

[g] Includes consulting firms, businesses, and other industry settings.

[h] Includes business, government, and other settings.

increase their salaries with additional experience. Table 9.6 demonstrates that in 1999 the median salaries of all doctoral-level psychologists ranged from $55,000 for faculty to $100,000 for administrators in applied settings (i.e., managing a firm specializing in market research).

Cautions for Clinicians: The Changing Roles of Psychologists

Concern about the supply and demand of psychologists has recently grown (Cummings, 1995; Frank & Ross, 1995; Robiner & Crew, 2000). The absolute number of psychologists, proportional to the population, has been growing

TABLE 9.6 **MEDIAN SALARIES OF ALL DOCTORAL-LEVEL PSYCHOLOGISTS IN 2001**

Position	Median Salary ($)
Faculty positions [a]	55,000
Educational administration [b]	90,000
Research positions [c]	65,000
Administration of research	85,000
Direct human services	
Clinical psychology [d]	72,000
Counseling psychology [e]	66,500
School psychology [f]	77,000
Other areas of psychology [g]	71,000
Administration of human services [h]	67,000
Applied psychology	
Industrial/organizational psychology [i]	96,000
Other areas of psychology [j]	79,000
Administration of applied psychology [k]	100,000
Other administrative positions [l]	85,500

Adapted from Singleton et al., 2003b.

[a] This is a 9- to 10-month salary for faculty at all ranks in the following settings: university psychology, education, business, and other academic departments, 4- and 2-year colleges, medical schools, and professional schools of psychology.

[b] Includes administrative offices of universities, 4-year colleges, and 2-year colleges.

[c] Includes the following settings: university psychology departments, university research centers, private research organizations, government research organizations, and other nonprofit organizations.

[d] Includes the following settings: elementary and secondary schools, hospitals, independent practices, group practices, community mental health centers, rehabilitation facilities, and other human service settings.

[e] Includes the following settings: university and college counseling centers, hospitals, independent private practices, group practices, and community mental health centers.

[f] Elementary and secondary school settings, school district system offices, and individual private practices.

[g] Includes the fields of health psychology, educational, developmental, rehabilitation, neuroscience, and behavioral medicine, community psychology, social, and the following settings: hospital, individual practice, group practice, rehabilitation facilities.

[h] Includes university and college counseling centers, hospitals, community mental health clinics, specialized health services, human service agencies, the criminal justice system, nonprofit organizations, and rehabilitation facilities.

[i] Where the major field is industrial/organizational psychology. Includes consulting firms, business, and industry.

[j] Consulting, business, and industry.

[k] Consulting firms.

[l] Business and industry, other nonprofit organizations.

(Robiner & Crew, 2000). There have been steady increases in the number of APA-accredited doctoral programs since the early 1980s (Robiner & Crew, 2000); in 1995 there were 253 accredited doctoral programs in the United States, reflecting a mean annual increase of 8.3 programs since 1981.

Internships, a required part of doctoral training for clinicians, are becoming more difficult to secure. Even some capable, well-trained applicants experience problems obtaining internships, leading many students to become distressed in anticipation of such difficulties (Robiner & Crew, 2000).

Many of the changes in opportunities for psychologists are the result of the movement toward managed care. Traditionally, psychologists have been trained to believe that therapy is a long, drawn-out practice and that the most prestigious practitioners see a limited number of clients over a long period of time. Managed care has an emphasis on brief therapy that is not compatible with this approach (Cummings, 1995), because research has shown that short-term therapy is effective (Bennett, 1994). We're seeing more group practices, as solo practices are becoming economically unfeasible (Cummings, 1995; Hersch, 1995).

Between 1988 and 1995 the increase in licensed psychologists exceeded 40%, even though the demand for psychologists and their earnings decreased (Robiner & Crew, 2000). Doctoral-level clinical psychologists are now "being underbid by master's-level social workers, marriage and family counselors, and psychological assistants, and will be increasingly supplanted in the role of psychotherapist by these master's level professionals" (Humphreys, 1996, p. 190). In the future, most hands-on behavioral treatment will be conducted by master's-level therapists working with focused, empirically driven interventions (Cummings, 1995).

Humphreys (1996) warns that psychologists will experience what has already happened in psychiatry: "Psychiatrists are still involved in psychotherapy, but their role has become circumscribed . . . cost-conscious payers prefer not to pay a psychiatrist's fee for anything other than what only a psychiatrist can do . . . such as brief diagnostic assessment and prescription of medications" (p. 192). Cummings (1995) predicts that similar economic factors will force psychologists out of psychotherapy practice as well. Master's-level professionals have been joining clinical psychologists in conducting therapy (Humphreys, 1996). Master's-level professionals are arguing for more autonomy, which makes sense in light of studies that show no difference between therapy provided by master's- and doctoral-level psychotherapists (Christensen & Jacobson, 1994). Humphreys (1996) warns that psychologists must adapt by allowing the roles of clinical and counseling psychologists to expand beyond direct service to include program development, health promotion activities, community intervention, and public advocacy (Himelein, 1999; Humphreys, 1996).

What do all these dire warnings mean? Should you give up on a doctoral degree in clinical or counseling psychology? No! Each of the doomsayers has received a substantial amount of criticism. We don't know where the field is going and how opportunities for psychologists will change in the coming years, but the *Occupational Outlook Handbook* reports that the employment of psychologists is expected to increase faster than average for all occupations through

2012 (U.S. Bureau of Labor Statistics, 2004b). These warnings are provided as encouragement for you to enter the field with your eyes open. There are many opportunities for new psychologists; however, the new psychologists who will be the most successful in the coming years will be those who have a mind open to change and who are not afraid to explore new and nontraditional avenues.

Suggested Readings

Keller, P. A. (1994). *Academic paths: Career decisions and experiences of psychologists.* Hillsdale, NJ: Erlbaum.

Kuther, T. L. (2005). *Your career in psychology: Clinical and counseling psychology.* Belmont, CA: Wadsworth.

Kuther, T. L. (2004). *Your career in psychology: Industrial/organizational psychology and human factors*. Belmont, CA: Wadsworth.

Kuther, T. L. (2004). *Your career in psychology: Psychology and law*. Belmont, CA: Wadsworth.

Kuther, T. L., & Morgan, R. (2004). *Careers in psychology: Opportunities in a changing world*. Belmont, CA: Wadsworth.

Morgan, R. D., Kuther, T. L., & Habben, C. J. (2005). *Life after graduate school: Opportunities and advice from new psychologists*. New York: Psychology Press.

Sternberg, R. J. (1997). *Career paths in psychology: Where your degree can take you*. Washington, DC: American Psychological Association.

Woody, R. H., & Robertson, M. H. (1997). *A career in clinical psychology: From training to employment.* Madison, CT: International Universities Press.

Web Resources

The following web sites are hot-linked at *The Psychology Major's Handbook* web site at *http://info.wadsworth.com/kuther*

Interesting Careers in Psychology

http://www.apa.org/science/nonacad_careers.html

Interested in a nonacademic career in psychology? Check out the links to case studies on this page.

Fields of Psychology

http://www.psichi.org/pubs/search.asp?category1 = 8

Psi Chi, the National Honor Society in Psychology, presents links to articles about a variety of career areas in psychology.

Early Career Psychologists

http://www.apa.org/earlycareer/

The American Psychological Association provides resources and links for new psychologists. Get a feel for the field by visiting this site.

Psychology Careers for the 21st Century

http://www.apa.org/students/brochure/brochurenew.pdf

This American Psychological Association brochure describes the field of psychology, including employment settings, job outlook, and career preparation.

Alternative Careers

http://www.apa.org/monitor/feb01/careerpath.html

This article from the February 2001 issue of *Monitor on Psychology* profiles the new and unusual careers of 21 recent graduates of doctoral programs in psychology.

JOURNAL EXERCISES

Is Graduate School Necessary?

Look through your journal and review past entries. Considering all that you've learned about yourself, what type of career would make you happy? Now consider the information in this chapter. Will a graduate degree help you to achieve your goals? Be honest with yourself.

Other Applications

Imagine that you have gone to graduate school and earned a doctoral degree in psychology, but that you will not practice therapy. What will you do? What other activities of psychologists appeal to you aside from therapy?

APPLYING TO GRADUATE SCHOOL IN PSYCHOLOGY

CHAPTER 10

CHAPTER GUIDE

At some point in their undergraduate education, most psychology majors seriously consider attending graduate school, but only about one-quarter actually attend graduate programs (National Center for Education Statistics, 2001). Graduate school isn't for everyone. A graduate degree isn't necessary to be employable. As we discussed in Chapter 7, psychology majors have a host of skills that employers want, and so a bachelor's degree in psychology doesn't automatically commit you to years of graduate study. Should you decide to apply to graduate school, however, you'll need to focus your energy because the application process is arduous and many applicants are not successful. During the 1999–2000 school year the acceptance rate for U.S. doctoral programs was 21%; accredited PhD programs had an overall acceptance rate of 10%, and PsyD programs had an acceptance rate of 34% (Pate, 2001). Master's programs had an acceptance rate of 59% (Pate, 2001). In this chapter we'll explore the graduate application process and offer advice to help you succeed in a difficult market.

SHOULD YOU GO TO GRADUATE SCHOOL?

Graduate study isn't the right choice for everyone. Is it right for you? Only you can answer this question. Don't make the decision lightly, because grad school isn't a given or an automatic choice for all psychology students. Take the time to thoroughly consider your interests, goals, dreams, and abilities. People often avoid this sort of in-depth soul-searching because it can be uncomfortable. It forces us to face uncertainty, which is stressful. But uncertainty about your educational and career goals is one stressor that you don't want to avoid. Careful consideration and soul-searching is vital to making a decision that you can live with for the next 2 to 7 years and beyond.

What kind of career do you want? Look back over your responses to the assessments in Chapter 2. Is it really necessary for you to go to grad school to achieve your goals? Are there alternative ways of achieving them? As we've discussed in Chapters 7 and 9, if your main goal is to work with people, there are lots of alternatives to a doctoral degree in psychology (and some are preferable to a psychology degree in terms of time and expense).

Are you considering graduate study for the right reasons? Some people attend graduate school for the love of learning; others seek career advancement. Most people attend graduate school for a variety of reasons and to satisfy a variety of needs. What are your reasons? Can you fulfill your goals with your bachelor's degree or is a master's degree needed? If you're considering pursuing a doctorate, why? Some students focus on the desire to be called "Doctor"—the prestige. A graduate degree is certainly prestigious, but that shouldn't be the only reason for attending grad school. Are you willing to take on the immense responsibilities that come with this prestige? Remember that just because your faculty advisor has a PhD doesn't mean that you need to earn one to be happy or respected. This is a personal decision. If you decide to attend graduate school, choose the level of education, whether a master's or a doctoral degree, that is compatible with your orientation and offers the training and course work to prepare you for the career to which you aspire.

Are you ready for the academic demands of graduate study? Think about your undergraduate psychology course work. How comfortable did you feel with those courses? Do you like writing papers? How about library research? Students who go on to graduate school tend to have been more satisfied with their undergraduate courses than were those who don't go on. Do you have the academic qualities to succeed in a graduate program? Generally, it is expected that students will maintain at least a 3.0 average during graduate school. Some programs deny funding to students with less than a 3.33 average. Can you juggle multiple tasks, projects, and papers at the same time? Can you manage time effectively? Look back over your responses to the assessments in Chapter 4. What did they reveal about your academic habits? Are your habits suited for graduate study?

Are you ready for more methodology and statistics courses? Remember that you'll need to take statistics at the graduate level. If you're weak in math, you may not be able to complete the basic statistical requirements for psychology. If you like math and have done well in your math courses (say, with grades of B or higher), then you will be better able to handle graduate-level math. Before you rule out graduate school based on these math requirements, do a little soul-searching. Is your ability in math really weak or do you just think so? Perhaps if you adjust your studying strategies or devote more time to it, you'll find that you're better at math than you think.

Do you have the motivation for two or more years of school? Grad school is different from college because it requires a higher level of commitment. You must enjoy and excel at reading, writing, and analyzing information. Gone are the days of skipping classes, waiting until the last minute to write papers, and late-night partying. Although you may have found it easy to excel in college, grad school has a whole different atmosphere. You'll be surrounded by students who performed just as well or even better than you did in college. The bar is set much higher, and you'll have to work harder and more consistently than ever before. Speak with professors and graduate students to get a better idea of what's involved in graduate study. Most first-year graduate students are overwhelmed and admit that they had no idea of what they were getting into. Seek a first-year student's perspective for a reality check (read a letter from a new graduate student in Box 10.1).

BOX 10.1

Letter From a First-Year Graduate Student

Dear Potential Graduate Student:

I am currently enrolled in Your State University's developmental psychology PhD program. I am writing to provide advice about how to prepare for admission and what grad school is really like.

As an undergraduate, there are many things you should do to prepare for graduate school. In selecting courses, take extra mathematics and science classes because graduate schools are looking for students with well-rounded backgrounds. Balance should also be reflected in your choice of major courses. Don't focus only on the fun classes (e.g., social, clinical, and child psychology); take the harder psychology classes too (e.g., physiological psychology, perception, and learning theory).

Try to obtain additional research experience beyond the methodology requirements. Speak to faculty about research opportunities if you are genuinely interested. Many faculty members are very much interested in student research; however, you need to express your desire. Thus, it is important to develop relationships with faculty members with whom you share interests because they can serve as role models or mentors.

It is also important to develop a solid background and understanding of statistics (especially if you're interested in a clinical program because they are the most competitive). Consider taking additional statistics courses in the mathematics department because they will improve your standing. In addition to monitoring your course selection, save all your class notes and books from your major courses. They will be helpful in preparing for the GRE as well as for later reference.

It's crucial that you prepare for the GRE. The GRE scores are used not only as entry criteria; competitive financial aid packages and assistantships are allocated on the basis of these scores. Therefore, you should do the best that you can to qualify for financial assistance. When applying to graduate school, be sure that you and each school that you apply to are a good fit. Don't apply hoping to be accepted anywhere. Consider the philosophy/orientation of the school with your career goals in mind or you might be unpleasantly surprised. For example, one student in our research-oriented developmental program recently dropped out because she had the false impression that with this degree she would be able to have a private practice providing clinical services. Learn more about current students' career goals and those of successful graduates.

As an undergraduate, I wish I had spoken with someone about what graduate school is really like. Grad school requires a higher level of dedication, time, professionalism, and maturity. Successful grad students constantly study or work on research 8 hours per day 6 or 7 days per week. In most graduate schools, professors don't read the material to you nor do they interpret it for you. Rather, you are required to read, understand, and discuss it intelligently. It's a whole other world compared to the innocence of undergraduate work. It's a lot of work and a life change, but I'm glad I'm here.

TABLE 10.1 **TOP 15 CHARACTERISTICS THAT DESCRIBE A SUCCESSFUL GRADUATE STUDENT ACCORDING TO A SURVEY OF 79 FACULTY MEMBERS**

Characteristic	Average Rating
1. Working hard	5.60
2. Getting along with others	5.17
3. Writing ability	4.83
4. Clinical and counseling skills	4.81
5. Doing research	4.74
6. Handling stress	4.72
7. Discipline	4.64
8. Good grades	4.61
9. High intelligence	4.53
10. Empathy	4.48
11. Establishing a relationship with a mentor	4.39
12. Getting along with peers	4.00
13. Broad knowledge of psychology	4.00
14. Specialized knowledge in one or two areas of psychology	3.88
15. Reflecting program values	3.78

Surveyed by Descutner and Thelen, 1989.

Do you have the personal characteristics needed to succeed in graduate school? Self-reliance, a desire to excel, commitment to scholarship, intellectual curiosity, and emotional stability are necessary to successfully navigate the rigor, stress, and often impersonal nature of graduate school. What personal characteristics do faculty think are important? Descutner and Thelen (1989) asked 79 faculty members from departments with graduate programs to rank 25 characteristics based on their importance for success in graduate school (1 = not important; 6 = very important). Table 10.1 displays the top 15 characteristics and their average scores.

As you can see, some of the characteristics are skill-based (like research and counseling ability); others are more intrinsic (like empathy and discipline). A quick perusal of the list reveals that hard work, social skills, and writing skills are vital to success in graduate school. Therefore, you should work on developing not only academic skills but also interpersonal (teamwork) and intrapersonal (emotional intelligence and self-management) skills. Learn how to manage stress because professors prefer to work with students who are emotionally mature, can consistently produce quality work, and can meet deadlines in an emotionally stable manner. Take Quiz 10.1 to see if graduate school is for you.

Finally, consider Fretz and Stang's warning (1988):

> Graduate work takes initiative, independence, perseverance, acceptance of responsibility, and a general freedom from emotional conflict and anxiety. The benefits of going to graduate school, especially a top-ranked school, are enormous, but they demand a high price in sweat and anxiety. . . . Succeeding in graduate school requires years of single-minded dedication, much energy, individual initiative, and responsible independent study (pp. 79–80.)

Does all this sound overwhelming? That's a normal response. This information is not meant to change your mind but to provide a more realistic picture of what attending graduate school really entails.

Going to graduate school affects the rest of your life. There are both pros and cons to continuing your education. Seek information from multiple sources—this book, the career counseling center, graduate students, professors, and your family. Take your time with the decision. More important, trust your judgment and have faith that you'll make the choice that's best for you.

Quiz 10.1
Is Graduate School for You?

Answer the following questions honestly (that's the hard part!)

1. Are you ready to live in near poverty for the next 2 to 7 years?
2. Does the thought of studying all the time make you ill?
3. Is writing term papers fun?
4. Does public speaking bother (or even terrify) you?
5. Do you like to read psychology books or articles even if they are not assigned?
6. Do you put off studying for tests or writing papers as long as possible?
7. Do you enjoy reading and studying?
8. Do you hate library research?
9. Will you give up a social opportunity (like a party) to study for a test or to finish a paper?
10. Are you sick of school?
11. Can you concentrate and study for hours at a time?
12. Are your grades mainly B's or lower?
13. Do you read recent issues of psychology journals?
14. Are there other careers aside from psychology that you'd like to explore?
15. Did you earn an A or B in statistics?
16. Does research bore you?
17. Are you comfortable competing with other students?
18. Do you frequently hand assignments in late or forget to do them?

Scoring:

Assign 1 point for each odd item to which you answered yes and 1 point for each even item to which you answered no. Sum the points to obtain a total score. Higher scores indicate a greater potential for successful graduate study.

Reflection:

How did you score? Given your score, how well do you think your characteristics and habits match those of successful graduate students? Is graduate study a realistic match to your characteristics? Why or why not?

Adapted from Appleby, 1997; Keith-Spiegel & Wiederman, 2000; Fretz & Stang, 1988.

Costs of Graduate Study

Attending graduate school entails emotional costs: It takes a great deal of time, is often stressful, and can put a strain on relationships with friends, family, and significant others. However, graduate study also involves financial costs. Many students underestimate the financial burden of graduate study in terms of years in the workforce lost and loans for tuition and living expenses.

What does graduate study cost? The median tuition in U.S. and Canadian graduate departments for the 1999–2000 academic year was $3,178 for state residents at public institutions, $8,416 for nonstate residents at public institutions, and $16,596 at private institutions (Pate, 2001). According to a survey conducted by the American Psychological Association (APA) (Singleton et al., 2003a), more than two-thirds of 2002 recipients of master's degrees in psychology had education-related debt. Of those with debt, 44% owed more than $30,000, 17% owed $21,000 to $30,000, 16% owed $16,000 to $20,000, 9% owed $11,000 to $15,000, 9% owed $6,000 to $10,000, and 5% owed $5,000 or less. Sixty-nine percent of 1999 doctoral degree recipients had education-related debt, with about three-quarters of graduates in the health provider subfields of clinical psychology, counseling psychology, school psychology, and so on, and about two-thirds of graduates in the research-oriented subfields reporting education-related debt (Kohout & Wicherski, 2004). Of those with debt, 36% owed $51,000 or more, 8% owed $41,000 to $50,000, 25% owed $21,000 to $40,000, 15% owed $11,000 to $20,000, and 16% owed $10,000 or less.

Keys to Graduate School Admission Success

Before we discuss the application process in detail, let's take a step back and consider the three basic keys to admission to graduate school: preparation, application know-how, and patience (Lunneborg & Wilson, 1987). Students often underestimate the importance of preparation (and the amount of time it takes). Graduate applications are quite different from those for college. Comparatively, there are fewer graduate than undergraduate programs, and graduate programs are highly specialized. Each application takes hours to complete, and the application fees range from $25 to $50 or more.

Invest the time required to prepare adequately. Doing so helps ensure that you're applying to programs that are realistic for you—they are those that you want to attend, and you have a reasonable chance of being accepted in them. Preparation entails thinking carefully about your own values and goals (remember the self-assessments from Chapter 2?), as well as ensuring that you've done all you can to broaden your background and make yourself an attractive candidate. The information provided throughout this book will help you in preparing for graduate programs and strengthening your overall background.

Application know-how involves understanding the application process, having a sense of what admissions committees are looking for, and knowing what information you are expected to provide in your application. The application process runs more smoothly when an applicant is familiar with the various components of the application. This chapter will familiarize you with the application process.

The final key to graduate school admission is patience. The admissions process is lengthy. It is hoped that you have begun planning for graduate school admission early in college and have spent years preparing and improving your application. Although most applications are due from December through February, students may wait until late March or April to receive word on the status of their applications. Patience is essential.

Choosing Graduate Programs

As you'll soon see, pursuing graduate study in psychology entails many decisions. You'll confront decisions concerning types of degrees, training models, and types of programs.

PhD vs. PsyD

Students are often perplexed about the differences between doctor of philosophy (PhD) and doctor of psychology (PsyD) degrees. Both are doctoral degrees, and both will allow you to practice psychology. They differ in their emphases. The PhD has a long historical tradition. Most of your college professors hold this degree; it is conferred in nearly all academic fields. A PhD in psychology provides training in research and methodology as well as in the content of your specialty area. PhD recipients find employment at universities, medical centers, and mental health centers, as well as in industry and government.

The PsyD is a practitioner degree that emphasizes clinical training or the professional model of training; it is sought by those who want to practice psychology. PsyD programs tend to be larger than traditional scientist-practitioner programs, so more students are accepted and your chances of being admitted are much higher (Mayne, Norcross, & Sayette, 1994). In 1999–2000, accredited PhD programs in clinical psychology had acceptance rates of about 6%, and accredited PsyD programs in clinical psychology had acceptance rates of about 39% (Pate, 2001). The PsyD degree is often offered at private and professional schools and is generally more expensive than a PhD. Most funding for PhD students comes from faculty research grants; little research is conducted in PsyD programs, so there are fewer opportunities for funding. Professional programs train students to be educated consumers of research rather than generators of research. Because there is less emphasis on research, PsyD students earn their degrees a little faster but usually graduate with more debt than do PhD students.

Practice-oriented students often find the curricula of professional programs to be better aligned with their own interests and career aspirations than those of traditional scientist-practitioner programs. Although some have argued that the PhD is more prestigious than the PsyD (Buskist & Sherburne, 1996) and that the PhD may be more flexible in terms of career options because of its research basis, you should choose the degree that will prepare you for the career you desire. If you're interested in practicing psychology and do not want to teach in a university setting or conduct research, the PsyD may be for you. Graduates from professional schools are at a disadvantage only when they apply for positions in research or academic settings.

Clinical vs. Counseling Psychology

Clinical and counseling psychology are very closely related fields. Generally speaking, clinical psychology involves a greater range of activities and subject populations than does counseling. Counseling psychology is limited to helping people solve problems related to everyday life, including marital problems, difficult transitions, and other personal problems that normal people experience. Clinical psychology includes all these activities, along with helping people who are experiencing more severe problems such as mental illnesses and health-related problems that interfere with daily living. In other words, clinical psychologists tend to work with more seriously disturbed populations, whereas counseling psychologists work with healthier and less pathological populations; counseling psychologists also conduct more career and vocational assessments (Norcross, 2000).

Although the preceding paragraph outlines the technical distinction between clinical and counseling psychology, in practice, this distinction has become blurred (Keith-Spiegel & Wiederman, 2000; Kuther & Morgan, 2004; Norcross, 2000). Graduates of clinical and counseling psychology programs are eligible for the same professional benefits such as licensure, independent practice, and insurance reimbursement. Generally speaking, counseling psychology programs have higher acceptance rates than clinical psychology programs. In the 1999–2000 academic year, accredited clinical psychology PhD programs admitted about 7% of applicants, whereas accredited counseling psychology doctoral PhD programs admitted about 13% (Pate, 2001). Note that both clinical and counseling psychology doctoral programs are quite competitive. Before deciding that you must apply to a graduate program in clinical or counseling psychology with the intent of becoming a practicing psychologist, take some time to really consider what it means to practice psychology. Quiz 10.2 will help you determine if you have the people skills needed to practice psychology.

Quiz 10.2
Do You Really Want to Work With People?

1. Are you naturally curious?
2. Do you enjoy asking questions?
3. Do you enjoy problem solving?
4. Can you listen without interrupting someone?
5. Can you listen without showing your perspective in your facial expression?
6. Are you naturally interested in people?
7. Do you get tired with dealing with others' needs?
8. Can you put your own problems aside?
9. Can you attend to someone who seems to be focusing on a problem that you don't feel is worthy of their attention?
10. Are you good at managing your emotions?
11. Do you communicate well?
12. Can you listen actively and acknowledge other viewpoints even when you don't agree with them?
13. Can you suggest creative solutions for resolving conflict?
14. Are you good at managing stress?
15. Do you cry easily?
16. Are you flexible?

Scoring:

Add 1 point for each yes response, except for items 7 and 15, in which a no response yields 1 point. The higher your score, the more likely you are to have characteristics that will help you to work with people.

Reflection:

1. Reflect on your score. What did you learn about yourself? Is working with people really for you?
2. How might an individual's score influence his or her decision about whether to attend graduate school or which type of program to attend? How has your perspective on your future and your goals changed?
3. Are there ways to improve your tolerance for working with people? Suggest three ways of improving your people skills.

Training Models

Most graduate programs follow one of three basic models of training. Choose a program whose model best fits your interests, because most psychologists engage in the same type of activities that they experienced in their graduate program of study.

Research-Scientist Model Programs that follow a research-scientist model focus on molding students into scholars who will make new discoveries and advance the knowledge in their field. From a historical perspective, this was the first training model to emerge. It characterizes PhD programs in the core academic areas of psychology such as experimental, social and personality, quantitative, physiological, and developmental psychology. Individuals trained in the research-scientist model conduct original research, teach, and write about their research findings. Training focuses on developing experimental methods, methodological skill, and a background in a particular content area. Graduates tend to be employed as researchers or college and university professors. Some work as consultants or conduct research for the government or corporations.

Scientist-Practitioner Model Programs adopting the scientist-practitioner model seek to train scholars who integrate their research training with human service; graduates engage in practice activities and conduct applied and basic research. This model is commonly found in PhD programs in clinical, counseling, school, and industrial psychology. Similar to the research-scientist model, students trained in the scientist-practitioner model receive training in research and methodology, but they take more courses in applied areas and complete more internships and practica than students trained in the research-scientist model. Graduates trained in the scientist-practitioner model are employed by hospitals and clinical practices, teach in colleges and universities, and own private practices. The extent to which a particular psychologist engages in each of these activities depends on his or her job setting and commitment to research; most practicing clinicians do little to no research.

Professional Psychologist-Practitioner Model Programs oriented toward the professional psychologist-practitioner model train students to provide psychological services. There is a greater emphasis on clinical practice than in the scientist-practitioner model, and much less emphasis on research. This model is applied in PsyD programs in which students are trained to be consumers of research rather than producers of it.

We have examined some basic decisions that you should make well before preparing graduate school applications. Now let's move on to the next step. Remember when you applied to college? Applying to graduate school is a bit more complex, requiring more research and preparation and resulting in more overall stress. Most graduate programs in psychology receive from 2 to 50 times as many applications as they have openings to fill. Some programs are more competitive than those in medical school. How do you excel during the admissions process? Choose programs that are appropriate to your interests, skills, and academic abilities.

Consider Your Priorities

Before you spend a great deal of time gathering information about potential programs, consider your priorities. Where does graduate school fit in your life? Are there geographical restrictions on where you live? What will you specialize in? This is a crucial question. Unlike college, where you majored in psychology and obtained a general degree, graduate school entails specializing in a particular area of psychology. Carefully consider your area of specialization (e.g., clinical, experimental, developmental, school, and others), because that will determine which schools and programs you should apply to as well as your likelihood of being accepted.

How do you choose? Examine your responses to the assessments in this book as well as your journal entries. Consider your interests. Do you want to work with people? Work in a laboratory? Teach college? Conduct research? What were your favorite classes in college? On what topics have you written term papers? Seek advice from professors in your department, especially from those in the areas in which you wish to specialize. Chapter 1 notes the major specialty areas of psychology. In order to apply to graduate school you must choose an area in which to specialize. Take your time in making this decision, because it will shape your education and your career.

Gather Program Information

Once you have a specialty area(s) in mind, it's time to gather program information. How do you get information about programs? Rely on a variety of resources in print and online. Several books have been published that offer information about programs; many resources are also available on the Internet. Peterson's Guides publishes a set of educational guidebooks each year; look for the volume entitled *Graduate Studies in Social Sciences and Work*. Most college libraries have a copy. This guidebook is organized by field, with universities listed alphabetically. It is a good general guide to help you find out about existing programs and their general requirements; compare the listed admission requirements with your own grade point average (GPA) and Graduate Record Exam (GRE) scores for an initial glimpse of what programs are within your range.

One of the best sources of information about graduate programs is the APA *Guide to Graduate Study in Psychology*. It describes every psychology graduate program in the United States and Canada. Organized alphabetically by state and by school, this guide provides the following information: criteria for admission; program emphasis; number of faculty; number of students enrolled; and additional admissions information, including the average GPA and GRE scores for each school. Most campus bookstores keep this volume in stock or will order it for you. It is updated every 2 years and is a very helpful, informative guide.

Peruse the bookshelves at the college bookstore and library, and you'll find several other guides. A list of helpful print and online resources is provided at the end of this chapter. Note that the material in each of these printed resources is usually at least 2 years old because of the time required to print and distribute books. The American Psychological Association web site has an online searchable database of graduate programs that contains the most up-to-date information. A 3-month subscription to this database costs about $20; visit http://www.apa.org/gradstudy/ for more information. Once you have a list of potential programs, your next step is to gather more detailed information. Visit the school's web site to get more information about admissions, and possibly an online application, as well as to review the department and program home pages for additional information.

Evaluate Programs

All too often when I ask undergraduates where they want to go to school, they respond, "Anywhere that takes me." It's understandable that you're stressed and want a graduate degree, but it's also important to be an educated consumer. While the admissions committee is evaluating you as a potential student, you should be evaluating the program to see whether it fits your needs. Is it someplace where you want to spend the next few years? Take the time to carefully review and evaluate each program. As you read the information about graduate programs, you'll probably notice that there are differences among graduate departments in goals, program philosophies, theoretical orientations, facilities, and resources. What are you looking for as you peruse the volumes of information obtained through your research? Basically you're trying to determine how well each program matches your goals and aspirations—the fit between you and the program. How do you determine fit? As you examine a program, consider the areas listed in the following sections. How well does each program fulfill your expectations of what graduate training should entail?

Department Emphasis and Program Philosophy What are the program goals? Do they fit with your own? Is the department heavily research-oriented or is it more directed toward theoretical or applied psychology? What's the program's theoretical orientation (e.g., cognitive-behavioral, psychoanalytic)? Is the program directed toward producing researchers? Is it heavily oriented toward theory? Are theory and practice united? Where does the program fall on the scientist-practitioner continuum?

- **Faculty Research Interests and Publications.** Do you share interests with any of the faculty? Do the faculty publish often and in refereed journals? Look up faculty members in PsychINFO to learn more about their work.
- **Teaching Goals and Style.** Can you find any information about how classes are run? Look at the web site. Do faculty have their own web pages? Do any of these web pages describe classes or provide resources for students? Try to find out what it's like to be a student in the program. Does it appear to be a student-oriented program?
- **Information About Students and Graduates.** Where do graduates go? Do they find jobs in academia, practice, or the real world?
- **Course Offerings.** Look over the program course book and requirements to get a feel of what courses you'll take and what you'll learn. This will give you a chance to see some of the program's inner workings so that you won't be surprised once you're admitted.

Program Quality Program quality is difficult to access because some of it is rather subjective. Here are some factors to consider in evaluating program quality.

- **Attrition.** What is the attrition rate? Some programs select only a handful of top students and lose a few of them; other programs take in more students than they can effectively manage and lose many of them. Some programs use comprehensive exams to weed out students.
- **Time to Completion.** What is the average time for completing the degree? In psychology, 5 to 7 years is a normal range. If a program's average time to completion is close to 7 years or beyond, you should examine it more closely to determine why.
- **Logistical Resources.** Are there adequate computer facilities, library resources, money for travel to conferences, and other forms of support?
- **Financial Support.** Are research and teaching assistantships used to fund students? Does it appear to be a quality program?

To help you evaluate the overall quality of the program, Checklist 10.1 presents some characteristics of quality PhD programs.

CHECKLIST 10.1

Characteristics of a Quality PhD Program

- ❑ Program faculty work closely with students.
- ❑ Faculty regularly publish in their field and attend conferences at the regional, state, national, and international levels.
- ❑ Faculty publish with students and graduates.
- ❑ Program is accredited by the American Psychological Association (APA) (if clinical, counseling, or school).

- ❑ Program emphasizes research productivity.
- ❑ Program faculty are tenured or on a tenure track.
- ❑ Department is large enough to have faculty who represent the major areas in psychology.
- ❑ Program is able to support or partially support students through assistantships and other means.
- ❑ Program has adequate facilities for research and practica.

Adapted from Buskist & Sherburne, 1996; Keith-Spiegel & Wiederman, 2000.

In addition to program quality, consider the prestige of the department. How much does prestige matter? That depends on what you hope do with your degree. There generally is a correlation between departmental prestige and job quality (Peters, 1992). Doctoral recipients from prestigious departments are more likely to land prestigious jobs (e.g., at research institutions) than are those from less distinguished institutions. In academia, the teaching load in your first job often predicts your career: Professors carrying heavy teaching loads have little time for research (and research institutions generally are more prestigious). Advisors and mentors in prestigious graduate departments often have excellent reputations and important connections that can help you advance in your career. Powerful mentors can write persuasive letters of recommendation, lend authority to student papers, and pull strings because their old classmates, friends, and former students often hold prestigious positions. But you should also realize that powerful mentors are often very busy and that you may have little direct contact with them.

Accreditation Many programs advertise that they are accredited by the American Psychological Association. What does this mean? The APA is a national association of psychologists. One of its many activities is to evaluate practice-oriented psychology programs to ensure that the educational criteria meet the public's needs. APA accredits doctoral programs in the practice areas of clinical, school, counseling, and combined professional-scientific psychology (e.g., some programs in applied developmental psychology seek accreditation).

In order to be accredited, a program must meet the minimum standards for clinical training established by APA. The criteria include faculty credentials, specific course work, eligibility for state licensure, adequate research and clinical opportunities, and internships for clinical and counseling students. A site visit confirms that these requirements are met, and they must be maintained over time. Note that programs in nonpractice areas, such as experimental and social psychology, are not part of the APA accreditation program. If you are applying to clinical, counseling, or school programs, it is in your best interest to be sure that they are accredited, because a degree from an APA-approved program carries more weight; students from accredited programs are more successful in competing for clinical internships and jobs. In fact, many states *require* doctoral degrees from APA programs for licensure.

WHAT DO GRADUATE PROGRAMS WANT?

Now that you know what to look for in choosing a graduate program, let's consider the flip side: What do graduate programs look for in applicants? Surveys of faculty members involved in selecting graduate students have shown the following to be *very important* criteria in evaluating applicants (Bonifazi, Crespi, & Rieker, 1997; Keith-Spiegel, Tabachnick, & Spiegel, 1994):

1. The fit or match between the applicant's interests and skills and the program's goals
2. Research experience (especially research resulting in the publication in a scholarly journal or a paper presented at a professional conference)
3. Interest expressed by one or more members of the selection committee in working with a particular applicant
4. The clarity, focus, and content of the applicant's admissions essays

As you can see, the fit among student, program, and faculty is essential, as revealed in the admissions essay and in prior research. Surveys of faculty have classified the following criteria as *generally important* in evaluating applicants (Bonifazi et al., 1997; Keith-Spiegel et al., 1994):

1. Experience as research assistant
2. Writing skills
3. Knowledge about and interest in the program
4. Number of statistics, research methodology, and hard science courses taken
5. Prestige and status of faculty in undergraduate department, especially of those writing letters of recommendation
6. Potential for success as judged by interview
7. Honors and merit scholarships

It appears that graduate programs want applicants who are interested in the program, have research experience, and have a background in statistics, methodology, and science. Appleby, Keenan, and Mauer (1999) examined recommendation forms from the application packages of 143 graduate programs in clinical, experimental, and industrial-organizational psychology. The applicant characteristics that recommenders were requested to discuss and rank were identified and categorized. About 40% of the 802 characteristics referred to personal characteristics; about one-third referred to acquired skills; and about one-quarter referred to intellectual abilities or knowledge. The top characteristics that recommendation forms asked faculty to discuss are listed in Table 10.2. As you can see, grad school programs are interested in more than your academic abilities. A large part of acceptance depends on whether you appear to be capable of fulfilling the needs of others:

> Because graduate faculties must be diverse enough to represent the breadth of the discipline within the department, any given faculty member may not have a single colleague in his or her area of expertise. The remedy for such isolation and

TABLE 10.2 TOP CHARACTERISTICS ASSESSED BY RECOMMENDATION FORMS

Motivation
Intellectual/scholarly ability
Research skills
Emotional stability and maturity
Writing skills
Speaking skills
Teaching skills or potential
Ability to work with others
Creativity
Knowledge of area of study

Adapted from Appleby et al., 1999.

> frustration is, of course, to attract students who will share an appetite for the professor's area. (Keith-Spiegel & Wiederman, 2000, p. 39.)

Faculty look for applicants who share their interests and are prepared to engage in collaborative research or scholarship. In addition, scholarly productivity in the form of publications in scholarly journals is the primary criterion by which faculty are evaluated and rewarded. Therefore, it's important for faculty to find students who fit their needs, who can work with them, and who enhance their productivity and reputation. Faculty want students who will thrive and bring respect to their program long after graduation. That's why it is important for you to know as much as possible about the program and faculty so that you can present yourself effectively.

THE APPLICATION

Once you have narrowed your choice of programs, you're ready to begin the application. Apply to enough programs to have a reasonable chance of being accepted given your credentials. There is a great deal of competition for entry into doctoral programs in psychology. Plan on applying to 6 to 10 programs and possibly more if you're applying to particularly selective programs (especially in clinical psychology). This can quickly become expensive; application fees run from $25 to $60 per program. In addition to investing money, plan on investing a significant amount of time in preparing each application.

Make copies of each application form before you begin. Neatness counts because you want to make the best impression possible. Instead of typing each application, scan your applications into a computer so that you can prepare professional-looking forms. If you don't have a scanner at home, plan on spending time in the computer lab at school. Many programs have online applications; check the web site for each program to which you're applying to determine whether you can submit your application via the Internet. Table 10.3 provides a timetable for applying to graduate school. Following that, we'll examine the typical components of a graduate application.

TABLE 10.3 TIME LINE FOR APPLYING TO GRADUATE SCHOOL

Sophomore Year

- Take a least one more math and science course beyond the general requirements.
- Learn about the research interests of the faculty at your school, read their articles, and get to know those whose work interests you.
- Request to assist professors with their research.
- Seek research experiences in psychology.
- Make contact with graduate students in psychology whom you may know. Ask them what graduate student life is like and what kind of study load you can expect in various specialties in psychology. Your professors may be able to help you locate graduate students, or you can check with the Career Services Office or the Alumni Office.
- Also, find out about regional psychological meetings, such as the meetings of the Eastern Psychological Association and the Midwestern Psychological Association, which are usually held in late March, April, or early May. Check the American Psychological Association web site (http:// www.apa.org/organizations/regionals.html) for links to each association.

Junior Year

- Take note of professors' research interests and talk with them about research opportunities.
- Participate in an independent research project with a faculty member. Talk with your professors about research opportunities.
- Get information about the Graduate Record Exam (GRE); use study guides to prepare.
- Take the GRE in the spring.
- Some programs require the Miller Analogy Test (MAT) (learn about the requirements of the programs to which you plan to apply).
- If you are interested in the clinical or counseling areas of psychology, get practical experience.

TABLE 10.3 **Time Line for Applying to Graduate School**

- Learn about graduate programs and begin considering programs to which to apply.

Summer Before Your Senior Year

- Examine graduate programs online. Request bulletins, brochures, financial aid forms, and departmental application forms from the schools to which you may eventually apply. Many schools place these materials online or have online request forms.
- Prepare and register for the GRE Psychology Test. Check the registration deadlines and be sure not to miss them.
- Begin drafting your resume.

Beginning of Your Senior Year

- Check with your advisor and the registrar to determine that you have fulfilled all graduation and departmental requirements.
- Ask professors for their opinions on what courses you should take beyond the requirements to help you prepare for graduate school.
- Take a list of your graduate school choices to your professors and ask them to recommend the schools they feel would be most appropriate for you. Take copies of your résumé and transcript with you and ask them if they will write letters of recommendation for you when the time comes.
- If you haven't already taken the GRE General Test and the GRE Psychology Test, do so.
- If you are applying for financial aid, pick up the necessary forms now. The same goes for fellowships and scholarships. The deadlines may be earlier than the actual applications for admission.

November of Your Senior Year

- Narrow down your list of graduate schools to which to apply (seek faculty assistance).
- List each school, noting the application deadline and what each school requires for a complete application.
- Ask your professors for letters of recommendation. Some prefer a deadline to work by, so be prepared to offer a firm date by which they should have the recommendation finished and sent. If they are writing directly to the school (i.e., the letter is not returned in a sealed envelope to you in order for it to be included with your application materials), be sure to offer to pay for the postage. Provide them with a copy of your résumé and with a list of the activities, clubs, or organizations you've been involved in, and talk to them about your future goals. Give them a clear

(Continued)

TABLE 10.3 TIME LINE FOR APPLYING TO GRADUATE SCHOOL (CONTINUED)

sense of where you are headed and what you intend to do in graduate school and afterward.
- Begin working on your personal statement. Always show it to at least one other person before you type it on the application and send it. Show it to someone who knows you and who is a good judge of writing skills. Be sure to write the statement carefully, answering the questions each graduate school wants you to comment on.
- Request that GRE and MAT scores be sent to all the schools to which you are applying.

December of Your Senior Year

- Finish application materials and mail them at least 2 weeks in advance of the deadline. Be sure to include letters of recommendation (if the school requests they be sent with your application) and the necessary application fees.
- If you are submitting the applications online, do so several days in advance (do not wait for the last minute, as computer problems often arise!).
- Keep photocopies of each application.
- Check back with the professors who are providing letters of recommendation to make sure they have finished them and sent them out.
- Request that the registrar's office and the financial aid office send out official transcripts to all the schools to which you are applying. Do this early, as it often requires 10 working days to send a transcript request.
- Be sure that GRE and MAT scores have been sent to all the schools to which you are applying.

Late January Through April

- Follow up to confirm that your completed applications and all letters of recommendation have been received.
- Most schools send a postcard on receipt of each application. Keep track of these. If you don't receive a postcard or letter, contact the admissions office by e-mail or phone to ensure that your application has been received before the deadline.
- Thank those who wrote letters of recommendation.
- Attend any interviews to which you are invited.

March and April

- Accept and decline offers.
- When declining an offer, be sure to phone the schools whose offers you are declining to let them know that you appreciate the offer but have

TABLE 10.3 **TIME LINE FOR APPLYING TO GRADUATE SCHOOL**

decided not to accept it. Schools wait for your decision in order to accept alternates.
- If you accept an offer, you have until April 15 to change your mind—after that, any reason besides illness, change of career plans, or dire circumstances will not impress the graduate school whose offer you have accepted. You should not accept any other offer until you are officially separated from your first acceptance.
- Call or write people who wrote letters of recommendation and inform them of the outcome, thanking them for their help.

THE GRADUATE RECORD EXAM GENERAL TEST

The Graduate Record Exam (GRE) is a standardized test that all applicants to graduate programs must complete. It's often a major source of stress for students. What is the GRE, and how can you prepare for it?

Overview

The GRE General Test is an aptitude test that measures a variety of skills, acquired over the high school and college years, that are thought to predict success in graduate school. It is only one of several criteria that graduate schools use to evaluate your application, but it is one of the most important. This is particularly true if your college grade point average (GPA) is not as high as you'd like. Exceptional GRE scores can open up new opportunities for grad school. Similarly, low GRE scores can cast doubt on a very good GPA.

The GRE General Test yields three scores: verbal ability, quantitative ability, and analytic ability. The verbal section assesses your ability to understand and analyze written material through the use of analogies, antonyms, sentence completions, and reading comprehension questions. The quantitative section tests basic math skills and your ability to understand and apply quantitative skills to solve problems. Types of questions include quantitative comparisons, problem solving, and data interpretation. The analytic writing section examines critical thinking and analytic writing skills. No specific content knowledge is assessed. This section examines your ability to explain and support complex ideas and engage in a focused, coherent discussion and analysis of arguments. The verbal and quantitative subtests yield scores ranging from 200 to 800. Graduate schools consider the verbal and quantitative sections to be particularly important in making decisions about applicants. Therefore, the total GRE score usually refers to the quantitative and verbal scores summed to a total of 1,600 possible points. The analytic writing section is the most recent addition to the GRE and is scored on a scale of 0 to 6 points (in half-point increments).

The GRE General Test is administered by computer year-round. Plan to take it well in advance of application due dates. Generally, you should take it in the spring or summer before you apply to grad school. Remember that it takes several weeks for scores to be reported to schools—if you take the GRE too late in the fall, the scores may not arrive in time for your application to be considered. Also, you will want to have enough time to retake it if necessary. You can always retake the GRE, but remember that you're allowed to take it only once per calendar month. Because all prior scores are sent to the institutions that you're applying to, never take the GRE as practice.

The GRE General Test takes 2¼ hours to complete, but you should allow an extra 1½ hours for reading instructions and taking tutorials. The verbal section consists of 30 multiple-choice questions to be answered within 30 minutes. That's not a lot of time, so it's important to be familiar with the test so that you can work quickly and efficiently. In other words, practice beforehand using the PowerPrep software provided by www.gre.org, as well as the books and web sites recommended at the end of this chapter.

Verbal Section of the GRE

In the verbal section, you will be asked to read passages and analyze information obtained from your reading, analyze sentences and the relationships among component parts of sentences, and recognize relationships between words and concepts within written material. The items that constitute the reading comprehension sections are meant to be answered without any particular knowledge or expertise other than the general knowledge and skills that an average graduate is presumed to have. Excelling on the verbal section of the GRE requires an advanced vocabulary.

There are four types of questions: analogies, antonyms, reading comprehension, and sentence completion. Let's take a closer look at each.

- Analogies examine your ability to understand the relationship between the words in a word pair and recognize a parallel relationship between the words in other word pairs. This requires determining how two words are related and then determining which word pair provided displays a similar relationship.
- Antonyms test your knowledge of vocabulary and your ability to identify the opposite of a given concept.
- Comprehension measures your ability to read analytically. You're asked to explore a written passage from several perspectives, recognize elements that are explicitly stated and inferred, and understand the assumptions underlying the passage as well as the implications of these assumptions.

- Reading comprehension questions assess six types of information: identify the main idea, identify explicitly stated information, identify implied ideas, apply the author's ideas to other situations, identify the author's logic or persuasive techniques, and identify the attitudinal tone of the passage.
- Sentence completion questions measure your ability to use syntax and grammar cues to understand the meaning of a sentence. This task requires that you analyze the parts of an incomplete sentence and determine which word or set of words can be substituted for the blank space in the sentence.

Quantitative Section of the GRE

The GRE General Test contains two quantitative sections (three if a new set of quantitative questions are being tested). Each quantitative section consists of 28 multiple-choice questions to be completed within 45 minutes. The quantitative sections measure "basic mathematical skills and understanding of mathematical concepts, as well as the ability to reason quantitatively and to solve problems in a quantitative setting" (GRE Bulletin, p. 5) (Educational Testing Service, 2004). They do not require math skills beyond the high school level (e.g., arithmetic, algebra, geometry, and data analysis); however, calculators are not permitted, so you must be prepared to complete problems only with the help of a pencil and scratch paper. The quantitative section is composed of three types of questions: problem solving, quantitative comparison, and data analysis. Let's take a look at each type of question:

- Problem-solving questions are word problems that assess your understanding of and ability to apply arithmetic, algebra, and geometry.
- Quantitative comparison questions ask you to compare two quantities, one in column a and one in column b. Your task is to determine if they are equal, if one is larger than the other, or if not enough information is presented to make the determination.
- Data analysis questions require the use of basic descriptive statistics, the ability to interpret data in graphs and tables, and a knowledge of elementary probability. Questions emphasize the "ability to synthesize information, to select appropriate data for answering a question, and to determine whether or not the data provided are sufficient to answer a given question" (GRE Bulletin, p. 8).

Analytic Writing Section of the GRE

The analytical writing section examines your ability to communicate complex ideas clearly and effectively, support your ideas, examine claims and supporting evidence, sustain a focused and coherent discussion, and effectively use the elements of standard written English. There are two subsections:

- **Present Your Perspective on an Issue**: In this 45-minute task, you are presented with an issue of general interest and asked to address it from any perspective, providing reasons and examples to support your views. Your job is to construct an argument and support it with reasons and examples.
- **Analyze an Argument**: This 30-minute task presents you with an argument. Your task is to critique the argument, assess its claims, and conclude whether or not it is reasoned.

Like the other sections of the GRE General Test, the essay tasks are delivered on a computer. The GRE software contains a simple word processor that includes basic functions such as cut and paste, insert text, delete, and undo, but does not include spelling or grammar checkers. Practice using the word processor in PowerPrep, the practice software sent to you when you register for the GRE (and downloadable from the GRE web site at www.gre.org).

Preparing for the GRE General Test

Begin preparing for the GRE early to ensure that you earn the highest score possible. This is not the time to cram!

General Preparation Tips

- Know the test. Your GRE preparation should emphasize getting to know the test and the types of questions that will appear. Be familiar with the time limit for each section and how many questions each section includes.
- Understand the directions for each question beforehand to save time, but remember that the directions for the actual test might be slightly different from the ones in your study material. So be sure to always read the instructions—quickly.
- Download GRE PowerPrep Software: Test Preparation for the GRE General Test, which is free software provided by the makers of the GRE. According to the online description, PowerPrep "includes test tutorials, practice questions with explanations, and two actual computer-adaptive tests for the verbal and quantitative sections. The software also includes sample topics and essays for the analytical writing section, and advice on how to write effective essays for the Issue and Argument tasks. PowerPrep lets you practice writing essays under simulated GRE testing conditions with the same GRE word processing and testing tools that appear on the test" (at www.gre.org/faqnew.html).
- Try a practice test under conditions similar to the actual GRE. Based on your practice score, devise a study plan to help you brush up on vocabulary, reading comprehension, analogies, algebra, and geometry.

- Download sample GRE tests.
- Buy a GRE review book—and use it.

Before the Test

- Arrive at the test center at least 30 minutes early to complete any paperwork. If you arrive late, you may not be admitted and your application fee will not be refunded. Remember to bring at least two forms of identification (with at least one containing a photo and a signature). For more information about identification requirements and policies, consult the GRE Information and Registration Bulletin.
- If you're taking the GRE at a test center other than at your college or university, do a test drive the week before to learn where the center is and how long it takes to arrive, because it's important that you arrive 30 minutes beforehand.
- Get enough sleep the night before. Don't study the night before. Instead, have a quiet night at home and do something that you find relaxing and enjoyable.
- Eat breakfast. Make sure that you're not hungry during the test, which can affect your performance.
- Wear comfortable clothes and bring a sweater in case the test center is cold.

On the Test Day

- Your previous practice should make you familiar with the test and the amount of time you need to complete each type of question. Don't get stuck on one particular question for too long because you'll lose time and may miss easier questions later on.
- Don't rush. The GRE isn't a race, so use your time judiciously, devoting just enough time to each question to complete it and maximize your score in the limited time allotted.
- The questions at the beginning of the exam are more important than those toward the end. Because the GRE is computer-adaptive, the difficulty level of the questions you receive later is determined by the difficulty of those you've answered correctly before.
- If you don't know the answer to a question, use the method of elimination to find alternatives that cannot be the answer to narrow down your guesses to two or three alternatives and improve the odds of choosing correctly.
- Don't leave questions unanswered—there is no penalty for wrong answers.
- Be very sure of your answer before proceeding, because a computer-adaptive test does not permit you to return to a question once you have attempted it. You cannot leave difficult questions for later, nor can you check your answers at the end even if you have extra time. So pace yourself properly and be very certain of your answers.

What score should you aim for? There is tremendous variation among programs, but most PsyD programs require a minimum score of 540 on each subtest; most scientist-practitioner programs require 580; and most research programs require 600 (Mayne et al., 1994). Norcross (1997) reports mean total GRE scores of incoming graduate students of 1206 for doctoral programs and 1033 for master's programs. Generally, more competitive programs require higher minimum GRE scores. The average GRE scores for incoming students are listed in program materials, in APA's *Guide to Graduate Study in Psychology*, and in the annual program rankings provided by *US News and World Report*.

THE GRE PSYCHOLOGY TEST

About one-half of doctoral programs require that applicants take the GRE Psychology Test (Matlin & Kalat, 2001). This test consists of about 215 questions that tap information from the core psychology courses required in most undergraduate programs. About 40% of the test consists of experimental and natural science questions from the areas of learning, language, memory, thinking, perception, ethology, sensation, comparative psychology, and physiological psychology. Social and social science areas of psychology account for an additional 43% of the test questions, including clinical, abnormal, developmental, personality, and social psychology. The remaining 17% consists of questions on history, applied psychology, measurement, research methodology, and statistics (Matlin & Kalat, 2001).

Unlike the GRE General Test, the GRE Psychology Test is administered only by pencil and paper three times a year: in April, November, and December. Ideally, you should take it in April so that you have time to retake it if necessary. If you are taking it as a senior, take it in November, not December, to allow enough time for your scores to be reported. Register for the GRE Psychology Test by phone (1-800-GRE-CALL or 1-800-473-2255) or by mail using the address and registration form found in the GRE Information and Registration Bulletin (at www.gre.org). Remember that seats are assigned on a first-come, first-served basis, so register early.

When you register for the GRE, you'll select from among several test administration centers at colleges, universities, and testing centers. For a complete list of these locations, consult the GRE web site. The instructions regarding arriving early and bringing proper identification provided earlier for the GRE General Test also apply to the GRE Psychology Test. The test takes up to 3½ hours to complete.

Since the GRE Psychology Test is designed to sample a broad overview of topics in psychology, the best way to prepare is by studying an upper-level introductory psychology textbook such as *Psychology* by A. J. Fridlund, D. Reisburg, and H. Gleitman, or *Psychology: In Search of the Human Mind,* by

R J. Sternberg. Take the GRE Psychology Test in November of your senior year (to benefit from all the psychology courses that you've taken beforehand).

Although GRE scores are an important part of your application, remember that graduate admissions committees consider many other factors. Many programs accept students with lower GRE scores if they have strengths in other areas, such as research. How do you communicate your strengths to graduate admissions committees? Admissions essays and personal statements offer you an opportunity to speak directly to the members of these committees.

Admissions Essays and Personal Statements

The admissions essay or personal statement is often the most difficult part of the application; this is because the task is somewhat ambiguous, yet very important. It's your chance to present yourself as an individual, a person behind the GPA and GRE scores. Because most of the other applicants have similar academic credentials, admissions committees need the additional information contained in admissions essays to narrow the pool of applicants. Your essays provide information about your ability to write, to stick to the task at hand, and to persuade readers. Your essay also informs the admissions committee about your interests, career aspirations, and values. This is the place where you can stand out.

Essay Topics

So exactly what do you write about? Usually programs give applicants a question or two to answer or a specific topic on which to write. Keith-Spiegel and Wiederman (2000) have noted that there is a remarkable similarity among essay topics requested by graduate programs. Most questions fall into one of several categories (Keith-Spiegel & Wiederman, 2000):

- **Career plans.** What are your long-term career goals? Where do you see yourself 10 years from now?
- **General interest areas.** What academic or professional areas interest you?
- **Research experiences.** Discuss areas in which you might like to do research, research experiences you have had, or both. Describe your research interests.
- **Academic objectives.** Why are you undertaking graduate study? Explain why graduate training is necessary to reach your goals.
- **Clinical or other field experiences.** Describe your clinical experiences. How have your field experiences shaped your career goals?
- **Academic background and achievements.** Discuss your academic background.

- **Personal.** Is there anything in your background that you think would be relevant in our evaluation of applicants? Describe your life up to now: family, friends, home, school, work, and particularly those experiences most relevant to you and to your interests in psychology. Write an autobiographical sketch.
- **Personal and professional development.** Describe your values and your approach to life.

Although there are many similarities among essay topics, you should not write a generic essay. Tailor your essay to the specific question and the program. The "old days" of writing a statement on a typewriter and then photocopying it are long gone. Saving your essay on a computer permits you to revise it and tailor it to each program. Be sure to save each version of your essay. Many applications essays ask the applicant to discuss how the program or faculty matches his or her individual needs. This means that you must demonstrate that you have researched the program and are familiar with its faculty and curriculum. Explain how the program will prepare you for the career you desire, offering specific examples. When writing your essay, remember that your goal is to come across as someone with the potential to succeed in graduate school.

Length and Content

Your essay should be about two single-spaced pages long. Shorter statements provide too little information, and longer ones tend to become wordy. Readers assess the content of your essay and your ability to express yourself effectively and succinctly. Be extra careful to correct any spelling or grammatical errors. Attention to detail is critical.

Be careful about the content of your essay. As Bottoms and Nysse (1999) advise, "Do not misinterpret the meaning of *personal* in the phrase *personal statement*!" The essay is a professional essay, not a place to discuss your own mental health, experiences with therapy, or heartaches. Instead, explain the experiences that have prepared you for graduate school and have led to your decision to apply. Use concrete examples whenever possible. Your essay should include at least these four components: your previous research experience, research interests, relevant experience, and career goals (Bottoms & Nysse, 1999).

Discuss the details of your involvement in previous research. Who supervised the work? Was the research part of a course requirement, for class credit, or part of an independent study? Discuss the purpose of the research, including the theory, method, and results. Explain your role. Rather than merely stating that you entered data for Dr. Smith's research study, for example, show that you have worked to understand the purpose of the research. If the research resulted in class papers, conference presentations, or publications, mention that. If you were an author on a conference presentation or publication, include a copy in your application packet. Discuss how your attitude about research has changed as a result of the experience.

Discuss the areas of psychology that interest you most now. You've already chosen the graduate programs to which you'll apply based on the fit between your interests and the faculty's research interests. For each program, identify faculty whose research interests you and tailor your personal statement so that it will entice faculty with whom you'd like to work. This entails doing your homework first. Read the faculty members' web pages and locate articles they have published. Explain what interests you about a professor's work. State your preferred research interests but also mention that you are open to studying related areas (if that is true). You are more likely to be accepted into a particular program if you discuss the research interests of several faculty (because not all professors look for new students each year).

Your statement should also include other relevant experience that pertains to your decision to go to graduate school or makes you qualified for graduate school. Internship experiences and volunteer experiences should be included here. Avoid personal emotional self-disclosures. Explain what you would like to do after graduation. What kind of career do you envision for yourself after receiving your degree? Illustrate how the specific program will prepare you for the career that you desire. Personal details that you include about yourself should be relevant to your ability to be a successful graduate student and reflect maturity, adaptability, and motivation.

Writing as a Process

Writing your admissions essay is a process, not a discrete event. The first step involves preparation—gathering the information needed to compose the essay. Conduct a thorough self-assessment to gather the information needed to compose a personal essay that sets you apart from the other candidates. Allow yourself plenty of time; you don't want to rush this process of self-exploration. Look back over your journal entries, especially your responses to the exercises in Chapter 2. Then sit down with a pad, or at the keyboard, and begin writing. Don't censor yourself in any way. Just write what feels natural. Begin taking notes on what drives you. Describe your hopes, dreams, and aspirations. What do you hope to gain from graduate study? Granted, not all of this information will make it into the essay, but your goal at this point is to brainstorm. Identify as much of your personal history as possible so that you can carefully sift through it and sort out events and personal items that will strengthen your essay. Consider the following:

- Hobbies
- Projects you've completed

- Jobs you've held
- Responsibilities
- Personal and academic accomplishments
- Challenges and hurdles you've overcome
- Life events that motivate your education
- People who have influenced you or motivated you
- Traits, work habits, and attitudes that will ensure your success

Carefully consider your academic record and personal accomplishments. How do the attitudes, values, and personal qualities that you've listed correspond to these experiences? Try to pair them up. For example, your curiosity and thirst for knowledge may have led you to conduct independent research with a professor. Consider how each pair of attitudes, personal qualities, and experiences show that you're prepared to excel in graduate school.

Once you have a master list, carefully examine the information. Remember that the information you choose to present can portray you as a positive, upbeat person or as a tired, discouraged student. Think about the image you want to portray and revise your master list accordingly. Use the revised list as a basis for all your admissions essays. Remember to be forthcoming about your weaknesses. If your early academic record is weak, explain why. Bright people will be evaluating your application, and they'll spot weaknesses. Don't force them to make assumptions about you. Instead, discuss your weaknesses and explain how you've overcome them.

There's still more information to consider in writing your admissions essays. Tailor your essay to each program. Show that you're interested and that you've taken the time to learn about each one. Put all the research you've done on programs to good use. Reread the program brochure; check the web site; gather all the information possible to help you determine what the admissions committee is looking for from potential students. Take careful notes on each program, observing where your personal interests, qualities, and accomplishments coincide. If you're truly interested in the graduate programs to which you're applying (and with a $50 application fee for most schools, you should be interested), take the time to tailor your essay to each program. One size clearly does not fit all.

As you write your essay, occasionally stop to make sure that you're answering the question posed by the admissions committee. Think about the question, the central theme asked, and how it corresponds to your master list of experiences and personal qualities. Some applications require you to answer a string of questions. Pay attention to your responses and try to avoid being redundant. Remember that this is your chance to present your strengths and really shine. Take advantage of it. Discuss your accomplishments, describe valuable experiences, and emphasize the positive. Show that you're motivated. The committee is composed of professionals who have read hundreds, even thousands, of such statements over the years. Make yours stand out.

Letters of Recommendation

Nearly every graduate program requires applicants to submit letters of recommendation. Don't underestimate the importance of these letters. Although your transcript, standardized test scores, and admissions essay are vital components of your application, an excellent letter of recommendation can make up for weaknesses in any of these areas. A letter of recommendation gives admissions committees information that isn't found elsewhere in the application. What is a letter of recommendation? It's a letter, written by a faculty member, that discusses the personal qualities, accomplishments, and experiences that make you unique and perfect for the programs to which you've applied.

Whom Should You Ask?

Most graduate programs require two or more letters of recommendation. Deciding who will write your recommendation letters is often difficult. Consider faculty members, administrators, internship or cooperative education supervisors, and employers. But remember that it's faculty who will be reading these letters (and they've been through graduate school), so faculty tend to write the most credible recommendation letters. The persons you ask to write your letters should:

- Know you well
- Have known you long enough to write with authority
- Know your work
- Describe your work positively
- Have a high opinion of you
- Know where you are applying
- Know your educational and career goals
- Be able to compare you favorably with your peers
- Be well known
- Be able to write a good letter

Keep in mind that no one person will satisfy all these criteria. Aim for a set of letters covering the range of your skills. Letters should include your academic and scholastic skills, research abilities and experiences, and applied experiences (e.g., cooperative education, internships, related work experience). When you approach potential recommenders, ask if they know you well enough to write a meaningful letter. Pay attention to their demeanor. If you sense reluctance, thank them and ask someone else. Remember that it is best to ask early in the semester. As the end of the semester approaches, faculty may hesitate because of time constraints.

Help Your Referees

The best thing you can do to ensure that your letters of recommendation cover all the bases is to provide your referees (those who will write your letters) with all the necessary information. Don't assume that they can remember anything about you. I know, you're quite memorable, but think about what it must be like to have 150 or more students each semester. Make an appointment to speak with each of your referees. Give them plenty of time (3 to 4 weeks at a minimum). Provide a file with all your background information:

- Transcript
- Résumé or vita
- GRE scores
- Courses you've taken with them and grades that you've earned
- Research experiences
- Internships and other applied experiences
- Honor societies to which you belong
- Awards you've won
- Work experiences
- Professional goals
- Due date for the application
- Copies of the application recommendation forms

Confidentiality

The recommendation forms supplied by graduate programs require you to decide whether to waive or to retain your rights to see the recommendations. As you decide whether to retain your rights, remember that confidential letters tend to carry more weight with admissions committees. In addition, many faculty members will not write a recommendation letter unless it is confidential. Other faculty may provide you with a copy of each letter even if it is confidential. If you are unsure of your decision, discuss it with your referees. As the application deadline approaches, check back with your recommenders to ensure that the letters were sent on time (but don't nag). Contacting the graduate programs to inquire whether your materials were received is also appropriate.

NOW WHAT?

It has been said that the keys to graduate school admission are preparation, application know-how, and patience (Lunneborg & Wilson, 1987). Now that you've submitted your applications, patience is essential. It is easy to start ruminating about the status of your application and wonder, "Do they like me? Am I good enough? Will I get in? Why haven't I heard anything?" Don't let these destructive thoughts overwhelm you. Instead, focus on what you can control—your schoolwork. Remember school? You've still got to graduate, and you don't want to let your grades slip now.

Should you ever make contact with graduate school programs? If you have not been notified that your application file is complete, a call or an e-mail to the admissions office is appropriate to determine that your application is complete. Incomplete files are not considered for admission, and not all programs notify applicants that their files are incomplete.

When can you expect to hear from programs? Every program has a different method and style of handling admissions. Some review applications and make decisions early, and others wait. How quickly applications are reviewed depends on a variety of factors, including the number of applications received, how many people are on the committee, academic demands, conferences, holidays, how well the members of the committee work together, and so on. Most programs inform applicants of their status by mid-April, but you might hear from programs earlier or later.

Acing the Interview

Some programs conduct phone interviews, some conduct on-site interviews, and some don't interview at all. What happens if you're invited to interview? How do you prepare? What are admissions committees looking for? An interview gives admissions committees an opportunity to meet candidates and see the people behind the GPAs and GRE scores. It's a chance for them to meet you, to see how you react under pressure, and to assess your verbal and nonverbal communication skills. The interview might range from a half-hour with one or two faculty to a full day or more filled with meetings with students and faculty. Activities might range from small group discussions to larger group interviews and even social hours or parties.

How do you prepare for the interview? Learn as much about the program as possible. Review the program description, department web site, and faculty web sites. Understand the program's emphasis and be aware of the faculty's research interests. Consider how you will answer common interview questions such as the following.

- Why are you interested in our program?
- What do you know about our program?
- What are your career goals?
- Why did you choose a career in psychology?
- What are your research interests? Describe your research experience. Regarding research, what are your strengths and weaknesses?

- What are your academic strengths? What was your favorite course, and why?
- What do you like best about yourself?
- Who would you like to work with? Why?
- Describe the accomplishment you're most proud of.
- If you were to begin a research project now, what would the topic be?
- Describe your theoretical orientation.
- Discuss your experiences in clinical settings. Evaluate your clinical abilities.
- What are your strengths and weaknesses?
- Tell us about yourself.

Consider how you might answer each of these questions but don't memorize answers. Instead, be prepared to speak extemporaneously so that you'll be ready for interview curveballs. To gain confidence, practice with family, with friends, or in front of the mirror.

Don't forget that this is your opportunity to ask questions too. In fact, admissions committees expect you to ask questions, so prepare some thoughtful questions about the program, faculty, and students. Use this opportunity to learn about the program and whether it meets your needs. During your visit, try to get a sense of the department's emotional climate. What do graduate students call professors? Doctor? Or do they use first names? Are students competitive with one another? Try to get a sense of whether the atmosphere matches your personality. Is it excessively formal? Would you be happy there?

BEING ACCEPTED

You've received good news. Congratulations! Most programs inform applicants of their acceptance from March through early April. In most cases, your decision on whether to accept an offer is due by April 15. Once you decline an offer, it can be passed along to someone else who is waiting, so don't hold on to offers that you don't plan to accept. As soon as you have two offers, decide which one to decline. Each time you receive a new offer, decline your least preferred offer so that you're not holding on to offers that you don't intend to accept. How do you decide which offer to decline? Consider your priorities. Know what you are accepting. Don't be surprised because you have made assumptions about financial support, housing, or assistantships. Ask about financial aid, housing, and assistantships. Compare acceptance packages to decide among programs. Don't be afraid to do some negotiating, because they've decided that they want you. Help them make it possible for you to accept by explaining any financial limitations that might impede accepting their offer. How do you decline a graduate program? E-mail or fax a letter explaining that you appreciate their interest but will not be accepting their offer. Mail a hard copy of the letter as well.

Dealing With Rejection

What if you're rejected? It is difficult to be told that you are not among a program's top choices. From a statistical standpoint, you have lots of company; most competitive doctoral programs receive 10 to 50 times as many applicants as they can take. You may find it particularly difficult if you were invited for an interview. As many as 75% of applicants invited for interviews are not accepted.

Why are students rejected? Most are rejected simply because there aren't enough slots; graduate programs in psychology receive far more applications from qualified candidates than they can accept. Why were you eliminated by a particular program? There is no way to tell, but in many cases applicants are rejected because they don't fit the program. For example, an applicant to a research-scientist program who doesn't read the program materials carefully might be rejected for indicating an interest in practicing therapy.

You might find it difficult to inform family, friends, and professors of the bad news, but it is essential that you seek social support. Allow yourself to feel upset, acknowledge your feelings, and then move forward. If you are rejected by every program you apply to, reassess your goals but don't necessarily give up.

- Did you select schools carefully, paying attention to fit?
- Did you apply to enough programs?
- Did you complete all parts of each application?
- Did you spend enough time on your essays?
- Did you have research experience?
- Did you have field experience?
- Did you know your referees well, and did they have something to write about?

Were most of your applications made to highly competitive programs? Your answers to these questions may help you determine whether to reapply to a greater range of programs next year or to apply to a master's program instead, as either a first step toward a doctoral degree or as an end in itself. Or you may want to choose another career path. If you are firmly committed to attending graduate school in psychology, consider reapplying next year, but don't send out the same applications. Use the next few months to improve your academic record, seek research experience, and get to know professors. Apply to a wider range of schools (including "safety" schools), select programs more carefully, and thoroughly research each program.

Suggested Readings

American Psychological Association (1993). *Getting in: A step-by-step plan for gaining admission to graduate school in psychology.* Washington, DC: Author.

American Psychological Association (2004). *Graduate study in psychology: 2005 Edition.* Washington, DC: Author.

Educational Testing Service (1999). *GRE PowerPrep software: Test preparation for the GRE General Test.*Version 2.0. New York: Warner Books.

Green, S. W., & Wolf, I. (2003). *How to prepare for the GRE Test (with CD-ROM).* Hauppauge, NY: Barron's Educational Series.

Keith-Spiegel, P., & Weiderman, M. W. (2000). *The Complete guide to graduate school admission: Psychology, counseling, and related professions.* Hillsdale, NJ: Erlbaum.

Kuther, T. L. (2004). *Getting into graduate school in psychology and related fields: Your guide to success.* Springfield, IL: Charles C Thomas.

Lurie, K. (2001). *Cracking the GRE 2005 (with four complete sample tests on CD-ROM).* New York: Random House.

Mayne, T. J., Norcross, J. G., & Sayette, M. A. (2004). *Insider's guide to graduate programs in clinical and counseling psychology.* New York: Guilford.

Web Resources

The following web sites are hot-linked at *The Psychology Major's Handbook* web site at *http://info.wadsworth.com/kuther*

Applying to Graduate School

http://www.psichi.org/pubs/search.asp?category1 = 7

At this site, you'll find articles about all aspects of the graduate admissions process; from Psi Chi, the National Honor Society in Psychology.

GRE Homepage

http://www.gre.org

Get information about the GRE from the source.

Psychology Graduate School Portal

http://www.psychgrad.org/

This site provides extensive coverage of all aspects of graduate admissions.

Applying to Psychology Graduate School Programs: The Application Process

http://psychology.okstate.edu/undergrad/gradbook/ApplyGradProg.html

Covers all parts of the admissions process.

About Graduate School

http://gradschool.about.com

I maintain this site, which is part of the about.com network. Here, you'll find information for graduate school applicants, current students, postdoctoral fellows, and faculty in all disciplines, including psychology.

JOURNAL EXERCISE

Why Graduate School?

Where does graduate education fit into your life? What goals will it help to accomplish? What are the costs of graduate school? It is sometimes said that as one door of opportunity opens, another closes. What door will close when you enter graduate school? What will you miss out on in your years of graduate study?

References

Actkinson, T. R. (2000). Master's and myth: Little-known information about a popular degree. *Eye on Psi Chi, 4*(2), 19–21, 23, 25.

Allen, M. J., Noel, R., Deegan, J., Halpern, D., & Crawford, C. (2000) *Goals and objectives for the undergraduate psychology major: Recommendations from a meeting of California State University psychology faculty.* Retrieved August 20, 2000, from http://www.lemoyne.edu/OTRP/otrpresources/otrp_outcomes.html

American Counseling Association (2000). *A comparative analysis of the educational preparation of the two professions.* Retrieved February 1, 2001, from http://www.counseling.org/resources/pc_sw.htm

American Psychological Association (1993). *Getting in: A step-by-step plan for gaining admission to graduate school in psychology.* Washington, DC: Author.

American Psychological Association (1996). *Psychology: Careers for the twenty-first century*. Washington, DC: Author.

American Psychological Association (1997). *The 1995 APA survey of 1992 baccalaureate recipients.* Retrieved August 13, 2001, from http://research.apa.org/95survey/homepage.html

American Psychological Association (1998). *Skills [that may be] obtained during graduate study in psychology.* Retrieved December 29, 2000, from http://www.apa.org/science/skills.html

American Psychological Association (2001). *Publication manual of the American Psychological Association.* Washington, DC: Author.

American Psychological Association (n.d.). Employed psychology PhDs by setting: 1997. Retrieved July 20, 2001, from http://research.apa.org/doc10.html

Amsel, J. (1997). *An interesting career in psychology: Acquisitions editor*. Retrieved February 1, 2001, from http://www.apa.org/science/ic-amsel.html

Appleby, D. (1997). *The handbook of psychology*. New York: Longman.

Appleby, D. (1999) Choosing a mentor. *Eye on Psi Chi, 3*(3), 38–39.

Appleby, D. (2000). Job skills valued by employers who interview psychology majors. *Eye on Psi Chi, 4*(3), 17.

Appleby, D. (2001). The covert curriculum: The lifelong learning skills you can learn in college. *Eye on Psi Chi, 5*(3), 28.

Appleby, D., Keenan, J., & Mauer, B. (1999). Applicant characteristics valued by graduate programs in psychology. *Eye on Psi Chi, 3*(3), 9.

Austin, J. T., & Calderon, R. F. (1996). Writing in APA style: Why and how. In F. Leong & J. Austin (Eds.), *The psychology research handbook: A guide for graduate students and research assistants* (pp. 265–281). Thousand Oaks, CA: Sage.

Balster, R. L. (1995). An interesting career in psychology: A research psychologist in a medical school. *Psychological Science Agenda.* Retrieved April 12, 2002, from http://www.apa.org/science/ic-balster.html

Bare, J. K. (1988). A liberal education. In P. J. Woods (Ed.), *Is psychology for them? A guide to undergraduate advising.* Washington, DC: American Psychological Association.

Bat-Chava, Y. (2000). *An interesting career in psychology: Research director for a non-profit organization.* Retrieved February 1, 2001, from http://www.apa.org/science/ic-bat-chava.html

Bennett, M. J. (1994). Can competing psychotherapists be managed? *Managed Care Quarterly, 2,* 29–35.

Bonifazi, D. Z., Crespi, S. D., & Rieker, P. (1997). Value of a master's degree for gaining admission to doctoral programs in psychology. *Teaching of Psychology, 24,* 176–182.

Borden, V. M. H., & Rajecki, D. W. (2000). First-year employment outcomes of psychology baccalaureates: Relatedness, preparedness, and prospects. *Teaching of Psychology, 27,* 164–168.

Bornstein, M. H., & Arterberry, M. E. (1999). Perceptual development. In M. H. Bornstein & M. E. Lamb (Eds.), *Developmental psychology: An advanced textbook.* Mahwah, NJ: Erlbaum.

Bottoms, B. L., & Nysse, K. L. (1999). Applying to graduate school: Writing a compelling personal statement. *Eye on Psi Chi 4*(1), 20–22.

Buskist, W., & Sherburne, T. R. (1996). *Preparing for graduate study in psychology: 101 questions and answers.* Needham Heights, MA: Allyn & Bacon.

Carroll, J. L., Shmidt, J. L., & Sorensen, R. (1992). Careers in psychology: Or what can I do with a bachelor's degree. *Psychological Reports, 71,* 1151–1154.

Christensen, A., & Jacobson, N. S. (1994). Who (or what) can do psychotherapy: The status and challenge of nonprofessional therapies. *Psychological Science, 5,* 8–12.

Chronicle of Higher Education (1999). *Earned degrees conferred, 1995–96.* Retrieved August 18, 2000, from http://chronicle.com/weekly/almanac/1999/facts/9stu.htm

Cummings, N. A. (1995). Impact of managed care on employment and training: A primer for survival. *Professional Psychology: Research and Practice, 26,* 10–15.

Dale, R. H. I. (1988). State psychological associations, licensing criteria, and the "master's issue." *Professional Psychology: Research and Practice, 20,* 56–58.

Davis, S. F. (1995). The value of collaborative scholarship with undergraduates. *Psi Chi Newsletter, 21*(1), 12–13.

DeGalan, J., & Lambert, S. (1995). *Great jobs for psychology majors.* Chicago: VGM Career Horizons.

Descutner, C. J., & Thelen, M. H. (1989). Graduate student and faculty perspectives about graduate school. *Teaching of Psychology, 16,* 58–60.

Educational Testing Service. (2004). *GRE information and registration bulletin.* Princeton, NJ: Author.

Edwards, J., and Smith, K. (1988). What skills and knowledge do potential employers value in baccalaureate psychologists? In P. J. Woods (ed.), *Is psychology for them? A guide to undergraduate advising.* Washington, DC: American Psychological Association.

Finney, P., Snell, W., & Sebby, R. (1989). Assessment of academic, personal, and career development of alumni from Southeast Missouri State University. *Teaching of Psychology, 16,* 173–177.

Flattau, P. E. (1998). *An interesting career in psychology: Policy scientist as an independent consultant.* Retrieved on February 1, 2001, from http://www.apa.org/science/icflattau.html

Frank, R. G., & Ross, M. J. (1995). The changing workforce: The role of health psychology. *Health Psychology, 14,* 519–525

Fretz, B. R. (1976). Finding careers with a bachelor's degree in psychology. *Psi Chi Newsletter, 2,* 5–9.

Fretz, B. R., & Stang, D. J. (1988). *Preparing for graduate study in psychology: Not for seniors only!* Washington, DC: American Psychological Association.

Fry, R. (1991). *Manage your time.* Hawthorne, NJ: Career Press.

Gardner, P. D. (2000). *Recruiting trends 1999–2000.* Collegiate Employment Institute, Michigan State University. Retrieved August 20, 2000, from http://www.csp.msu.edu/ceri/pubs/rectrends9899.htm

Garfein, R. (1997). *An interesting career in psychology: International market research consultant.* Retrieved February 1, 2001, from http://www.apa.org/science/ic-garfein.html

Grocer, S., & Kohout, J. (1997). *The 1995 APA survey of 1992 psychology baccalaureate recipients.* Retrieved August 21, 2000, from http://research.apa.org/95survey/homepage.html

Hayes, N. (1996). What makes a psychology graduate distinctive? *European Psychologist, 1,* 30–134.

Hays-Thomas, R. L. (2000). The silent conversation: Talking about the master's degree. *Professional Psychology: Research and Practice, 31,* 339–345.

Hersch, L. (1995). Adapting to health care reform and managed care: Three strategies for survival and growth. *Professional Psychology: Research & Practice, 26,* 16–26.

Himelein, M. J. (1999). A student's guide to careers in the helping professions. *Office of Teaching Resources in Psychology.* Retrieved January 3, 2001, from http://www.lemoyne.edu/OTRP/otrpresources/helping.html

Holland, J. L. (1959). A theory of vocational choice. *Journal of Counseling Psychology, 6,* 35–45.

Holland, J. L. (1994). *Self-Directed Search®.* Retrieved July 5, 2001, from http://www.self-directed-search.com

Holloway, J. D. (2004). A win-win for health-care providers and consumers. *Monitor on Psychology, 35*(11), 30.

Humphreys, K. (1996). Clinical psychologists as psychotherapists: History, future, and alternatives. *American Psychologist, 51,* 190–197.

Jalbert, N. L. (1998). *Publication and award opportunities for undergraduate students. Office of Teaching Resources in Psychology.* Retrieved August 8, 2001, from http://www.lemoyne.edu/OTRP/otrpresources/otrp_undergrad.html

Jessen, B. C. (1988). Field experience for undergraduate psychology students. In P. J. Woods (Ed.), *Is psychology for them? A guide to undergraduate advising* (pp. 79–84). Washington, DC: American Psychological Association.

Kahn, N. B. (1992). *More learning in less time: A guide for students, professionals, career changers, and lifelong learners*. Berkeley, CA: Ten Speed Press.

Karlin, N. J. (2000). Creating an effective conference presentation. *Eye on Psi Chi, 4*(2), 26–27.

Keith-Spiegel, P., Tabachnick, B. G., & Spiegel, G. B. (1994). When demand exceeds supply: Second order criteria used by graduate school selection committees. *Teaching of Psychology, 21,* 79–81.

Keith-Spiegel, P., & Wiederman, M. W. (2000). *The complete guide to graduate school admission: Psychology, counseling, and related professions*. Hillsdale, NJ: Erlbaum.

Kierniesky, N. C. (1992). Specialization of the undergraduate major. *American Psychologist, 47,* 1146–1147.

Keyes, B. J., & Hogberg, D. K. (1990). Undergraduate psychology alumni: Gender and cohort differences in course usefulness, post baccalaureate education, and career paths. *Teaching of Psychology, 17,* 101–105.

Kohout, J., & Wicherski, M. (1999). *1997 Doctoral employment survey*. Retrieved January 4, 2001, from http://research.apa.org/des97contents.html

Kohout, J., & Wicherski, M. (2004). 2001 Doctorate Employment Survey. Retrieved April 7, 2004, http://research.apa.org/des01.html

Krannich, R. I. (1991). *Careering and re-careering for the 1990's: The complete guide to planning your future.* Woodbridge, VA: Impact Publishers.

Kraus, S. J. (1996). *An interesting career in psychology: Market research consultant.* Retrieved February 1, 2001, from http://www.apa.org/science/ic-kraus.html

Kressel, N. J. (1990). Job and degree satisfaction among social science graduates. *Teaching of Psychology, 17,* 222–227.

Kuther, T. L. (1996). Doctoral training in applied developmental psychology: Matching graduate education and accreditation standards to student needs, career opportunities, and licensure requirements. In C. B. Fisher, J. P. Murray, & I. E. Sigel (Eds.), *Applied developmental science: Graduate training for diverse disciplines and educational settings* (pp. 53–74). Norwood, NJ: Ablex.

Kuther, T. L., & Morgan, R. D. (2004). *Careers in psychology: Opportunities in a changing world.* Belmont, CA: Wadsworth.

Landrum, E., Davis, S., & Landrum, T. (2000). *The psychology major: Career options and strategies for success*. Upper Saddle River, NJ: Prentice Hall.

Landrum, R. E., Harrold, R. & Davis, S. F. (2003). What employers want from psychology graduates. Teaching of Psychology, 30, 131–133.

Levant, R. F., Moldawsky, S., & Stigall, T. T. (2000). The evolving profession of psychology: Comment on Hays-Thomas' (2000) "The silent conversation," *Professional Psychology Research and Practice, 31,* 346–348.

Littlepage, G., Perry, S., & Hodge, H. (1990). Career experiences of bachelor's degree recipients: Comparison of psychology and other majors. *Journal of Employment Counseling, 27,* 50-59.

Lloyd, M. A. (1997a). *Entry level positions obtained by psychology majors.* Retrieved August 18, 2000, from http://www.psywww.com/careers/entry.htm

Lloyd, M. A. (1997b). *Graduate school options for psychology majors.* Retrieved February 15, 2001, from http://www.psywww.com/careers/options.htm

Lloyd, M. A. (2000). *Master's- and doctoral-level careers in psychology and related areas.* Retrieved February 1, 2000, from http://www.psychwww.com/careers/masters.htm

Lloyd, M. A., & Kennedy, J. H. (1997). *Skills employers seek.* Retrieved August 20, 2000, from http://www.psywww.com/careers/skills.htm

LoCicero, A., & Hancock, J. (2000). Preparing students for success in fieldwork. *Teaching of Psychology, 27,* 117–120.

Lock, R. D. (1992). *Taking charge of your career direction.* Pacific Grove, CA: Brooks/Cole.

Lowe, R. H. (1993). Master's programs in industrial/organization psychology: Current status and a call for action. *Professional Psychology: Research and Practice, 24,* 27–34.

Lunneborg, P. W. (1985). Job satisfactions in different occupational areas among psychology baccalaureates. *Teaching of Psychology, 12,* 21–22.

Lunneborg, P. W., & Wilson, V. M. (1987). Three keys to graduate psychology. In P. J. Woods & C. S. Wilkinson (Eds.), *Is psychology the major for you? Planning your undergraduate years* (pp. 89–104). Washington, DC: American Psychological Association.

Matlin, M. W., & Kalat, J. W. (2001). Demystifying the GRE Psychology Test: A brief guide for students. *Eye on Psi Chi, 5*(1), 22–25.

Mayne, T. J., Norcross, J. C., & Sayette, M. A. (1994). Admission requirements, acceptance rates, and financial assistance in clinical psychology programs. *American Psychologist, 12,* 806–811.

McGovern, T. V., & Carr, K. F. (1989). Carving out the niche: A review of alumni surveys on undergraduate psychology majors. *Teaching of Psychology, 16,* 52–57.

McGovern, T. V., Furumoto, L., Halpern, D. F., Kimble, G. A., & McKeachie, W. J. (1991). Liberal education, study in depth, and the arts and sciences major–psychology *American Psychologist, 46,* 598–605.

Meyer, M. (1985). *The Little, Brown guide to writing research papers.* Boston: Little, Brown and Company.

Murray, T. M., & Williams, S. (1999). Analyses of data from graduate study in psychology: 1997–98. *APA Research Office.* Retrieved February 15, 2001, from http://research.apa.org/grad98contents.html

National Association of Colleges and Employers (2000). *Ideal candidate has top-notch interpersonal skills, say employers.* Retrieved August 19, 2000, from http://www.naceweb.org/press/display.cfm/2000/pr011800.htm

National Center for Education Statistics (2001). Postsecondary institutions in the United States: Fall 2000 and degrees and other awards conferred: 1999-2000. Washington, DC: US. Department of Education.

National Center for Education Statistics (2003a). *Bachelor's degrees conferred by degree-granting institutions, by discipline division: Selected years, 1970–71 to 2001–02.* http://nces.ed.gov/programs/digest/d03/tables/dt252.asp

National Center for Education Statistics (2003b). *Earned degrees in psychology conferred by degree-granting institutions, by level of degree and sex of student: Selected years*

1949–50 to 2001–02. Retrieved on January 19, 2005, at http://nces.ed.gov/programs/digest/d03/tables/dt293.asp

National Science Foundation (2001). *Primary education and employment status and median salary of 1999 and 2000 science and engineering bachelor's degree recipients, by major field of degree: April 2001.* Retrieved December 31, 2004, from http://www.nsf.gov/sbe/srs/nsf04302/pdf/tabs1a.pdf

Norcross, J. C. (1997). GREs and GPAs: The numbers game in graduate admissions. *Eye on Psi Chi, 1*(2), 10–11.

Norcross, J. C. (2000). Clinical vs. counseling psychology: What's the diff? *Eye on Psi Chi, 4*(3), 20–22.

Norcross, J. C., Hanych, J. M., & Terranova, R. D. (1996). Graduate study in psychology: 1992–1993. *American Psychologist, 51,* 631–643.

Pate, W. E. (2001). *Analyses of data from graduate study in psychology: 1999–2000.* Retrieved January 19, 2005, from http://research.apa.org/grad00contents.html

Pauk, W., & Fiore, J. (2000). *Succeed in college!* New York: Harper & Row.

Peters, R. L. (1992). *Getting what you came for: The smart student's guide to earning a master's or a PhD.* New York: Noonday Press.

Powell, J. L. (2000). Creative outlets for student research or what do I do now that my study is completed? *Eye on Psi Chi, 4*(2), 28–29.

Psi Chi. (2000). *Tips for paper/poster presentations.* Retrieved May 18, 2001, from http://www.psichi.org/content/conventions/tps.asp

Quereshi, M. Y., & Kuchan, A. M. (1988). The master's degree in clinical psychology: Longitudinal program evaluation. *Professional Psychology: Research and Practice, 19,* 594–599.

Rittle, R. (2000). *Career options with a master's degree.* Retrieved February 1, 2001, from http://www.nsm.iup.edu/pc/jobs3ma.html

Robiner, W. N., & Crew, D. P. (2000). Rightsizing the workforce of psychologists in health care: Trends from licensing boards, training programs, and managed care. *Professional Psychology: Research and Practice, 31,* 245–263.

Robinson, F. P. (1970). *Effective study*. New York: Harper & Row.

Rosnow, R. L., & Rosnow, M. (2001). *Writing papers in psychology*. Belmont, CA: Wadsworth.

Scott, J. M., Koch, R. E., Scott, G. M., & Garrison, S. M. (1999). *The psychology student writer's manual*. Upper Saddle River, NJ: Prentice Hall.

SCRD (1991) Ethical standards for research with children. Retrieved April 4, 2005 from http://www.srcd.org/ethicalstandards.html

Seligman, M. E. P. (1995). The effectiveness of psychotherapy: The Consumer Reports Study. *American Psychologist, 50*, 965–974.

Seton Hall University (2000). *Beyond the BA: Making career choices*. Retrieved December 29, 2000, from http://artsci.shu.edu/psychology/hbook4.html

Sheetz, P. I. (1995). *Recruiting trends: 1995–1996*. East Lansing, MI: Collegiate Employment Research Institute, Michigan State University.

Singleton, D., Tate, A. C., & Kohout, J. L. (2003a). *2002 master's, specialist's, and related degrees employment survey*. Retrieved January 19, 2005, from http://research.apa.org/mes2004contents.html

Singleton, D., Tate, A. C., & Kohout, J. L. (2003b). *Salaries in psychology, 2001: Report of the 2001 APA salary survey.* Retrieved January 19, 2005, from http://research.apa.org/01salary/index.html

Stapp, J. (1996). *An interesting career in psychology: Trial consultant.* Retrieved February 1, 2001, from http://www.apa.org/science/ic-stapp.html

Sternberg, R. J. (1993). *The psychologist's companion.* New York: Cambridge University Press.

Taylor, M. S. (1988). Effects of college internships on individual participants. *Journal of Applied Psychology, 73,* 393–401.

Trent, J. T. (1993). Issues and concerns in master's-level training and employment. *Journal of Clinical Psychology, 49,* 586–592.

Tsapogas, J. (2004). *Employment outcomes of recent science and engineering graduates vary by field of degree and sector of employment: Science resources statistics info brief.* Retrieved December 31, 2004, from http://www.nsf.gov/sbe/srs/infbrief/nsf04316/start.htm

University of Tennessee (n.d.). *Major and career information.* Retrieved July 5, 2001, from http://career.utk.edu/students/holland/holland.asp

University of Texas at Austin (2000). *Career opportunities for psychology majors.* Retrieved August 18, 2000, from http://cwis.uta.edu/psychology/dept/careers.htm

U.S. Bureau of Labor Statistics (2004a). *Wholesale and retail trade: Industry at a glance.* Retrieved January 1, 2005, from http://www.bls.gov/iag/wholeretailtrade.htm

U.S. Bureau of Labor Statistics (2004b). *Occupational outlook handbook.* Washington, DC: Author.

U.S. Bureau of Labor Statistics (2004c). More education: Lower unemployment, higher pay. *Occupational Outlook Quarterly Online.* Retrieved January, 1, 2005, from http://www.bls.gov/opub/ooq/oochart.htm

Winter, D. G., McClelland, D. C., & Stewart, A. J. (1981). *A new case for the liberal arts: Assessing institutional goals and student development.* San Francisco: Jossey-Bass.

Woods, P. J. (1971). A history of APA's concern with the master's degree: Or "Discharged with thanks." *American Psychologist, 26,* 696–707.

Index

TO THE OWNER OF THIS BOOK:

I hope that you have found *The Psychology Major's Handbook,* Second Edition useful. So that this book can be improved in a future edition, would you take the time to complete this sheet and return it? Thank you.

School and address: ______________________________

____

____

Department: ______________________________

Instructor's name: ______________________________

1. What I like most about this book is: ______________________________

____

____

2. What I like least about this book is: ______________________________

____

____

3. My general reaction to this book is: ______________________________

____

____

4. The name of the course in which I used this book is: ______________________________

____

5. Were all of the chapters of the book assigned for you to read? ______________

   If not, which ones weren't? ______________________________

6. In the space below, or on a separate sheet of paper, please write specific suggestions for improving this book and anything else you'd care to share about your experience in using this book.

____

____

____

DO NOT STAPLE.
TAPE HERE.

DO NOT STAPLE.
TAPE HERE.

FOLD HERE

THOMSON

WADSWORTH

NO POSTAGE NECESSARY IF MAILED IN THE UNITED STATES

BUSINESS REPLY MAIL

FIRST-CLASS MAIL PERMIT NO. 102 MONTEREY CA

POSTAGE WILL BE PAID BY ADDRESSEE

Attn: Vicki Knight / Psychology Publisher

Wadsworth/Thomson Learning
60 Garden Ct Ste 205
Monterey CA 93940-9967

FOLD HERE

OPTIONAL:

Your name:____ Date: _______

May we quote you, either in promotion for *The Psychology Major's Handbook,* Second Edition or in future publishing ventures?

Yes: ________________ No: __________

Sincerely yours,

Tara L. Kuther

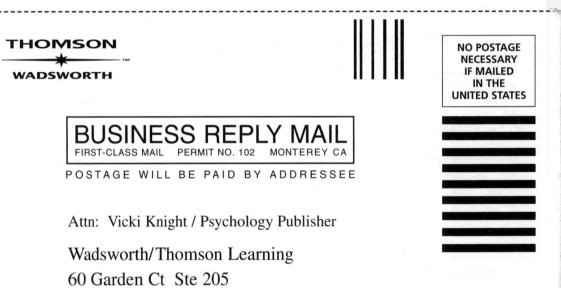